S0-ADV-995

# Building the
# Operational Data Store

# Building the
# Operational Data Store

## Second Edition

W. H. Inmon

**Wiley Computer Publishing**

**John Wiley & Sons, Inc.**

NEW YORK · CHICHESTER · WEINHEIM · BRISBANE · SINGAPORE · TORONTO

Publisher: Robert Ipsen
Editor: Robert M. Elliott
Managing Editor: Angela Murphy
Text Design & Composition: Publishers' Design and Production Services, Inc.

Designations used by companies to distinguish their products are often claimed as trademarks. In all instances where John Wiley & Sons, Inc., is aware of a claim, the product names appear in initial capital or all capital letters. Readers, however, should contact the appropriate companies for more complete information regarding trademarks and registration.

This book is printed on acid-free paper. ♾

Copyright © 1999 by W. H. Inmon. All rights reserved.

Published by John Wiley & Sons, Inc.

Published simultaneously in Canada.

No part of this publication may be reproduced, stored in a retrieval system or transmitted in any form or by any means, electronic, mechanical, photocopying, recording, scanning or otherwise, except as permitted under Sections 107 or 108 of the 1976 United States Copyright Act, without either the prior written permission of the Publisher, or authorization through payment of the appropriate per-copy fee to the Copyright Clearance Center, 222 Rosewood Drive, Danvers, MA 01923, (978) 750-8400, fax (978) 750-4744. Requests to the Publisher for permission should be addressed to the Permissions Department, John Wiley & Sons, Inc., 605 Third Avenue, New York, NY 10158-0012, (212) 850-6011, fax (212) 850-6008, E-Mail: PERMREQ@WILEY.COM.

This publication is designed to provide accurate and authoritative information in regard to the subject matter covered. It is sold with the understanding that the publisher is not engaged in professional serves. If professional advice or other expert assistance is required, the services of a competent professional person should be sought.

***Library of Congress Cataloging-in-Publication Data:***

Inmon, William H.
    Building the operational data store / W.H. Inmon. — 2nd ed.
      p.     cm.
    ISBN 0-471-32888-X
    1. Database management. 2. Management information systems.
    I. Title.
    QA76.9.D3I5374 1999
    658.4′038′028574—dc21

                                   99-14291

Printed in the United States of America.

10 9 8 7 6 5 4 3 2 1

*To Carol, who brightens each day.*

# Contents

# Preface

My first exposure to an operational data store (ODS) came long ago. It was a Sunday afternoon and my good friend John Zachman called me on the phone. We chatted for a while and then John told me that he had seen something that looked like a data warehouse, walked like a data warehouse, but didn't seem quite like a data warehouse. John then went on to describe what he had seen. He said he had been talking with an insurance company that had a problem. The insurance company had, over the years, collected a large number of policy management systems, about 14 to be precise. The applications had been acquired through a variety of means—by writing the application, by rewriting the application, by acquiring another insurance company, by buying package solutions, and so forth. These fourteen applications for the management of policies caused the insurance company no small amount of grief. When a customer called up and asked a simple question—how much coverage and what types of coverage do I have—the insurance company took an inordinate amount of time to answer the question. Furthermore, getting answers to simple questions was no small task. Answering such basic things as how many policies are in force was a singularly difficult undertaking. To make matters even worse, maintenance on the 14 applications was consuming far more resources than anything else. And the maintenance burden never seemed to get better. It was eternally increasing. In short the insurance company had a problem on its hands.

The information technology staff knew there was a problem. The answer the IT staff had was to call a local consulting firm with a national reputation. Sure enough, the consulting firm nodded its head and agreed there was a problem. The consulting firm hired on to solve the problem. First there was a massive modeling effort, then the consulting firm did a strategic plan, then the consulting firm set out to do reengineering. After several years and tens of millions of dollars paid to the consulting firm, there were no concrete results to show for a whole lot of shuffling, unless studies that sit on shelves count as results. But studies that sit on shelves were not what the insurance company had in mind. There were still no solutions to the problems created by the 14 applications that managed the policies for the insurance company.

Then one day, in desperation, an IT manager took destiny in his hands. Tired of spending huge amounts of money and having a small army of consultants that never produced anything useful, the manager built a simple file. The file broke all the rules of database design (as conventionally understood at the time). The manager simply didn't care if he got style points or faced derisive remarks from the database design staff. The manager wanted something simple—he wanted tangible results.

The file that the manager built was an amalgamation of lots of things. It centered around a customer. It had some basic information about the customer on the file and there was a reference to any and all policies that a customer might have. If there was a need to see further policy information, the users of the file knew right where to go. The file that was created could be accessed and updated online, and response time was good. In many ways the file was a glorified organization index to the policies that a customer might have.

The database designers laughed. The data administrators held their noses. The systems programmers said that the file could not be tuned. And all the while the clerical staff that had to respond to customers needs flocked to the file. To the users it was a huge success.

John Zachman said that it looked like a data warehouse but he didn't think it really was a data warehouse. Since people were doing OLTP processing against the file and since updates were being done, it did not appear that the file was a data warehouse. John was right (as he almost always is). This was something else; it was an ODS. This then was my first introduction to an ODS. Since then I have had the opportunity to observe many (and be a participant in a few) ODSs. As important as data warehouses are, they are not the only structure in the world of decision support systems (DSSs).

ODSs are interesting in that they have one foot in the world of operational, transaction processing and another foot in the world of DSS processing. They are truly a hybrid structure. Because of this dichotomy, ODSs are complex structures and systems. ODSs attempt to serve two masters at the same time, and this they cannot do. Therefore the design and the implementation of an ODS is always (and as a writer I do not used the word "always" lightly) a compromise. Of necessity, in every case, the design and implementation of an ODS is a compromise.

The fact that an ODS is a compromised structure bothers people, especially technicians. Technicians like to have things set out in black and white. There is a certain comfort in knowing that there is an inviolable set of rules that describes how things should be. Unfortunately the fundamental nature of ODSs is that there are multiple sets of rules. Sometimes the ODS conforms to one set of rules, on other occasions it conforms to another set of rules. This mandated compromise bothers designers and technicians, but that is the way ODSs are.

When the first edition of this book was written, the notion of an ODS was sketchy. I and my fellow authors freely admit that. We tried to draw a picture of a vision in the first edition of this book. But a few years have passed now and ODSs have gone from being an idea to a very concrete architectural entity. Now ODSs in one form or another are popping up everywhere. In a recent conference where 10 executives described their architecture, every one of the executives described an ODS as a prominent part of their architecture. So ODSs are here today and here to stay.

One of the significant events in the life of ODSs is that a commercial form of ODS has arisen. Since the first edition of this book, we now have such well-known packages as SAP, Oracle Financials, PeopleSoft, and BAAN, just to name a few. In one form or another these software packages represent a form of ODS. Some packages fit the form of being a classical ODS. When the first edition was written I had no idea that there would be a commercial manifestation of ODSs. The commercial form just suddenly appeared.

One of the really interesting aspects of ODSs is that they are sort of a stealth architectural structure, if there ever was such a thing. There are international conferences on data warehouses, national conferences and seminars on data marts, vendors selling data mining products, and major new advances being made in near-line storage. Everywhere you look there is some major and very public activity occurring for other parts of the data warehouse environment, but not for ODSs.

To date, ODSs have had no vendor pushing it as an agenda. There are no conferences on ODS, and the only seminar given on ODSs has been by Claudia Imhoff and Joyce Montanari, and that seminar has had only modest attendance. The only public utterance on ODSs has been the first edition of this book. Occasionally there will be a magazine article about ODSs. *Data Management Review* has been diligent in following advances in ODSs, but no other journal comes to mind when it comes to keeping the public informed as to the progress and happenings in the world of ODSs.

But a lot has been happening. Some very sophisticated ODSs are available, and these augment the data warehouse and the operational environment. The world of ODSs is just taking off.

What are the motivations for building and operating an ODS? There are many motivations, but three motivations stand out above all the rest:

**Operational integration**. Organizations find that it is not realistic to think that they are going to go back in time and rewrite or do major surgery to all their old applications. It was hard enough making changes for the year 2000 problems. Changing key structures, record layouts, and procedures is simply beyond the scope of most organizations. Building an ODS on top of older applications is like having your cake and eating it too. The organization has operational integration without rebuilding or retooling old legacy operational applications.

**DSS processing on operational data**. DSS processing and applications processing simply do not mix well, especially when it comes to transaction processing. One of the glories of an ODS is that it supports both kinds of processing, although admittedly with compromise.

**Staging area for eclectic analytical processing**. Occasionally there is the need for analyzing data in a heuristic manner without disturbing the workload of applications. An ODS provides an ideal platform for allowing that sort of analysis to be done. In addition, an ODS is a good platform for receiving preanalyzed data and making that data available to the world online.

These reasons represent only the tip of the iceberg. There are undoubtedly many other reasons for the existence of an ODS environment.

To the best of my knowledge there are no other books on ODSs. That places this second edition in a precarious position. That makes this both the best book in the world on the subject and the worst book in the world, since it is the only book in the world. This book has many features, including:

- Architectural evolution to the ODS
- The definition of the ODS
- The architectural description of the corporate information factory, the structure in which the ODS sits
- The different classes of ODS
- Designing the ODS
- Managing the ODS
- Technology in support of the ODS
- The role of standards
- Reengineering and the ODS
- Case studies
- Metadata and the ODS

This book is written for students of computer science, managers, designers, developers, users, system architects, and others. In short this book is for anyone needing to understand what the issues of ODSs are.

Special thanks to Valerie Anderson and Craig Dawson, Catalyst Partners; Bob Butchko, Barry Fisschel, Alice Lubowicz, Dennis McCann, and Ken Richardson, Pine Cone Systems; Cheryl Estep, Chevron; Jeanne Friedman, Vality Corp.;

Kevin Gould, Sybase; Dave Imhoff, Intelligent Solutions; Melba Inmon, Forest Rim Technologies; Don Parsons, Centennial Funds; Mark Sheppard, Morningside Funds; and John Zachman, Zachman International.

A special thanks goes to Claudia Imhoff, Intelligent Solutions, my friend and colleague, who revised the ODS development methodology in the appendix from the first edition of this book. As usual, Claudia is incisive and cogent. Thanks.

# Evolving to the Operational Data Store

In the beginning of the information systems profession were applications. The design of these early applications was shaped by an understanding of the requirements of the business at the time the applications were designed. For the most part, early applications focused on the day-to-day clerical needs of the organization. The applications were built, or otherwise acquired, one application at a time in a piecemeal, unintegrated fashion. Figure 1.1 shows day 1 of the genesis of the information systems that exist today.

Soon the business needs of the corporation changed and the corporation began doing maintenance on these applications, as seen in day 2 of the progression (Figure 1.1). The applications required a lot of changes for a variety of reasons, among them:

- New requirements that were only recently recognized
- Changing business requirements
- New opportunities that only became apparent with the advent of the implementation of the application

At the same time that the original applications were being maintained, there arose a request to get more information from the applications. The significance of this request for information from an existing base of information systems was not recognized at the time it was made. But history has shown that, indeed, the desire to obtain further information from an existing base of information systems was a very profound request.

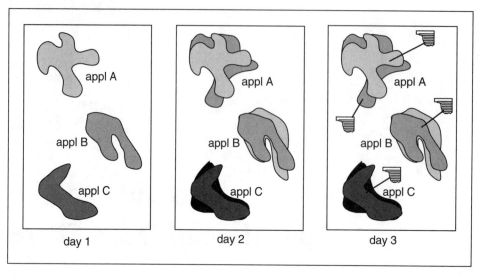

**Figure 1.1**  There is a predictable progression in the way systems and technology are implemented.

The first attempt to satisfy the request for more information resulted in the writing of programs that created reports, as seen on day 3 (Figure 1.1). These reports were typically written in COBOL, and were written in a customized fashion. The theory was that getting more information out of an existing base of information systems was as simple as writing reports. Unfortunately there were some major limitations with writing reports as a way to satisfy the information needs of an organization.

The first limitation was that when a report was written it was limited to the data that resided in any one given application. If there was a desire to get further information from other applications for the report, then merely writing a report would not suffice. A second limitation was that once the reports were written, they were constantly being changed and maintained. Considerable effort was required in order for the end-user analyst's changes to be accommodated. A third and very obvious limitation of using reports to try to get information out of a base of existing information systems was that the reports themselves required a large, customized, and often complex effort to be written in the first place. A fourth limitation was that when similar data was retrieved from different sources, the data was inconsistent. In short, the practice of writing customized reports as the only means of satisfying the information needs of the corporation passed quickly.

The next step in the progression of satisfying the information needs of the corporation was to "interface" the applications together, as seen in day 4 of the progression shown in Figure 1.2. This means that when one application needs data from another application for the purpose of reporting, the requesting appli-

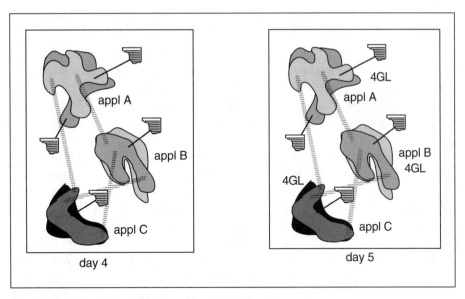

**Figure 1.2**   The thirst for information drives the progression.

cation sends a transaction or notification to the application holding the data. Once the holding application receives the request for data, the data is located and is passed back to the requesting application.

While interfacing data from one application to another works well in theory, there are some major drawbacks. The first is that the application holding the data that is being requested may not welcome interruptions in its processing pattern. For example, if the application holding the data that has been requested is a high-performance application that is processing many transactions per second, a request for 100,000 records in the middle of the high-performance processing window will not be welcome. A second drawback to interfacing applications is that even if the data is received back at the requesting application with no fuss, there is the task of integrating the requested information with the information that already resides at the application. Such integration is traditionally very difficult to do.

The next step in the progression of the thirst for information was to use 4GL products, as seen on day 5 of Figure 1.2. The notion behind 4GL products was that information was difficult to acquire because reports could not be written fast enough. There were claims that 4GL products would increase the productivity of an organization by as much as 1,000 percent. There was no question that 4GLs provided a significant gain in the writing of code over COBOL. But the speed of code production was not the main reason why organizations had such a difficult time in getting information out of an existing base of systems. Even if the 4GL products could create code very quickly, the reports that were produced were subject to the same limitations as reports that were produced on a customized basis. Very quickly, 4GLs were unveiled as the panacea to the problem of gathering information from an existing base of systems.

But soon reality dawned and the limitations of 4GLs were discovered. The next step in the progression toward getting information out of an existing base of information systems was the introduction of the extract program, as seen on day 6. The extract program is one in which a program moves data from one application to the next on a wholesale basis. Figure 1.3 shows this step in the progression.

An extract file is created by rummaging through data and looking for units of data that meet some predetermined criteria. Once having found data that meets the criteria, the qualified data is moved off onto an extract file and shipped to another application. In some ways, extract files represented an advance over interfaces, in that there is a minimal disruption to the processing window of the application holding the data that has been requested. But there were some major problems associated with extract files. The first problem with extraction is that the data put into the extract file is never more current than the moment it is extracted. As soon as the extraction process completes, the extracted file starts aging. A second problem with extraction is the considerable amount of machine resources required for doing the extraction. A third problem is that once the data is extracted, it has to be integrated with the data that already resides in the application where the extracted data is being sent. This integration process is a very complex activity. Either the data that is extracted retains its definition and context from the originating application or the extract

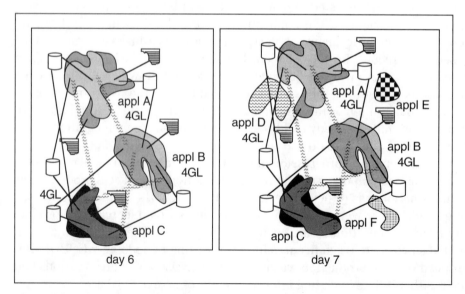

**Figure 1.3**  The progression continues as new applications are built and extract processing becomes a reality.

process must transform the data to the definition and context required by the requesting application. And finally, in the face of many extraction files, there soon was a massive proliferation of redundant data. For these reasons, the extract approach was not a good long-term solution. The progression toward accessing information from a base of existing information systems continued.

At this time in the progression there had grown to be a large number of older applications, and the difficulties manifest in these applications became apparent. New theoreticians sprang up and declared the development techniques of the past to be ineffective. They declared that new applications should be written in a new and improved manner. Once written, the natural superiority of the new applications would be so apparent that they would displace the older, "bad" applications. So fresh applications were written in a new and improved fashion, and soon they were implemented. But for a variety of reasons, these newer applications had a difficult time supplanting older legacy applications, whatever difficulties and whatever shortcomings the older legacy applications had. Day 7 in Figure 1.3 illustrates the introduction of new and improved applications.

Into the fray came the personal computer (PC). The theory behind the personal computer was that the reason why there had been a general failure to successfully pull information out of the existing information environment in a timely, usable form was that the wrong organization had been in control of information processing all along. The IT organization had been making promises for the delivery of information for many years and had not delivered. Figure 1.4

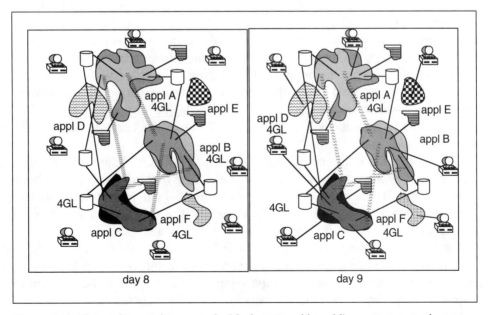

**Figure 1.4**  The end user takes control with the PC and by adding gateways to the corporate computing environment.

shows day 8, where the PC is brought into the information processing organization and is given to the end-user community so that the end-user community can take control of its own destiny.

With the arrival of the PC, the end user was freed from the tight control of the IT organization. The PC proved to be immensely popular. But merely bringing the PC into the organization hardly sufficed to satisfy the hunger of the end user for information. Very quickly the end user found that, with no data to operate on, having the PC on the desk was an exercise in futility.

The next step in the progression was to allow the end user to hook the PC up to the systems of the corporation. This hookup to the "official" corporate systems was accomplished through gateways and simple networks, as seen on day 9 of Figure 1.4. But soon the end user discovered that it was one thing to have access to official data and it was quite another to make sense of that data. Once allowed into the corporate systems, the end user was subject to the same lack of integration, the same lack of consistency, and the same limitations that everyone else was subject to prior to the advent of the PC. A few end users persevered and were able to succeed in accessing and analyzing data. But technology itself stymied many users. The result was a stratification of users into a new business social order—information-starved users or information-rich users. The illusion that getting information was as simple as buying a PC and turning the end user loose with the equipment faded quickly.

The next step in the progression of trying to get information out of existing information systems was to buy ever more powerful personal computers, which were called "workstations." The workstations first ran on a 286, then a 386, and then a 486 chip. Soon there were Pentium chips. Powerful spreadsheets were added as well as desktop database management systems. Soon there were gigabytes of data that were economical to store and manipulate on these workstations, as shown on day 10 of Figure 1.5. But for all the power that was being added to the desktop, there was general frustration with information processing because the data that was going into the desktop was no better than the data that was available before. Figure 1.5 shows the addition of powerful tools to the desktop.

The progression continued because there was still a real demand for information even though the past record for delivering that information had been unsuccessful. If anything, over the years the demand for information had increased rather than abated. The next step in the progression was toward interlinking all of the workstations, as seen in Figure 1.6.

Figure 1.6 shows that workstations and PCs were interlinked in a network, as seen on day 11. While there were certainly some advantages toward establishing a network of this variety, making communications easier did nothing to improve the quality of the data that was available for analysis.

Over the years there has been a wide variety of technological band-aids placed over a very serious wound. All the technological band-aids in the world

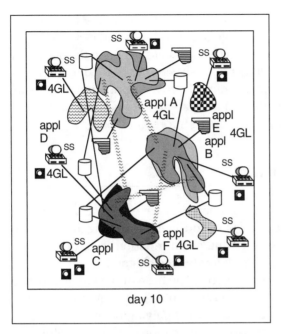

**Figure 1.5**  Spreadsheets and powerful workstation technology are added.

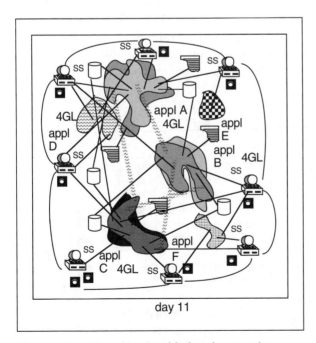

**Figure 1.6**  Networking is added to the equation.

will do nothing to address the fundamental problems at the root of the inability to access information. Adding more technological band-aids to the chaos shown on day 11 does nothing for an organization other than to heighten the desire for information. Nothing short of a fundamental restructuring of the base applications will suffice to form a foundation on which effective information processing can be done. The technological band-aids have patently not addressed the root problems of getting information from an existing information base.

## At the Heart of the Matter

To understand just how the old legacy applications have to be changed, it is necessary to understand the root causes of the difficulty in getting information. What, then, are the root problems of getting at information from an existing base of information systems? Figure 1.7 illustrates the obstacles.

The first difficulty in getting information from the base of old applications is that those old applications were shaped around business requirements that were relevant as many as 30 years ago. All thriving, living businesses change over a quarter-century, but the information applications are still profoundly shaped by their early requirements. The second reason why older applications are so hard to use as a basis for information is that those applications were shaped around the clerical needs of the corporation. Shaping application requirements around clerical needs inevitably focuses on repetitive processes that are concerned only with very current data, which the clerical community needs in order to run today's business. By focusing on today's data, the opportunity to store and use archival data preempts management of the opportunity

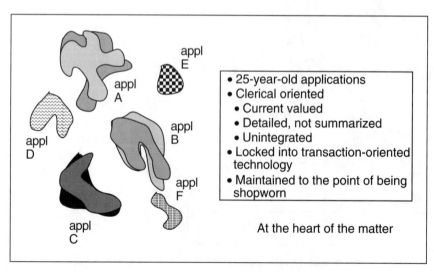

**Figure 1.7**  Rethinking the architecture of applications.

to examine data over the spectrum of time. In many cases, management would like to compare today's results with last month's, or last quarter's, or even last year's similar results. But a clerically focused application of necessity does not have the historical foundation required to support a long-term view.

The second reason why the clerical perspective does not support management's needs for information is that the clerical community focuses on detailed data. While detailed data is fine for the day-to-day clerical needs of the organization, management needs to see summary data in order to identify trends, challenges, and opportunities. And summary data was never designed as an integral part of the legacy application environment. Of course, detailed data is required in order to calculate and reshape summarizations. While management needs to look at things on a summarized basis, the detail that supports the summary allows the data to be looked at with flexibility.

The third reason why the clerical perspective does not suffice for management's need for information is that the clerically oriented applications were built one application at a time, and there was little or no integration from one application to the next. The result is that the old legacy applications cannot easily and reliably be combined to produce a unified perspective of data.

The fourth reason why the older legacy applications are not viable as a foundation for informational processing is that the older applications were built on a foundation of older transaction-oriented technology. While it was fine for the purposes for which it was originally intended, older transaction technology is not appropriate for today's informational processing.

A further reason why older legacy applications are not appropriate as a foundation for informational processing is that in many cases the older legacy applications have been maintained to the point that they are fragile. Many organizations are reluctant to do any large or complex amount of maintenance to applications that have been altered to the point of being threadbare.

# A Change in Architecture

For these and other reasons, the older foundation of applications will not suffice as a basis for the important informational processing that organizations need to do in order to become efficient, competitive corporations. Nothing short of an entire change in architecture and a fundamental restructuring of the applications foundation will suffice. Fortunately, there is an alternative architecture, which consists of a separation of processing into two broad categories—operational processing and decision support system (DSS) processing. Figure 1.8 depicts the classic architecture that companies discover they need in order to bring about fundamental changes to their legacy systems environment. The architecture outlined in Figure 1.8 is one that has been well described in other books and articles. See the references for a complete description of the literature that describes this architecture.

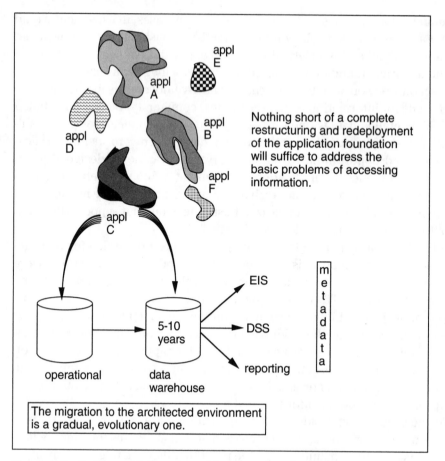

Nothing short of a complete restructuring and redeployment of the application foundation will suffice to address the basic problems of accessing information.

The migration to the architected environment is a gradual, evolutionary one.

**Figure 1.8**  Further rethinking the architecture of applications.

## The Data Warehouse

The centerpiece of the architecture is the data warehouse, which positions an organization for informational processing. Furthermore, a data warehouse can be built quickly and tangible results can be achieved and demonstrated to the sponsor of the data warehouse effort. The data warehouse environment has many very positive aspects. A simple view of the data warehouse concentric architecture is shown in Figure 1.9.

After the data warehouse was built, the need for departmentalized data arose. This departmentalized data took the form of a data mart, and the source of the data mart was the data warehouse. There was a fundamental transformation of data as it passed into the data mart. It went from a state of granular corporate data to aggregated departmental data as it passed into the data marts of the corporation.

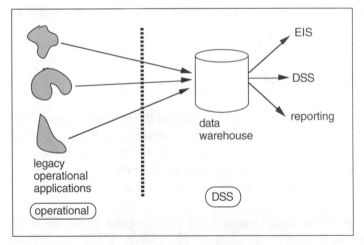

**Figure 1.9**   For all the advantages of the data warehouse, it did nothing for the integration of the operational environment.

Figure 1.9 shows that older, disparate applications feed the data warehouse, where data is integrated and stored over a lengthy period of time. There are many advantages to the data warehouse. But for all of the advantages, there are some disadvantages or limitations that deserve to be mentioned. The major drawback to the data warehouse concentric architecture is that it does nothing for the organization seeking operational integration. As long as the organization is seeking integration for informational processing, then the data warehouse is ideal. But when the organization requires operational integration, the data warehouse is not the proper architectural construct. Figure 1.10 shows that

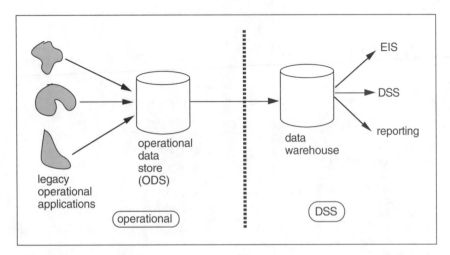

**Figure 1.10**   An alternative to the classical integrated informational architecture is one in which there is an architectural construct—the operational data store.

there is an alternate configuration or architecture that does take into consideration the need for operational integration.

## The Operational Data Store

Figure 1.10 shows that the unintegrated applications of the legacy systems environment feed what can be termed an operational data store (ODS). The ODS is a basis for doing integrated operational processing and, in turn, it feeds the data warehouse. There is still a clear line between operational processing and informational processing. The ODS is a separate architectural entity from the data warehouse.

The ODS serves the needs of the operational environment while the data warehouse serves the needs of the informational community. For those organizations requiring operational integration, the ODS is the architectural entity that fulfills their needs.

### What Is an Operational Data Store?

An ODS is an architectural construct that in some ways looks very much like a data warehouse, but in other important ways the ODS is very different from a data warehouse. Figure 1.11 illustrates the definition of an ODS. An ODS is an architectural construct that is subject oriented, integrated (i.e., collectively

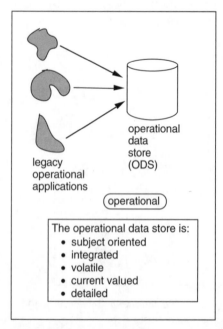

**Figure 1.11**   Operational data store characteristics.

integrated), volatile, current valued, and contains only corporate detailed data. Each of these aspects of an ODS deserves an explanation.

## Subject Oriented

An ODS is designed and organized around the major subjects of the corporation. The major subjects of the corporation are typically such things as CUSTOMER, PRODUCT, ACTIVITY, POLICY, CLAIM, and SHIPMENT. The ODS is *not* organized around any specific application or function. The subject orientation of the ODS is one of the ways in which it represents a collectively integrated image of data across the corporation.

## Integrated

The data found in the ODS is an aggregation of detailed data found in the legacy systems that feed it. As the data is pulled into the ODS from the legacy systems, the data is fundamentally transformed into a consistent, unified whole. The transformation and integration of detailed legacy data results in a truly integrated, corporate-wide understanding of data as it resides in the ODS. The transformation of data into the operational data store is very similar to the transformation and integration of data that occurs as legacy data flows into the data warehouse. As the older legacy application environment becomes integrated over time, the interface to the ODS becomes cleaner and more straightforward. Indeed, over time some data may be entered into the ODS directly.

## Volatile

Data in the ODS is updated on a regular basis. Every time the data in the foundation source systems—the legacy systems—changes, the ODS needs to be updated. In some cases, the update of the ODS occurs very quickly—second by second and transaction by transaction. In other cases, the update of the ODS occurs only periodically—every hour or every day. In still other cases, the update of ODS data is casual, happening every 24 hours or even longer. In any case, however the ODS is updated, the data in it is very much subject to change. Because data is volatile in the ODS, true transaction response time is a possibility. The user has a right to expect two- to three-second response times out of an ODS.

## Current Valued

Data in the ODS is quite up-to-date; there is very little, if any, archival data found in it. If, for whatever application need, archival data is found in the ODS, it is never more than a few days old (or at most, an accounting cycle's worth of data). If the designer finds that data older than a few days is being placed in the ODS, the question needs to be asked, Why?

## *Detailed*

Data in the ODS serves the operational community and as such is kept at a detailed level. In most cases, storing detailed data is straightforward and easy, but in other cases, what constitutes detailed data is not clear. For example, suppose that a corporate executive wants to look at the collective account status of an international customer that is found in the ODS. The collective account balance of the corporate customer is calculated as the result of many individual account balances (which are constantly changing).

In that sense, the ODS collective account balance is very much a calculated piece of information. However, in the eyes of the corporate executive, the col-

---

### THE ODS: A TRANSITORY STRUCTURE?

There have been some suggestions that the ODS is a transitory structure. Some database theoreticians have even suggested that there may be no need for an ODS. I beg to differ on both counts.

The ODS is as permanent a structure as a data warehouse, a legacy application, or any of the other forms of architecture. The great charm of the ODS is that it is integrated and that it can support both decision support and operational transaction processing. As long as there is a need for operational integration there will be ODSs. And as long as there is a need for the hybrid capabilities of transaction processing coupled with DSS analytical processing, there will be ODSs. If, by some chance, an organization does not have those capabilities, then an ODS may be a transitory structure. But organizations universally need the kinds of capabilities provided by an ODS.

Another alternative suggested is to build ODS functionality into a data warehouse or into the legacy applications themselves. Neither of these alternatives are acceptable for any amount of industrial data and processing. An ODS cannot simply be appended onto a data warehouse. An ODS entails very complex and intricate technologies that mandate that transaction processing be mixed with analytical processing. This mixture is very difficult to accommodate under the relatively heavy loads of data and processing that pass through the ODS. When the volumes of data found in a data warehouse are placed inside an ODS, the result is a functionally unworkable technology.

The other alternative is to attempt to construct an ODS in the legacy application environment. This too is an unworkable alternative. Once an application is written and is used for some of the processing done in the corporation, that application simply cannot be extended to include a very different view of the world. In order to reshape the application to make it hospitable to the ODS, key structures, definitions of data, data layouts, calculations, reference tables, etc., all have to be completely redone. In a word, the application must be rewritten from scratch to allow the ODS to be integrated into it.

While it is true that not all organizations need an ODS and while it is also true that some organizations need an ODS to an extent far less than other structures, there nevertheless is a need for an ODS. And once the ODS is built and in full operation, the odds of the ODS disappearing are slim to none.

lective account balance is a single piece of information that is constantly changing. From the perspective of the end user—the corporate executive—the collective account balance of the international company is very much a detailed piece of data. (Said another way, what may be detailed to one community may well be summary to another community.) Furthermore, even though the decisions that result from the data in the ODS are being made at the executive level, they are nonetheless operational decisions. Thus the ODS represents a uniform collective view of data.

## Comparing the Data Warehouse and the Operational Data Store

The ODS is similar to the data warehouse in some respects, but is very different from it in other respects. The ODS and the data warehouse are *identical* when it comes to being subject oriented and integrated. There are no discernible differences between the two constructs with regard to those characteristics. However, when it comes to volatility, currency of information, and detail, the ODS and the data warehouse are very different. Data in the ODS is subject to change every time one of its underlying details changes. If an ODS represents a collective bank account for a large international customer, then every time any of the customer's individual bank accounts change, the collective account changes as well. In the case of a data warehouse, changes are created by taking a snapshot. Each snapshot is placed in line with other snapshots, creating an historical record of data.

The second way that the ODS and the data warehouse diametrically differ is in the currency of data. The ODS contains very fresh and current data. In most cases, there is no archival data whatsoever. If archival data must be placed in the ODS, it must be very current. For example, an ODS designer may place data that is no older than 24 hours in an ODS for reasons known only to the designer, but nowhere would data of any significant age be found in an ODS. The data warehouse, on the other hand, contains data that is rich in history. The data warehouse contains data that may be as much as 10 years old.

The third major difference between the ODS and the data warehouse lies in the summary data that is found in each. The ODS contains data that is detailed, while the data warehouse contains much summary data. (For an in-depth discussion of the different kinds of summary data, refer to the Prism Solutions Tech Topic on summary data listed in the Reference section of this book.) Of course, data in the ODS can be summarized, and a summarized value can be calculated. But because the summarized value is subject to immediate change, it has a short effective life. Such summary data is called "dynamic summary data."

Summary data that is found in the data warehouse, on the other hand, is data that is static. Because it is static, it can be (and often is) stored for long periods of time. This difference in the types of summary data found in the data warehouse and the ODS thus forms the third major difference between the two environments.

There are many other ways to think about the differences between an ODS and a data warehouse. Perhaps the most profound way to envision the differences is in terms of basic record update. Figure 1.12 shows the fundamental difference between the two environments.

When an ODS needs to be updated, a simple update is made to a single record. Throughout the day, as updates are made, a single record is the repository for all activity. Updates are made in the normal way, where a value of data is altered as a result of the update. In the data warehouse, there is a very different approach in that when it comes time to alter a record, a new snapshot is created. In such a manner, an historical record is kept.

As an example of the differences between an ODS and a data warehouse, consider a customer address record. On January 1 a customer lives at 14 High Street; this is shown in the ODS record. In the data warehouse, there is a very similar record which looks like

```
Jan 1 to present - 14 High Street
```

On March 25 the bank discovers that the customer has changed her address to Apt B, Austin, TX. In the ODS the customer record now looks like

```
Apt B, Austin, TX.
```

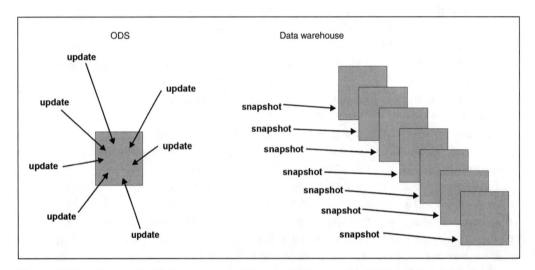

**Figure 1.12**   One of the other important differences between the ODS and the data warehouse is that of update versus snapshots.

But the ODS contains two records:

```
Jan 1 to Mar 24 - 14 High Street
Mar 25 to present - Apt B, Austin, TX
```

On October 10 the customer moves again—this time to 8913 Dirk, El Paso, TX. There is now one record in the ODS which shows 8913 Dirk, El Paso, TX. In the data warehouse there are three records:

```
Jan 1 to Mar 24 - 14 High Street
Mar 25 to Oct 9 - Apt B, Austin, TX
Oct 10 to present - 8913 Dirk, El Paso, TX
```

Therefore, there is a very fundamental difference in the way the update is handled between the data warehouse and the ODS.

# Two Types of ODS

There are two distinct types of ODS: commercial and custom built. Both types of ODS are common and both can exist in the same environment at the same time.

## Commercial ODSs

Commercial ODSs include such popular software packages as SAP, Oracle Financials, PeopleSoft, JD Edwards, and BAAN. There is a good reason for the popularity of the commercial implementation of ODS. Consider the state of many shops prior to the advent of these software packages. Many companies had a motley collection of applications which were unintegrated and had many deficiencies. For the longest time organizations thought that they were going to replace their older, shop-worn applications, so these organizations tried modeling, they tried reengineering, and they tried strategic planning. But the older applications lived on, despite the best attempts to get rid of them. At some point organizations came to realize that it was no simple matter to replace an old established application, whatever its faults.

Finally there was a change in strategies. Instead of attempting to replace old applications, organizations found it was easier to create an operational data store and feed the ODS from the older applications. By building the ODS, the organization could satisfy many needs without having to replace an old application. In some cases there actually was a replacement of older systems. In other cases there was no replacement. Two characteristics of commercial ODSs are that they take a long time to implement and that they are brittle, that is, they have a set of rigid requirements to which the organization must adhere.

## SAP

The most widespread of the commercial ODS is Germany's SAP. SAP began as a financial application package primarily for manufacturers. Today SAP's applications extend well beyond financial applications into shipment scheduling and routing, freight cost management, shipment processing, inbound/outbound processing, aerospace and defense, banking, chemicals, consumer products, engineering and construction, health care, insurance, metal, paper, wood, pharmaceuticals, public sector, real estate, retail, service provider, telecommunications, transportation, utilities, and others. SAP consists of one or more base modules that are then attached to (or provide a foundation for) other modules such as real-time enterprise management of data, data warehousing, and so forth. SAP's architecture is a classical ODS. There are elements of class I, II, and III ODS found in SAP.

SAP has announced a separate data warehouse facility that operates on all of the ODS components with tight integration of SAP application data and SAP's data warehouse. There are alternative strategies for getting to and using SAP data from independent vendors such as the SAS solution and D2K, among others.

SAP operates on standard database management system packages such as Oracle, SQL Server, and others. In addition SAP operates in both the UNIX and the NT environment. Several versions of SAP are available, depending on the environment that is needed. R/3 is the newest version of SAP's application/ODS technology. R/3 operates on client/server technology. R/2 is SAP's earlier technology which operates on mainframe technology.

Regardless of the release or version of SAP, the core of SAP is an ODS, with interfaces to other architectural entities such as data warehouses and data marts. One of the challenges of SAP as an ODS is the accessing and movement of data out of SAP. SAP's standard interface is something called BAPI. The ability to use BAPI for all the needs of the warehouse and ODS environment is questionable because of the gross inflexibility of the interface.

## Other Commercial Products

There are of course other ERP packages that have elements of an ODS. In the financial arena there is Oracle Financials. In the general application space is BAAN. In the general application AS400 space is JD Edwards. And in the personnel and human resources space is PeopleSoft. Each of these packages have their own idiosyncrasies as an ODS. Some packages make no distinction between an ODS and a baseline application. Other packages have only a limited scope of functionality. Almost all of the packages are easier to implement and allow easier access to their data than SAP.

## Custom-Built ODSs

The other type of ODS is one that is custom built. In this case the organization strikes out and builds its own ODS, going through design, programming, implementation, and installation. Given that the organization has complete control of the requirements going into the ODS, there is no problem with fitting the organization's needs to the ODS. However, the organization faces the challenges of designing the ODS and creating the infrastructure, two formidable challenges.

# Dynamic Data

One of the salient features of the ODS environment is that it contains what can be termed dynamic data. There are several ways in which data is dynamic in the ODS environment. The first sense is that data in the ODS is subject to change. Of course, just because it is subject to change does not mean that it will necessarily change. However, it is possible for any value in the ODS to be altered by a transaction. The transaction may enter the ODS directly or the transaction may come from the operational environment. In any case, there is a certain dynamism to the data found in an ODS.

Contrast the dynamism of data in the ODS with the historical nature of data in the data warehouse. In the data warehouse, when changes need to be made they are made by means of a snapshot. As an example of the fundamental differences in data between the ODS and the data warehouse, consider an ODS record that shows that Bill Inmon has a balance of $832 in his bank account. The ODS receives a transaction that shows that Bill Inmon now has $961 in his account. The record is changed in the ODS as quickly as possible.

Now consider the same type of activity in a data warehouse. In a data warehouse, there is a record showing that Bill Inmon has an account balance of $832 in his account as of November 15. A record is entered into the data warehouse on November 19 showing that Bill Inmon now has a balance of $961. A record is written in the data warehouse showing that as of November 19 Bill's balance is $961. The difference is that the data warehouse contains snapshot information. An historical record is made of activities in the data warehouse. As such, data warehouse data is static. But ODS data contains up-to-the-second accurate information. In the ODS there is no historical record of the activity of an account. Therefore data in the ODS can be updated and as a consequence is dynamic.

Another way that data is dynamic in the ODS environment is through the calculation and creation of dynamic summary data. Dynamic summary data is data whose accuracy depends on the moment of calculation. One value is calculated at 8:13 A.M. and another value is calculated at 3:58 P.M. One cannot use dynamic summary data without making reference to the moment of calculation.

Dynamic summary data that is found in the ODS is in contrast to static summary data which is found in the data warehouse. Static summary data is summary data whose value does not vary with the moment of calculation. On Monday the boss asks how much departmental expenses were for last month. The answer is created. Then, for reasons known only to the boss, the boss asks that the same calculation be made on Friday. The answer comes out the same as it did on Monday. Changing the day the calculation is made does not affect the outcome of the calculation when the calculation is made on static data.

## Summary

There has been a predictable progression from the early applications that were developed up to the point of the building of the operational data store. Driving the progression is the desire to get information out of an existing older legacy base of information. In the early days, reports were written. Then, interfaces between applications were created. Next, extracts were created along with the usage of 4GLs. PCs were added, as well as communications and sophisticated software. The net result was a technological mess. Organizations discovered that a fundamental change in architectures was the only effective way to address the problem. Soon, the data warehouse was created; but it was good for only the informational aspects of processing. For organizations desiring to achieve operational integration, the data warehouse did nothing. Thus was born the architectural entity known as the operational data store. The ODS is subject oriented, integrated, volatile, current valued, and detailed.

**CHAPTER**

**2**

# The Corporate Information Factory

The ODS, data warehouse, and older legacy applications combine to create a common architecture that can be called a "corporate information factory." Figure 2.1 shows the most common form of the corporate information factory.

## Corporate Information Factory

Figure 2.1 shows that raw, detailed data is put into the corporate information factory by means of data capture, entry, and transaction interaction with older legacy applications. The raw, detailed data is integrated and transformed and then passed into the ODS or the current detail level of the data warehouse. As the refined data passes out of the ODS it goes into the current level of the data warehouse. Once the refined data is summarized, it passes from the current detail level of the data warehouse into the summarized level of data, that is, the data marts, in the data warehouse. Informational processing can be done throughout—at the ODS level, at the current level of detail, or at the data mart level of detail. The corporate information factory provides the context and infrastructure in which the ODS resides and interacts with the other components of the architecture. As will be discussed in this chapter, there are variations in the corporate information factory. The corporate information factory that has been described is in its most general state, as shown in Figure 2.1.

In some cases, the corporate information factory has an ODS and a data warehouse. In other cases, the corporate information factory has only a data ware-

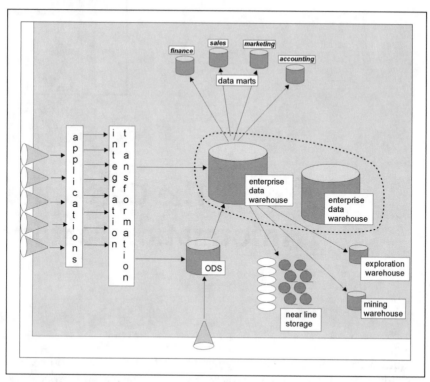

**Figure 2.1** The corporate "information factory" " of which the ODS and data warehouse are a prominent part.

house. When there is an ODS there is always a data warehouse, but the converse is not true. The flow of data from the older legacy systems environment within the context of the corporate information factory is illustrated in Figure 2.2. In one case, data flows from the applications into the data warehouse. In the other case, data flows from the applications into the ODS, then once it is in the ODS, the refined data flows into the data warehouse. Both flows of data are normal and acceptable. Based on the simple lines of flow that have been described, the two most common forms of the corporate information factory are shown in Figure 2.3.

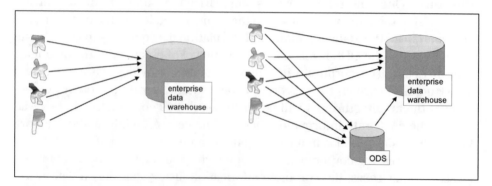

**Figure 2.2** The normal flow of data in the different environments.

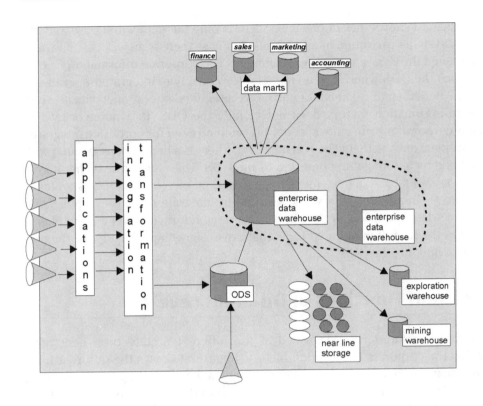

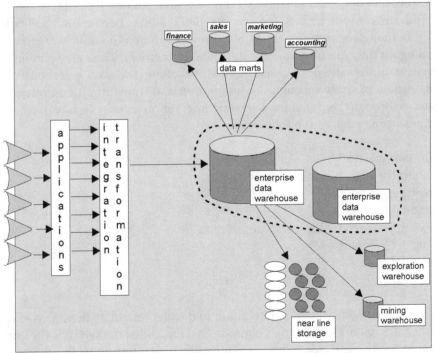

**Figure 2.3**  Two variations on the same theme—both are valid architectures.

Figure 2.3 shows that in one case there is only the data warehouse and the legacy systems environment and in the other case there is an ODS, a data warehouse, and the legacy systems environment. The corporate information factory includes the ODS where there is a need for collective, integrated operational data. Where there is no need for corporate integrated operational data, the corporate information factory does not include the ODS. It is noteworthy that many corporations run quite successfully with no need for corporate integrated operational data. In that vein, it is noted that there is a high cost associated with the building and ongoing operation of the ODS. The underlying technology—hardware, database management system, and so on—of the ODS is typically expensive. In addition, the work required to integrate the legacy application system's data into a cohesive, collective integrated form is never easy or cheap, even in the face of automated tools that are designed specifically for the purpose of building the ODS.

## Different Functions at Different Levels

Different functions are performed at the different architectural constructs within the corporate information factory. Figure 2.4 shows the different functions that are found at different levels of data and processing. The application layer of the corporate information factory serves the purpose of collecting raw data, editing that data, and performing the basic and routine function of interacting with the customer. Once the raw detailed data has been edited and collected, it is then prepared for entry into the ODS and/or the data warehouse (depending on the type of corporate information factory). The entry and integration of data into the operational data store and/or the data warehouse is done by means of going through the integration and transformation layer. As data passes through the transformation and integration layer, a variety of transformations occur, such as the following:

Reformatting data
Changing the key structure of data
Converting data
Recalculating data
Choosing between multiple sources of data
Changing technologies
Summarizing data
Filtering data

After the raw detailed data is integrated and transformed, it then passes to either the ODS and/or the data warehouse. As data passes to the ODS, the corporation is able to use the data in an operationally integrated, collective manner.

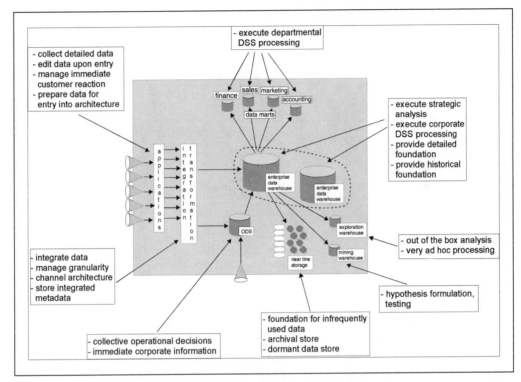

**Figure 2.4** The different kinds of functions that are fulfilled by the various components of the architecture.

The ODS is the architectural construct that enables operational, integrated corporate information processing to occur. Refined, integrated data passes into the data warehouse from both the ODS and the integration/transformation layer. Once the integrated data enters the data warehouse, classical informational processing is enabled. At the higher levels of summarization of the data warehouse, management-level analysis and reporting occurs.

# Different Functions in Different Components

Different functions occur at different places within the corporate information factory. Another way to understand the fundamental differences between the data and the processing that occur at each architectural construct of the corporate information factory is in terms of typical transactions and activities that are executed at each level. Figure 2.5 depicts the different types of activities that occur throughout the information factory.

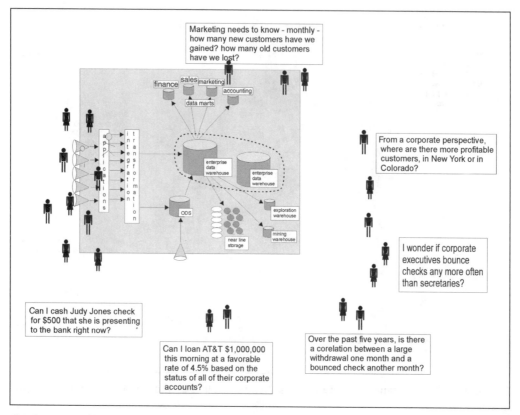

**Figure 2.5** Different types of questions are answered at different places in the corporate information factory.

At the direct customer interaction level, individual customers engage in detailed and up-to-the-second transactions with the bank using online applications. During the direct customer interaction, it is determined whether a check can be cashed for an individual customer—Judy Jones.

At the ODS level, an entirely different kind of interaction occurs. Here the online operational collective account for a large customer—AT&T—is managed. A corporate officer decides on the interest rate to be given to AT&T based on the collective balance and status of *all* of AT&T's accounts as of the instant the decision is made. The analyses and decisions made here are up to the second, operational in nature, and collective.

The current detailed data of the data warehouse is used for yet another purpose, that of ad hoc analysis of the branch banks. The analyses and the decisions made here are long term and strategic in nature.

At the historical summary level of the corporate information factory data is used for even higher, longer-term functions. Identifying and analyzing patterns of data are typical analyses done here, such as the determination of the common profile that emerges among customers that leave the bank. There are, then, very different functions and communities of interest being satisfied at the various levels of the corporate information factory.

# Redundancy of Data

One of the comments typically made when a person first looks at the flow of data within the corporate information factory is that apparently there is much redundancy of data. Such is not the case at all, but the lack of redundancy is hardly apparent at first glance. Figure 2.6 illustrates the flow of data from one corporate information factory component to another.

Data is originally entered into the factory in a detailed, raw state. Once the data passes through the applications and into the integration/transformation layer (where a significant transformation of data occurs), the data enters the ODS. Figure 2.6 shows that only very fresh data finds its way into the ODS. Once the data ages more than a few days in the ODS, the data is moved to the

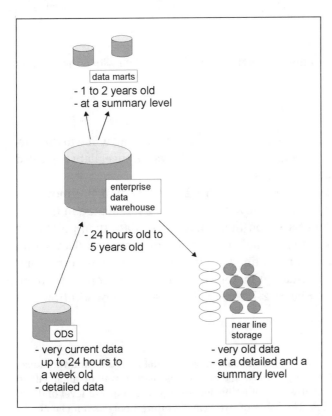

**Figure 2.6**   From the standpoint of timeliness and detail of data, there is little or no overlap among the different architectural constructs.

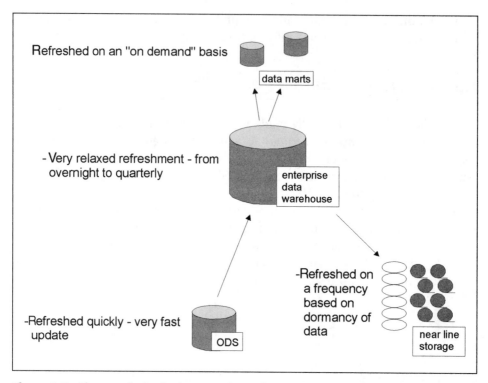

Refreshed on an "on demand" basis

data marts

- Very relaxed refreshment - from overnight to quarterly

enterprise data warehouse

-Refreshed on a frequency based on dormancy of data

near line storage

-Refreshed quickly - very fast update

ODS

**Figure 2.7**    The speed of refreshment reflects the timeliness of data within the different constructs of the architecture.

data warehouse current level of detail. The data ages for a long while in the current level of detail—up to two years*. From the data warehouse, data is passed to the data mart on an as needed basis.

After the data is no longer needed in the current level of detail, it is moved to archival storage and/or the data mart levels of storage, as indicated in the diagram. The movement of data based on the timeliness of data then points out that indeed there is an absolute minimal amount of redundancy of data within the corporate information factory. In line with the age of data within the components of the corporate information factory is the reconstitution and replenishment cycle of the data. Figure 2.7 shows the rate of reconstitution and

*The length of time the detailed data ages in the current level of detail of the data warehouse is a function of the business of the enterprise. Some businesses need current detailed data to contain data no more than six months old. Other businesses need the current level of detail to contain data as old as 10 years. The value of two years is offered only as a mean across many lines of business.

replenishment for the operational data store and the current level of detail of the data warehouse.

In most cases, data is moved into the ODS very quickly, but it is moved into the current level of detail of the data warehouse on a relaxed basis. The movement of data and the reconstitution and replenishment of the different levels relate to the timeliness of the data found in the various components of the corporate information factory.

One of the anomalies of the diagram of the corporate information factory is that the components are not at all drawn to scale. If the components of the corporate information factory were drawn to scale, they would look something like the components shown in Figure 2.8, which shows that the ODS contains a relatively small volume of data, certainly very little data in comparison with the current level of detail. The data marts are smaller than the current level of detail but larger than the ODS. And the current level of detail contains a huge amount of data.

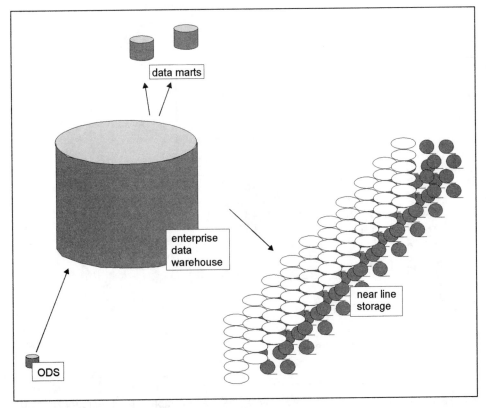

**Figure 2.8**   The different components of the architecture drawn to scale.

# The Integration/Transformation Layer

One of the interesting aspects of the corporate information factory is that of the integration/transformation layer. The integration/transformation layer is the mechanism that allows the detailed applications to communicate with the ODS and the data warehouse. The integration/transformation layer consists of code, data, procedures, and metadata. When the ODS and the data warehouse are being supported by the world of old, unintegrated systems, the integration/transformation layer is complex, as seen in Figure 2.9.

The sheer number of interfaces going into and out of the integration/transformation layer presents its own problems and adds to the complexity of that layer. The age of the older legacy applications and the fact that the applications were never designed with integration as a priority also contribute mightily to the complexity of the interface. Yet another complicating factor is the mixture of software packages along with custom in-house applications. All of these factors add up to a very complex interface between old legacy systems and ODS and data warehouses. But when the application component of the corporate

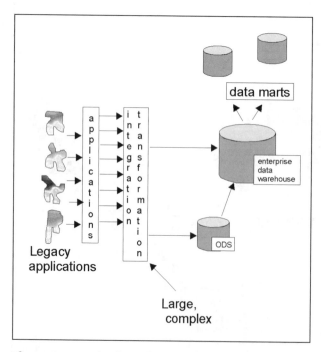

**Figure 2.9**  In the face of many old, unintegrated applications, the integration/transformation process is large and complex.

information factory is highly integrated (an infrequent occurrence at best!), where the applications are subject oriented and highly integrated, then the integration/transformation layer is straightforward and relatively simple, as shown in Figure 2.10.

Of course, where integration is achieved, there is the issue of maintaining integration over time as well. Even where the complexity of the application interface is not an issue, there is the issue of the volume and speed of movement of data through the integration/transformation mechanism.

In some circles, there is the notion that if the application layer is subject oriented and integrated then the integration/transformation layer is not needed. Such is not the case at all. The integration/transformation layer is needed even if the application layer is perfectly integrated. Much more occurs in the integration/transformation layer than straightforward integration, for instance:

The changing of technology

The summarization of data

The routing of data for movement to the ODS or the data warehouse

The creation of the metadata infrastructure

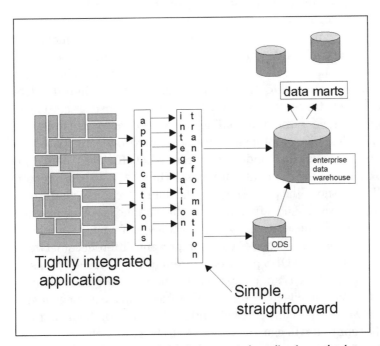

**Figure 2.10**  In the face of tightly integrated applications, the integration/transformation layer is relatively simple.

## Differences in Technology

Using conventional technology when the different components of the corporate information factory are built, different platforms are used for each of the different components. In such a manner, the very different operating characteristics of the various components can be accommodated, and any given component can be optimized for the type of processing that occurs on it. However, on occasion the ODS and the data warehouse may be built on the same technological platform. When the ODS and the data warehouse are built on the same platform, the technology that houses them is internally separated by what can be termed "firewalls." The data that is physically housed on one side of the firewall serves one environment and the data that sits on the other side of the firewall serves the other environment. As long as there is the firewall separation of the data, then it is possible for a single technology to serve both ODS and data warehouse purposes. Using conventional technology, it is not normally a good idea to physically combine the ODS and the data warehouse on the same platform.

One reason why the ODS and the data warehouse do not combine well on conventional technology is the significant difference in the requirements for underlying technology needed to support the ODS and the data warehouse. A conventional technological platform is able to optimize one set of tasks. When a platform attempts to optimize on diametrically opposed sets of tasks at the same time, it ends up being nonoptimal for any task.

Figure 2.11 illustrates some of the basic differences in the requirements for technology that underlie each of the various environments found in the corporate information factory. It also shows that the world of the data warehouse is a world of load and access technology. Data is periodically loaded into the data warehouse. Once loaded there, it is accessed. General-purpose, record-level update is not normally done within the confines of the technology that houses the data warehouse. The absence of general-purpose, record-level update processing makes data warehouse load-and-access processing efficient. There is no need for log tapes or journaling in a data warehouse. There is no need for record locking or COMMITs. In short, the processing on the data warehouse platform is very simple, straightforward, and efficient. But the simplicity of processing within the data warehouse does not end with the absence of a need for a high-level of integrity of database processing. Other important differences between data warehouse processing and ODS processing are that the physical blocks of data can be loaded so that there is no freespace in the data warehouse. (Since no update will occur, no space needs to be reserved for future space management.) And data in the data warehouse can be heavily indexed since no individual transaction update will occur that will cause the indexes to be rewritten.

In addition, the data in the data warehouse can be organized to accommodate the large transactions that will be used to read and analyze it. It is normal

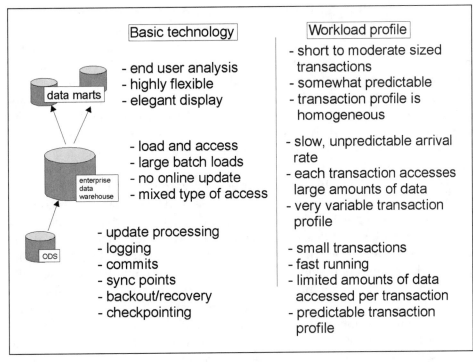

**Figure 2.11**  The technological requirements for the various environments are very different.

for a single data warehouse transaction to issue tens of thousands of calls (or more!), something that would never be accommodated in an ODS. The workload that is formed by transactions also constitutes a major difference between the technological requirements in the ODS and the data warehouse. The data warehouse typically has a very variable workload run against it. The transactions that run against the data warehouse are of the very large variety. It is normal for as many as 10 million records to be read during a data warehouse transaction. In addition, the transactions vary in size radically within the data warehouse. The variability of the size of the transactions and the variability of the rate at which the transactions arrive at the processor form another difference between the technological requirements of the data warehouse and the ODS.

Still another (and perhaps most important) reason why the data warehouse and the ODS requirements don't mix well technologically speaking is that the ODS requires a physical organization optimal to the flexible update processing of data and the data warehouse requires a physical organization optimal to the flexible access of data. Normally optimizing flexibility of the physical organization of data implies that data of like varieties is physically aggregated. (In other words, the data is normalized.) Data in the ODS—where transaction access efficiency is optimized—is organized quite differently physically. In the ODS, data is organized so that efficient access may be made on an individual transaction basis. This entails bringing together some of the data in an eclectic collection of data in a single physical unit; the exact opposite physical organization of data that is optimal for the data warehouse. (In this case, the data is physically denormalized.) And at the end of the day, data can physically be organized in only one of two ways, either optimally for the data warehouse or optimally for the ODS. Yet, other data in the ODS retains its normalized structure if it is not being regularly accessed. For these reasons (and plenty more that are not mentioned here), the underlying technology that is optimal in the support of the data warehouse is very different from the underlying technology required to support the ODS.

The ODS is typified by general-purpose, record-level update processing, where many transactions have a need to access the ODS and update records in it with no chance of an integrity conflict. For this reason, ODS processing must be managed with a high degree of locking, COMMITs, and checkpointing. The transaction profile in the ODS during the peak period day is very stable. The peak period transaction accesses a small number of units of data—typically from 2 to 10 units of data. Furthermore, the pattern of arrival in the ODS environment during peak period is reasonably uniform, with predictable peaks and valleys. From the standpoint of internal physical data organization, the ODS requires that different types of data commonly related by a single key value be physically stored in a single physical location in order to make performance acceptable.

# Near-Line Storage

One of the most useful components of the corporate information factory is that of near-line storage. Figure 2.12 illustrates the extension of data past disk storage onto optical or tape storage. At some point data warehouses grow large, while the actual amount of usage shrinks, thus introducing dormant data into the equation. When a warehouse contains essentially idle data (or at least a large portion of idle data), it makes sense to push much of the data off to other storage media. In doing so, two very beneficial things happen to the warehouse: the cost of the warehouse shrinks dramatically and performance in the warehouse gets better.

One issue that arises when moving data off to near-line storage is what to do about queries that need to access data that is stored off to both disk storage and near-line storage. Another issue is how does an administrator determine what data is safe to move from disk storage to near-line storage. Yet another issue is when does a company move data backup to disk storage. Despite these issues, the cost benefit of moving some of the data found in the data warehouse environment to near-line storage far outweighs simply stacking data on disk storage indefinitely.

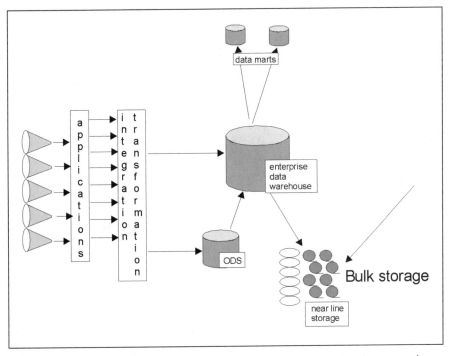

**Figure 2.12**   The near-line component of the data warehouse is an important but passive part of the corporate information factory.

## Other Architectural Constructs

The exploration warehouse shown in Figure 2.13 is an architectural structure designed for very ad hoc queries. When the data warehouse infrastructure is up and running, there is seldom room and capacity for data exploration.

When an analyst engages in "out of the box" thinking, the data warehouse resources are continually too busy to allow the analyst the capacity to prove or disprove the hypotheses that are of interest. In order to provide an opportunity for the analyst to do analysis, a separate exploration warehouse is created.

The exploration warehouse is usually physically much smaller than the actual data warehouse. There are two reasons for this:

- Only subsets of data are needed for the exploration warehouse.
- Exploration warehouses are usually housed in nonrelational technology, such as token-based or "in memory" technology, that allows data to be stored very compactly.

Because of the reduced volume of data in an exploration warehouse, queries are able to be run very quickly. The exploration warehouse is usually quickly

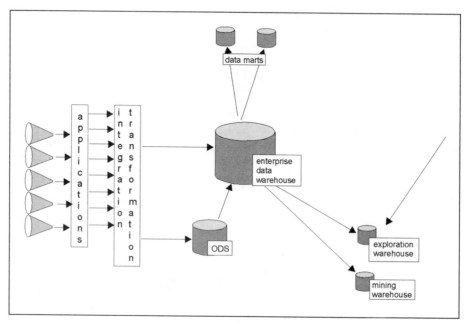

**Figure 2.13**   The exploration and mining component of the corporate information factory.

created on a temporary basis and is able to be re-created very quickly so that the analyst is free to do iterative analysis.

A second, related architectural structure found in the DSS environment is that of the data mining data warehouse. The data mining data warehouse is similar in content and purpose to the exploration warehouse, the primary difference being the exploration warehouse is used for truly random thinking and analysis, while the data mining warehouse is used for the proof or disproof of a single thought where many different sets of data are analysed based on the same or very similar hypotheses. In other words, the same data is used in an exploration warehouse to analyze many different hypotheses. But in a data mining data warehouse the reverse is true. In a data mining warehouse many sets of data are analyzed in relation to a single hypothesis.

A third interesting component of the corporate information factory is that of multiple enterprise data warehouses. Figure 2.14 depicts multiple enterprise data warehouses. Multiple enterprise data warehouses appear when

- A company is widely dispersed geographically
- A company has very diverse product lines
- A company is very large

Multiple enterprise data warehouses present both opportunity and challenge. With multiple enterprise data warehouses a company can truly map its data to its business. But in creating multiple enterprise data warehouses there is the possibility of data overlap. As long as data overlap is of the key/foreign

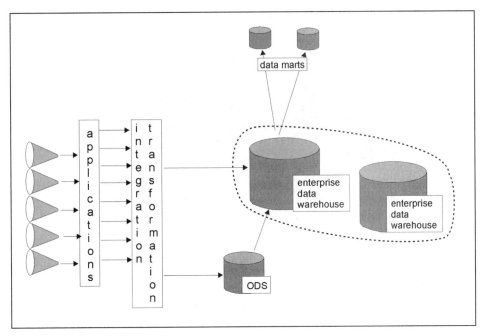

**Figure 2.14**   In some environments there are multiple enterprise data warehouses.

key variety, then there is no problem. But when the overlap in a multiple enterprise data warehouse is of the nonkey/foreign key variety, then there is a real potential for problems. In addition, when there are multiple enterprise data warehouses, secondary databases, such as reference tables, become a challenge to manage across different environments.

## What Happens to Legacy Applications?

Over time it is natural for complicated legacy systems environments to be rewritten and replaced. The corporate information factory is the architecture that results from the eventual rewrite and replacement of the production environment. Figure 2.15 shows the legacy systems environment being replaced over time, a step at a time, by the corporate information factory.

Part of the older legacy application goes to the data warehouse. Typically data that is summarized and data that is old—six months or more—is placed in the data warehouse. In addition, reports that are produced for management find their way into the data warehouse. The removal of summary data and old archival data, and the removal of massive amounts of reporting have the effect of greatly simplifying and streamlining the production/legacy environment. Figure 2.15 illustrates the effect of building the data warehouse from the legacy systems environment.

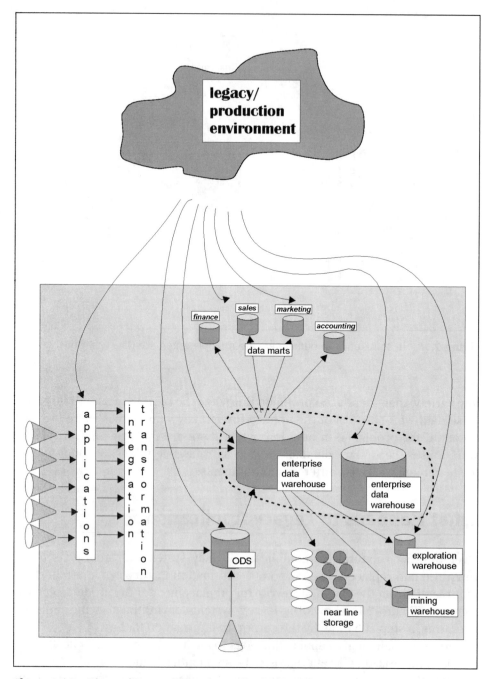

**Figure 2.15**  Dismantling an old legacy application in order to create the corporate information factory.

In fact, the legacy environment is so streamlined and simplified by the building and populating of the data warehouse that the building of the data warehouse is considered to be the precursor to successful reengineering of the legacy environment. Because of its very salubrious effect, building the data warehouse is usually the first step in going from the legacy systems environment to the corporate information factory.

The second step in the dismantling of the legacy environment is the building of the ODS, if an ODS is to be built at all. The ODS will contain collective integrated data and will be used for corporate integrated decisions. In almost all cases, the ODS will *not* contain the edit, capture, and direct end-user interface. (This topic will be discussed later in this book.) The ODS is usually built after the data warehouse is well under way. As in the case of the data warehouse, the building of the ODS has the effect of greatly simplifying the legacy environment. After the ODS is designed and populated (assuming that the ODS is built at all), the front-end collection and editing application systems are now in a position to be integrated. The progression of development of the data warehouse and the ODS is seen in Figure 2.16.

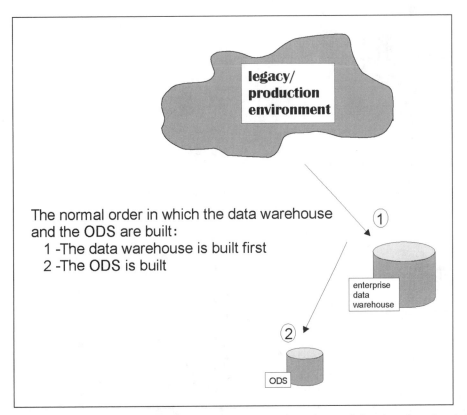

**Figure 2.16** By building the data warehouse first, the volume of data is reduced and the workload is greatly simplified and streamlined.

Figure 2.17 shows that each construction of the different components of the corporate information factory has a profound and healthy effect on the management of the production/legacy systems environment. Not until the data warehouse and the ODS have been built will the legacy systems environment be

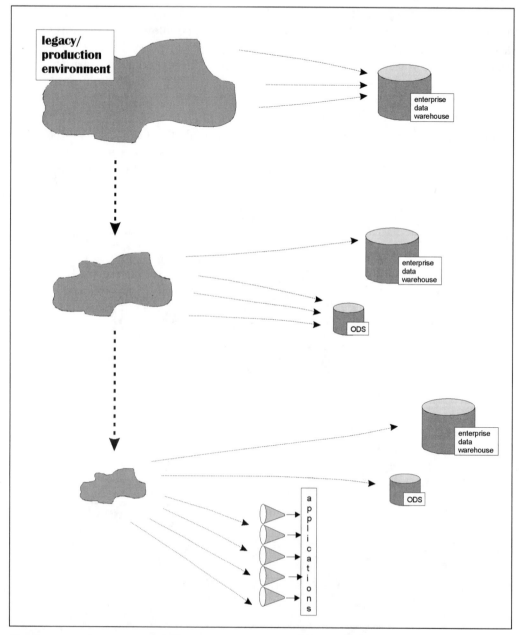

**Figure 2.17**   The recommended sequence of building for the different components of the corporate information factory environment.

reduced to a point of smallness and simplicity of data and processing that the production environment will be able to be effectively integrated.

# Building the ODS Before Building the Data Warehouse

Under most conditions it is normal to build the data warehouse before the ODS is built because data is integrated, there is a minimal amount of data, and the workflow is streamlined. Is it possible to build the ODS first? It indeed is possible to build the ODS first, but there are some pitfalls the designer should be aware of.

- If you are going to build the ODS first, you need to make sure that you understand where the separation between the ODS and the data warehouse is. When you build the ODS first there is the temptation to incorporate much of the data warehouse into the ODS.

- If you are going to build the ODS first, you need to mentally prepare management for the length of time from the onset of development to the moment when tangible results are obtained. An ODS requires a long development cycle in order for there to be payback. A data warehouse requires the minimal amount of time in order to show payback.

# Corporate Information Factory and Metadata/Metaprocess

One of the interesting aspects of the corporate information factory is that the entire environment is intellectually unified by a single data model. Figure 2.18 shows the unifying effect of the enterprise data model with regard to the corporate information factory.

The enterprise data model sets the stage for how the different components of the corporate information factory are to be shaped and related. The enterprise data model is translated into several forms of metadata. The metadata, in its several forms, is then used as a basis for design for the data warehouse, the ODS, and the integrated edit and collection applications. The enterprise data model then provides the basis for a cohesive and unified view of the components of the corporate information factory.

In addition to the corporate information factory requiring metadata, the corporate information factory also requires metaprocess information. Metaprocess information applies to the processing that is done in the ODS and the legacy systems (or capture and edit) processing. The metaprocess information identifies and codifies the repetitive activities that surround the corporate

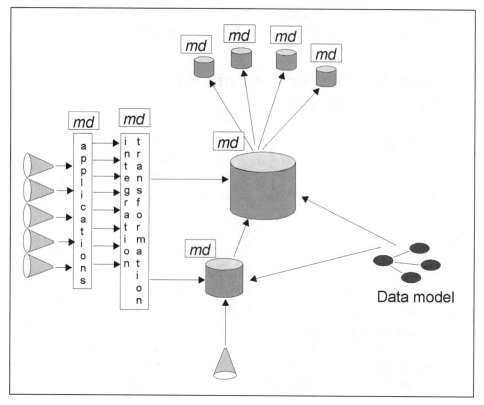

**Figure 2.18**    The role of the data model and metadata in the corporate information factory.

information factory. The metaprocess model in conjunction with the metadata model defines the unified information paradigm that serves as a roadmap for the data and system architect.

## Data Marts and the ODS

One of the interesting architectural constructs of the corporate information factory is that of the data mart. As a rule data marts sit above data warehouses. The data marts are fed data exclusively from the data warehouse. Data marts take on a very departmental (e.g., finance, sales, marketing) flavor.

The question is often asked, Do data marts fit with an ODS? If a data mart fits neatly and naturally with a data warehouse, why wouldn't the data mart fit with an ODS? The answer is that a data mart can be made to fit with an ODS, but the fit is not a comfortable one. The data mart can be force fit inside the confines of an ODS, but the result is a very unhappy marriage.

There are a variety of reasons why data marts do not fit well with an ODS. Perhaps the most important reason is that an ODS contains units of data that are in constant motion. Just because data can be lifted from an ODS and put into a data mart does not mean that the data will remain stable. When data is placed inside a data mart that has come from the ODS, the data is accurate and meaningful *only* as of the instant that the movement of data was made. In other words, suppose a data mart has pulled data from an ODS as of 2:15 P.M. on a Wednesday afternoon. The analysis done inside the data mart is relevant and accurate only to 2:15 P.M. The data in the ODS may have changed drastically by 4:12 P.M., to the point that any analysis done by the data mart is invalid. Furthermore, the data mart cannot go back to the ODS and re-create the data as of 2:15 P.M. If a reload of any part of the data is necessary at 5:35 P.M., then *all* of the data from the ODS must be reloaded into the data mart. It is because of this tremendous difference in the understanding of the relevancy of the timeliness of the data that ODS and data marts do not mix well.

Another good reason why data marts and ODS do not mix well is because, during the online day, the ODS does not care to have any long jobs in operation. During primary processing, the ODS is very sensitive to online transaction processing. During these hours, the processing done by the ODS is a series of small, faster running transactions. The ODS simply does not want anyone asking for huge amounts of data during these hours. By the same token, the data mart assumes it can be refreshed on an as needed basis. This "as needed" assumption is true for the world of data warehouses. But this assumption is not true for the ODS environment.

## Summary

The corporate information factory is made up of several components—the ODS, the data warehouse, the integration/transformation layer, and the edit and collection applications. There is a different flow of data throughout the corporate information factory depending on the application and the contents of the information factory. The corporate information factory may or may not contain an ODS, depending on whether there is a need for collective, operational, integrated information. The different components of the corporate information factory serve to fulfill the different information needs of various communities.

Because of the transformation of data that occurs as data passes to the operational data store or the data warehouse and because of the aging of data as it passes from the ODS to the data warehouse, it is said that there is little or no redundancy of data between the data warehouse and the ODS. There is a real difference in the reconstitution and replenishment time for the ODS and the data warehouse.

If the legacy environment is large and unintegrated, then the integration/transformation component will be large and complex. But if the edit and collection environment is integrated, then the integration/transformation component will be very straightforward.

**CHAPTER**

**3**

# Metadata in the ODS Environment

Metadata is data about data. In the case of the ODS, ODS metadata is descriptive information about the data that actually resides in the ODS. In the ODS environment, metadata can include many types of data. Some of those types are illustrated in Figure 3.1.

In Figure 3.1 it is seen that there are two basic categories of metadata: business metadata and technical metadata. Business metadata contains metadata of primary interest to the end user who needs to use the ODS for decision support. Technical metadata is of primary interest to the technical developer and designers as they maintain and update the ODS environment. Technical metadata is of primary use in the operational activities that take place in the ODS. For example, because the ODS environment supports both decision support and operational processing, it is no surprise that the ODS contains a wide variety of metadata types, including

- Table and column descriptions
- Table definitions
- Attribute definitions
- Subject area definitions
- Business entity definitions
- Metrics
- Refreshment scheduling

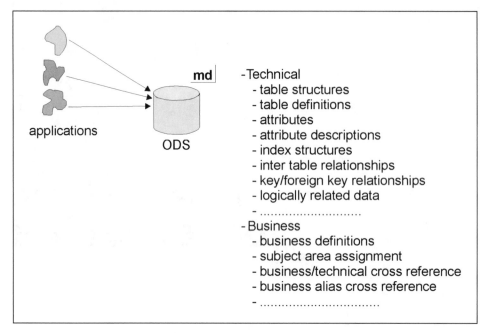

**Figure 3.1** Some likely candidates for ODS metadata.

- Ownership information
- System of record information
- History of changes

Another type of metadata found in the ODS includes business metadata. Business metadata includes metadata useful to the businessperson, not just the technician. Business definitions, business formulas, and business relationships are all forms of business metadata that are sometimes found in the ODS.

Compared to other parts of the DSS environment, data has a short life in its ODS state. But in order to use the ODS environment most effectively, another dimension of data is necessary—that of metadata. Because of the time sensitivity of data that resides in the ODS, it is helpful if the metadata that describes the ODS resides on the same database management system platform that the ODS resides on. There are several reasons for this:

- Any tool that can access the ODS can also access ODS metadata
- The end user can always be directly exposed to the ODS metadata
- There is one less technology to maintain

Thus formed is a "metadata store" on the ODS itself. For example, if the ODS is on Oracle, then the ODS metadata belongs on Oracle as well. Figure 3.2 shows this circumstance.

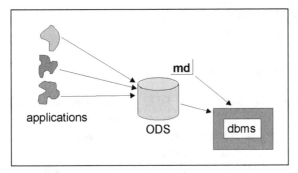

**Figure 3.2**    It helps if the metadata that belongs to the ODS is in the same database management system as the data that resides on the ODS.

# Data Model Metadata

One of the most useful types of metadata found in the ODS environment is that of the data model specifications for the ODS environment. The data model specifications include such things as table descriptions, attribute descriptions, physical descriptions of the attributes, and business descriptions of the tables and attributes. Figure 3.3 shows how the ODS data model contributes metadata to the ODS metadata collection.

The ODS data model simultaneously serves two masters—an operational master and a decision support system master. Serving multiple masters at the same time may cause compromises in design, which need to be well thought out and documented. As a result, designers and end users who come upon the

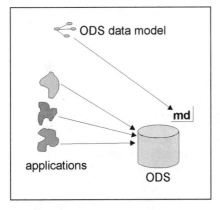

**Figure 3.3**    The information contained in the ODS data model should be reflected in the metadata belonging to the ODS.

ODS well after the ODS has been built and populated will have sufficient documentation of those decisions made at the design stage.

## Different Users of ODS Metadata

Because there is such a dichotomy of usage of the ODS and because the ODS design is usually complicated, there are different communities who will have a vested interest in the metadata that describes the ODS. Both the technical community and the end users will need to view ODS metadata, as seen in Figure 3.4. Typically technical metadata is used in the development process by the technician. End users seldom see technical metadata when doing operational processing. Conversely, end users freely use ODS metadata when doing analytical activities, and the technician is only indirectly involved in using ODS metadata for decision support.

# ODS Metadata Sources

The sources of metadata for the ODS environment are many. Figure 3.5 shows the rich variety of sources of metadata. There are several sources of metadata for the ODS, such as database management system catalogs, tools of automation, metadata exchange standards, free form text, and others. Each of these external sources of metadata may submit their contributions to the metadata store that resides at the ODS.

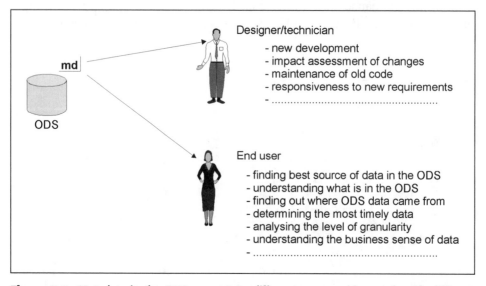

**Figure 3.4**  Metadata in the ODS serves two different communities, each with different agendas.

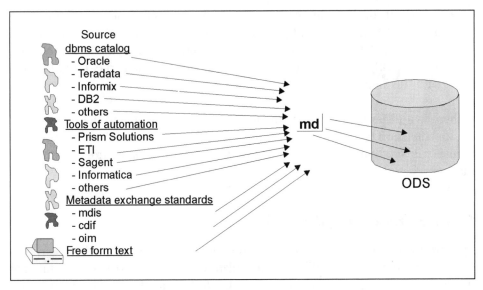

**Figure 3.5** The sources of metadata for the ODS.

The entry of metadata into the ODS metadata store is most often done by an administrator responsible for the ODS metadata. Seldom does the legacy environment volunteer any metadata outside of its environment. Legacy applications do not have metadata useful for the DSS environment for several reasons. The first is that many legacy applications have no metadata to begin with. The applications designer simply never thought metadata was important. Second, even if the legacy environment has metadata, the metadata found there is likely to be useful for administrators and developers. Operational metadata is not designed for end users. However, when crossing over into the DSS environment, metadata is primarily for the end user, not the administrator.

There is a third reason why ODS structures do not have metadata—the classical repository metadata environments do not recognize the existence of an ODS. With these considerations in mind, it is no accident that the legacy environment seldom provides any metadata for the ODS.

## Entering Metadata into the ODS Metadata Store

Metadata may be entered into the ODS metadata store in one of several ways:

- Manually, where the metadata is copied over
- Semiautomatically, where the metadata may be automatically captured then manually entered into the ODS metadata store

- In a synchronized manner, where the manager of the metadata store periodically "wakes up" and goes and gets the metadata from the source, hauls it back to the ODS metadata manager, then compares the metadata in the ODS manager byte for byte with the metadata recently obtained with the metadata in the ODS manager.

If there is a difference in the metadata, then a new version of the metadata is created in the ODS manager. In such a manner the metadata in the ODS manager is kept current with the metadata in the source in a purely automated manner.

## Synchronization of Entry

Synchronization is easily the most interesting of the forms of loading data into the ODS metadata store. With synchronization, there is no need for manual intervention after the metadata has first been described to the ODS metadata store. However, not all sources can be synchronized. Only those sources of metadata that are *persistent* can be synchronized. There are many sources of metadata that will appear either on a one time only basis or on a very infrequent basis. These sources of metadata cannot be synchronized in any meaningful way to the ODS metadata store. Figure 3.6 describes how synchronization works.

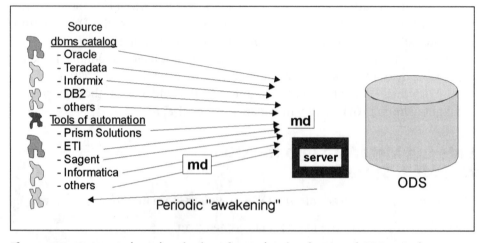

**Figure 3.6**  Automated synchronization of metadata is a feature of ODS metadata.

The entry of metadata from the external sources into the ODS metadata store entails some amount of editing as the metadata passes from the source into the ODS metadata store. Editing occurs more frequently and more heavily where the source of data is unstructured.

## Other Metadata Sources

The sources of metadata described in Figures 3.5 and 3.6 are not the only useful sources of metadata for the ODS metadata store. Figure 3.7 shows some other highly useful types of metadata that belong in the ODS metadata store. It also shows that information about the actual population of the ODS belongs in the ODS metadata store. The ODS metadata store can usefully contain types of metadata such as

- The source of a field of information found in the ODS
- The database or table the data element comes from
- The attribute(s) that forms the basis of the ODS data element
- The transformation that occurs as the source data passes into the data warehouse
- The route the source data goes through in order to reach the ODS
- The speed of the passage of the source data

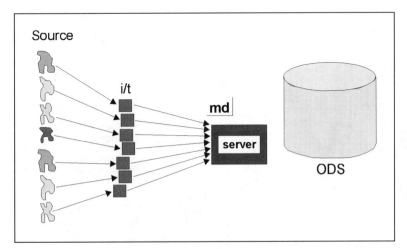

**Figure 3.7** Other useful metadata included the source of date as it flows into the ODS and the logic of integration and transformation.

The end user and the technician will find these types of metadata very interesting as the ODS matures.

## Accessing Metadata

The accessing of metadata in the ODS can be done in several ways, as seen in Figure 3.8:

- Directly from the database management system the ODS metadata resides in through native SQL calls to the database management system.
- Indirectly through end-user access and analysis tools. In this case, the end users move the ODS metadata into the end-user access and analysis tool, then incorporate the metadata into the reports issued by the tool.
- Through a Web graphical user interface (GUI).

The sophistication of the end user, the task at hand, and the permanency of the reporting being done will dictate which method of access to ODS metadata the end user will choose.

In conjunction with access of the ODS metadata by different channels, the issue of security arises. Figure 3.9 illustrates the fact that not all end users in the ODS environment should have access to all the ODS metadata. There are many ways the security of the ODS environment can be implemented, including

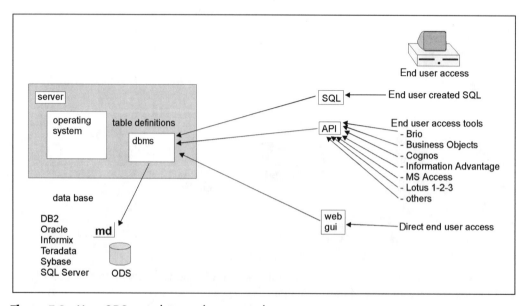

**Figure 3.8** How ODS metadata can be accessed.

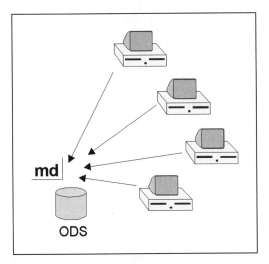

**Figure 3.9**   Security and authorized access to the ODS metadata is an issue as well.

access by type of metadata, by date of metadata entry, by ownership of metadata, or by predetermined levels of security. In the same vein, access privileges to the ODS metadata can be assigned according to different criteria—access by department type, access by organizational position, and access by "need to know" clearance.

## Metadata as Data Exits the ODS

Another type of metadata function that is unique to and useful in the ODS environment is that of the movement of metadata out of the ODS and into the enterprise data warehouse. Figure 3.10 shows this type of metadata that belongs in the ODS metadata store.

The movement of data from the ODS to the enterprise data warehouse is usually a fairly straightforward process. However, there are several variables that are of interest to the technician and the end user:

- When does movement take place?
- Is there any transformation done during movement?
- Is there a mechanism set up to signal that an incomplete or improper movement has occurred?
- Is there any data that is lost during movement?

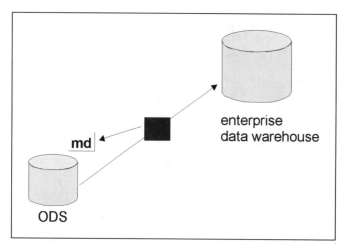

**Figure 3.10** The logic of extraction and condensation as data passes from the ODS into the enterprise data warehouse is another useful form of metadata.

# The Enterprise System of Record for Metadata

Perhaps the most interesting aspect of metadata in the ODS environment is that the metadata in the ODS environment is part of a larger network of metadata across the enterprise. In particular the ODS metadata has direct connections and interactions with the metadata found in the legacy applications and the enterprise data warehouse. Figure 3.11 shows the interactions of metadata between the ODS and the legacy applications enthronement and the ODS and the enterprise data warehouse.

The metadata found in the ODS comes from what can be called a system of record for the metadata. The system of record for the metadata implies that only the ODS manager of the metadata is allowed to access, update, create, and delete the metadata found in the ODS metadata store. The ODS metadata manager can grant access to external agencies that might have a need to see the ODS metadata, but control of the contents and usage of the metadata in the ODS is strictly a decision of the ODS manager.

The ODS manager can request access to external metadata that is stored or resides elsewhere, such as at the legacy application environment or the enterprise data warehouse. But once the ODS manager has accessed or brought external metadata into the ODS metadata store, the external metadata is marked as being shared. This means that the ODS metadata manager can analyze the shared metadata, but can take no actions to alter the shared metadata in any way. In creating an environment where there is local ownership of meta-

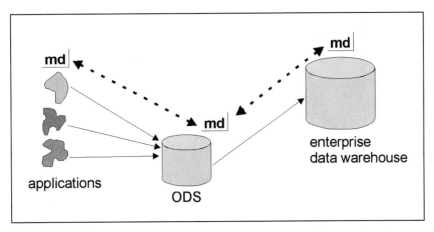

**Figure 3.11**   The metadata that resides in the ODS participates in a larger network of metadata.

data in the ODS and where external shared metadata can be accessed and shared with discipline, the ODS participates in an enterprise network of metadata that has integrity across the enterprise.

## Summary

Metadata is an important component of the ODS environment. ODS metadata is stored inside the ODS itself, in the best case on the ODS database management system. Both business and technical metadata occur in the ODS, which corresponds nicely to the dual usage of the ODS. Other types of metadata found in the ODS includes data model metadata, source metadata, transformation and integration metadata, and metadata about the movement of data out of the ODS.

The sources of metadata that flow into the ODS include database management system catalogs, tools of automation, metadata exchange standards, and free-form capture of metadata. Metadata can be entered into the ODS metadata manager either manually, semiautomatically, or in a fully automated synchronized state. Metadata can be accessed in several ways: by native SQL calls to the database management system, by end-user access and analysis tools, or by a Web GUI.

# Class I, II, III, and IV Operational Data Stores

The ODS is an architecturally recognizable entity, but within that entity are distinct classes of ODS. In addition, the ODS has some operating characteristics that are unique. This chapter explores some of the more interesting aspects of the architectural characteristics of the ODS.

## The Operational Data Store Within the Information Factory

The corporate information factory may or may not have an ODS as mentioned earlier. Figure 4.1 illustrates what the corporate information factory looks like when there is and is not an ODS. If an operational data store is optional, then what characterizes a corporation that needs one as opposed to one that does not?

## Operational Data Store Discriminators

The first discriminator between corporations that do and do not need an ODS is size. The larger the corporation, the greater the chance there will be a need for an ODS. The smaller the corporation, the smaller the chance one will be needed. Size plays an important role when it comes to integration. Very small

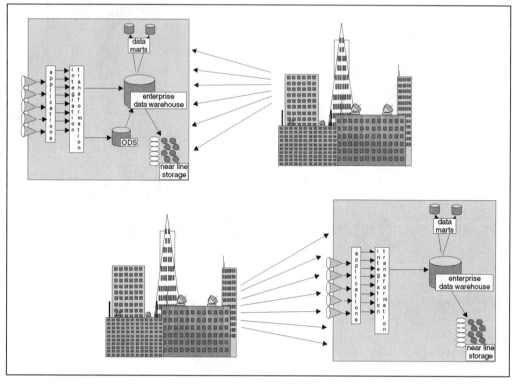

**Figure 4.1**  Some companies need an architecture that includes an ODS; other companies only need a data warehouse.

organizations rarely experience any great distress because of a lack of integration. But the larger the corporation, the greater the chance that a lack of integration has caused or will cause problems.

The second factor leading to the need for an ODS is the nature of the business of the corporation. If the corporation has an immediate need for information—typically because of direct customer interaction—then there is a good chance that an ODS will be needed. Some corporations may have little direct customer interaction but still have an immediate need for information, such as information in the manufacturing process. If there is a need for immediate information, then there will likely be a need for an ODS.

The third characteristic of a company that needs an ODS is that it has a large and messy application legacy systems environment. The larger the legacy systems environment and the less integrated it is, the better the chance that there will be a need for an ODS. Conversely, if the legacy systems environment is small and/or very integrated, then the need for an ODS is not as great.

It is this set of needs that typically drives corporations to the commercially available ERP packages such as SAP, PeopleSoft, Oracle Financials, and BAAN. These appeal to companies with particularly weak and unintegrated older applications.

Corporations that need an ODS share three common characteristics: size, immediacy of information, and status of the legacy information systems. When the three conditions intersect in a corporation and an ODS is in order, the need for one can often be expressed in terms of a business opportunity. The business opportunity is able to be exploited only when the ODS is built. While the ODS certainly has a technological justification, there is an equal business justification for it. (This phenomenon—of the ODS having equal value in both the technological and the business community—has long been observed in the data warehouse environment.)

## Four Classes of ODS

There are four classes of ODS (Figure 4.2). One class of ODS is updated synchronously (class I). Class I ODS have updates entered into them within two to three seconds after the update has entered and transacted with the operational world. In many cases in class I ODS, very little if any transformation occurs as the data passes from the operational environment into the ODS. In extreme cases (and there are some real dangers in this case), the data flows into the ODS at the same time that the transaction flows into the operational environment. In this extreme case, there is no synchronization of data after operational update as there is throughout all other components of the environ-

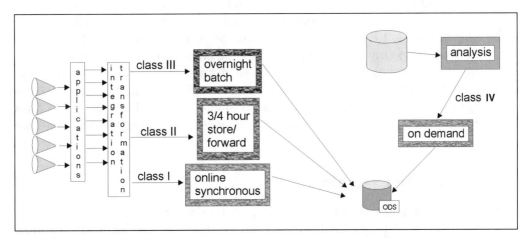

**Figure 4.2**  There are four very different classes of ODS based on the speed of refreshment.

ment. Class I ODS are used for extremely high-performance, transaction-dominated environments.

In the second class of ODS (class II), data is stored and forwarded into the ODS. The flow of the store and forward is done on an hourly or even half-hourly basis. There is not nearly the immediacy of the data as is found in class I ODS systems. Usually a fair amount of integration and transformation is accomplished as the data flows into the class II ODS.

The third class of ODS (class III) is the asynchronous class, where data is trapped in the operational environment and is loaded into the ODS on a 24-hour or more basis. In almost every case a significant amount of integration and transformation is done as the data passes into the class III ODS.

The fourth class of ODS is one where data is loaded on an unscheduled basis into the ODS in a composite form, usually from analysis created in the data warehouse. The detailed data at the data warehouse is then consolidated and aggregated into a form that is immediately usable in the ODS. The net result is the immediate availability of sweeping amounts of data and processing at the fingertips of the ODS user.

The primary distinguishing feature of the four different classes of ODS is the speed with which the data is moved from one environment to another. Class I refreshment speed is blinding. class II refreshment speed is not slow, but it is not as up-to-the-second as class I. Class III ODS refreshment occurs on a relaxed basis. Class IV refreshment is very slow.

Because of the significant differences in speed of refreshment in the four classes of ODS there is a corresponding difference in costs. Class I ODS are much more expensive than class II ODS, and class II ODS are more expensive to build and operate than class III ODS. The expense differential comes in the hardware platform and the operating systems that are required to support the different classes of ODS. Simply stated: Speed of refreshment costs, and it costs a lot! When the decision is made as to what class of ODS is required, there need to be compelling business and economic reasons why class I is chosen over class II or class III. Indeed, there are some cases where the speed of class I produces a competitive advantage such that the business case can be made to justify the expenditures. But because speed costs, it should not be assumed that the ODS will be class I without a stringent investigation into both the business advantage that will be gained and the possibility of doing business with a class II or a class III ODS. Ironically, some of the most compelling business cases are for class IV ODS.

## Class I: An Example

As an example of a class I ODS, Figure 4.3 depicts a banking environment where a bank has many individual accounts for a large multinational customer. As each of the individual accounts change, the corporate ODS is updated. Or,

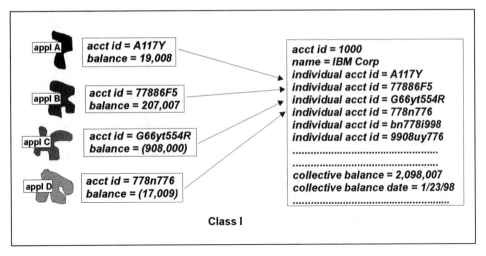

**Figure 4.3**    A fast form of update—synchronous update.

periodically—every minute or so—the individual accounts are swept and an update as to the status of the account is sent to the ODS. However the update mechanism is triggered, the update quickly finds its way into the ODS. Once it's there, the corporate manager is able to manage the customer on a collective, up-to-the-second basis.

Note that in the class I example described in Figure 4.3 there is a back reference to the account number as the account number is known in the legacy application. This is one way of handling disparate keys.

## Class II: An Example

When the update of the ODS is handled by store and forward techniques, the data in the ODS is not quite as fresh as it is in a class I ODS, but it still can be reasonably fresh. The individual banking example in Figure 4.4 shows that data is stored and forwarded to the ODS.

In Figure 4.4, an integrated individual bank account is kept on a weekly basis. The daily transactions that occur during the week are stored and forwarded to the ODS on an hourly basis. Once in the ODS, a composite picture of the customers' weekly activities is formed. The individual transactions and activities are not reflected separately. Instead, the individual activities are transacted against the ODS record in such a way that a composite record of the account is formed throughout the week as the detailed data is collected.

The technique shown in Figure 4.4 for the class II ODS is a common way of aggregating and "profiling" an account. The technique shown has the advantage

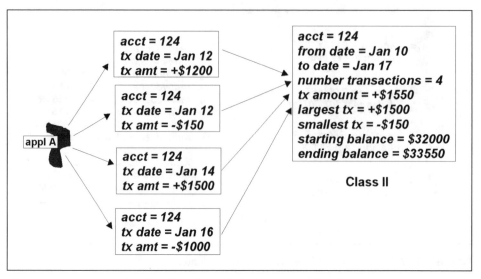

**Figure 4.4**    An example of loading the ODS from activities that have been stored and forwarded.

that many individual transactions can be represented in the ODS without taking up an enormous amount of storage. However, in order to create a useful profile, the designer must have a good feel for the usage of the data. Creating the profile without understanding the audience and the ultimate usage of the ODS is like flying a plane in a fog bank with no radar.

## Class III: An Example

The third class of ODS is one in which the refreshment from the operational environment occurs in a relaxed manner, typically every 24 hours or so. Consider the customer profile created in an ODS as shown in Figure 4.5. This figure shows that a customer record is created in the ODS. Data from different applications are merged in order to create a composite customer record. Note that there are back references that enable the user to go from the ODS record back to the legacy application if necessary.

The data that is in this class of ODS is updated in a casual fashion. For one thing, the customer data changes very slowly. When the data does change, the immediacy of the data is not paramount. There just is no business case for the immediate update of the ODS in the example shown. Therefore a relaxed (and inexpensive!) refreshment strategy can be employed for this class of ODS. The choice, then, of class I, II, III, or IV ODS depends in no small part on the data that

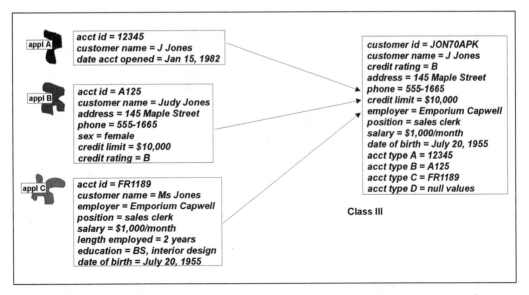

acct id = 12345
customer name = J Jones
date acct opened = Jan 15, 1982

appl A

acct id = A125
customer name = Judy Jones
address = 145 Maple Street
phone = 555-1665
sex = female
credit limit = $10,000
credit rating = B

appl B

acct id = FR1189
customer name = Ms Jones
employer = Emporium Capwell
position = sales clerk
salary = $1,000/month
length employed = 2 years
education = BS, interior design
date of birth = July 20, 1955

appl C

customer id = JON70APK
customer name = J Jones
credit rating = B
address = 145 Maple Street
phone = 555-1665
credit limit = $10,000
employer = Emporium Capwell
position = sales clerk
salary = $1,000/month
date of birth = July 20, 1955
acct type A = 12345
acct type B = A125
acct type C = FR1189
acct type D = null values

Class III

**Figure 4.5**  Creating the integrated record from the various applications—a form of asynchronous batch update.

will be contained in the ODS and the usage of that data. The class is chosen to fit the data.

## Class IV: An Example

In Figure 4.6 it is seen that a data warehouse has several analytical programs that are written. The analytical programs are written by marketing and analyze a customer's past activity. The data warehouse data that is analyzed is eclectic in that many different kinds of data go into the analytical mix, resulting in the ODS receiving the composite results of the analysis. Sometimes the analytical results are passed to the ODS on a unscheduled basis, and sometimes the results are passed as frequently as daily. On other occasions it may be months before the results are passed back to the ODS. In any case, once loaded into the ODS, the end user is able to access the data in its composite form almost immediately.

It is noteworthy that a single data structure can contain data that is class I, II, III, and IV all at the same time. In other words, in the same physical ODS structure, some data elements are class I, some data elements are class II, some data elements are class III, and some elements are class IV. The mixing of classes among different data elements within the same physical structure is natural and normal.

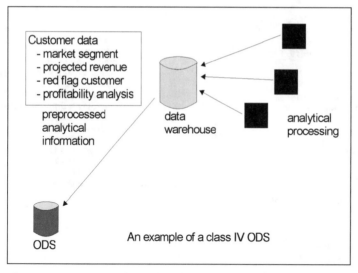

**Figure 4.6** An example of data that has been loaded from the analytical activity done in the data warehouse in a capsulized format into the ODS.

## Trapping the Incremental Operational Data

The refreshment of the ODS from the operational environment is a very important topic because it is an act that every ODS designer must consider and because, if not done properly, it can cost an inordinate amount of money. There are considerable technical and economic considerations to the refreshment of the ODS from the operational environment.

The ODS is fed from the results of transactions being executed in the operational environment. Only very rarely is the operational database read directly, then used as input to the refreshment process. Instead, the refreshment process is fed by the trapping of the results of updates that have occurred in the operational environment. Note that operational transactions are trapped *after* they have been executed. It normally does no good to trap operational transactions *before* they have executed because the results of their execution are unknown. What may happen is that the transaction may not pass edit and may abort in the operational environment. In that case, erroneous results occur when the ODS traps the transaction before it has executed. The techniques for trapping the results of an execution are shown in Figure 4.7.

Figure 4.7 shows that databases can be read if necessary to feed the ODS refreshment process. The (rarely occurring) instance of reading operational databases is done when transactions are stored in the operational databases. In most other cases, this is a very ineffective and expensive strategy for refreshment of the ODS.

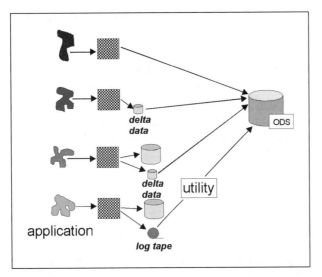

**Figure 4.7**  Common ways that legacy application data is trapped prior to refreshing the ODS.

The second strategy is to use delta files for the purpose of trapping the changes that have occurred. Delta files are sometimes written at the application level, usually for the purposes of auditing. On occasion, these delta files will contain the data and the element of time necessary to feed the ODS environment. When a delta file exists, it usually is an efficient and effective source of data for ODS refreshment. Unfortunately the creation of delta files is not a normal application practice.

The third strategy for trapping data for the purpose of refreshing the ODS is to trap database changes at the database management system level. Some database management systems are very amenable to this trapping and provide easy to use EXITs. Other database management systems are very difficult to tailor for this purpose. When this approach is used, there should be an awareness that there will be an input/output (I/O) impact on the online environment when the data is trapped. In some cases, this I/O interference may cause *severe* performance interruptions.

A nice aspect of trapping changes to an operational database at the database management system level is that there is no interruption to application programs or transactions. The trapping occurs entirely independently of the legacy code and for this reason alone is a popular option when the database management system is amenable.

The last option is the usage of the online application log tape (or journal) for the purpose of trapping changes that have occurred in the operational environment. When the log tape is used, in almost every case a utility is run that selects the data off of the log tape and prepares the data for inclusion into the ODS refreshment job stream.

The use of a log tape is desirable because it is entirely independent of application code and because there is no I/O impact on the system. In addition, once the log tape has been written, it can be processed off-line, on a processor far away from the operational platform. Removing log tape processing to a platform other than the one doing operational processing is usually a cost-effective strategy. In whatever way the changes to the operational environment are trapped, they are then batched together and transmitted to the integration/transformation layer in order to be prepared for entry into the ODS.

## The System of Record

Under most conditions, the ODS is fed from the operational environment. The data that is used as the source in the operational environment is called the "system of record." Defining the system of record for the ODS is a very important part of its development process. The system of record is the definition of exactly what operational data is needed in order to support the ODS environment. Figure 4.8 illustrates the system of record environment.

There are many considerations in choosing the correct system of record. Some of these include the following:

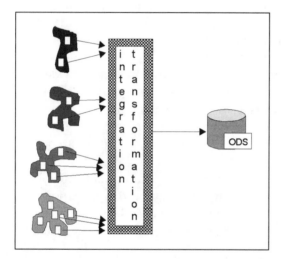

**Figure 4.8**    The system of record resides in the applications environment and provides the basis for loading data into the ODS.

- If there is more than one source, under what conditions is one source better than another?

- What reformatting/conversion must be done to prepare the source for entry into the ODS?

- What if the key structure of the source data is incompatible with the key structure of the data in the ODS?

- What if the source data has too many occurrences for inclusion in the ODS (such as transaction files often have)?

- How accurate is the source?

- How up-to-date is the source?

- How old is the source data?

- How complete is the source data?

- How compatible is the source structure of data with the ODS structure of data?

- What will be required to integrate the source data into the mainstream?

- What technology is the source data in?

- How efficiently can the source data be accessed?

- How does the source data compare with the enterprise data model?

There are a multitude of considerations in selecting the best source of legacy data with which to populate the ODS. Given that there are a multitude of considerations, the designer will not make the correct choice in every case. In other cases, the correct choice as to the best source of data will change over time. Fortunately the establishment of the ODS is an iterative process, much like the development of the data warehouse. The ODS is built in small, fast increments where periodic corrections to the design are made. One of the corrections that is commonly made is in the definition of the system of record for the ODS.

## Auditability of the Operational Data Store

The ODS contains much valuable information. It forms a foundation on which to make important corporate decisions. But the ODS is *not* the place for detailed corporate auditability and adjustments. Figure 4.9 makes this important point. It shows that corporate auditability—detailed adjustments to operational records—is done in the legacy applications, at the source record level. For all of the usefulness of the ODS, the auditability of data does not move with the legacy data as it is transformed and integrated into the ODS. Adjustments, billing records, audit trails, detailed accounting, and other such functions

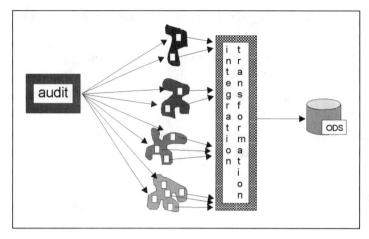

**Figure 4.9**  Auditability of the system of record is an essential feature of the decision support architecture.

remain at the legacy environment. It is patently a mistake to try to shift auditability and adjustments to the ODS.

Of course, if incorrect data is found in the ODS it needs to be corrected. A company certainly should not be making important corporate decisions based on poor data. There is, however, a correct procedure for the correction of bad ODS data. Figure 4.10 outlines that procedure.

An error is found in the ODS. The source of the data that feeds that part of the ODS is located. Then the transformation and integration logic that governs the movement of data from the legacy systems environment to the ODS is examined. The correction is then made in the legacy source environment and the data is moved into the ODS. In this way, corrections are made in the ODS environment; it is improper to make the corrections directly in the ODS without first correcting the data in the source record environment. If, by chance, corrections are made independently in the ODS, then the integrity of the relationship between the source systems and the ODS is compromised and reconcilability of data is lost.

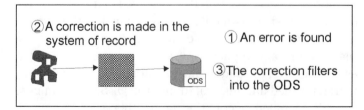

**Figure 4.10**  The mechanics of making corrections and adjustments.

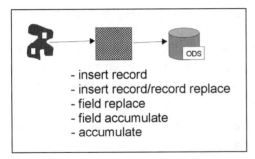

**Figure 4.11**   Typical types of inserts/updates found in the ODS environment.

There are many different ways in which data is moved from the source environment to the ODS. Figure 4.11 identifies five different common ways in which data is moved into and manipulated within the ODS. The simplest way in which the data is moved and manipulated is in terms of a simple record insertion. The system of record data record is moved to the ODS and inserted verbatim. A variation of simple record insertion is record insertion/replacement. In the record insert/replace mode, data is moved to the ODS. If data with the same key is found in there, it is replaced by the new value that has just been brought over. On the other hand, if there is no key of identical value in the ODS, the record is inserted into it.

The field replace mode is similar to the record replace mode that has been discussed except that only a field is replaced instead of an entire record. The field accumulate mode is one in which the data from a single field going into the ODS is accumulated. In the accumulate mode, more than one field is accumulated.

Another possibility is the field count mode, where the number of records being moved to the ODS is tallied. The field count mode can be modified so that, for example, only fields within a certain domain are counted. There are countless variations on the different ways in which data can be moved from the source environment into the ODS environment.

## The Operational Data Store Workload

The ODS workload is important because its demeanor has a great effect on the type and size of the platform on which the ODS is housed. And, of course, the size and type of the platform that houses the ODS has a great effect on the budget required. For that reason alone it is necessary to understand at least the rudiments of the platform the ODS resides on.

Of the different classes of ODS, the most workload-sensitive environment is that of class I. Class II, III, and IV ODSs have an interesting workload, and certainly their platform is important. But there is much less latitude for error when dealing with class I ODSs. For that reason, the discussion will center around the class I ODS insofar as the profiling of the ODS workload is concerned.

Figure 4.12 shows some of the aspects of class I workloads on ODS platforms. There are at least three main concerns of the capacity planner when dealing with the class I ODS workload:

- The rate at which legacy transactions flow into the ODS and the nature of the transformation that occurs once in the ODS environment
- The amount and rate of the two- to three-second transactions that are sent by the end users into the ODS
- The rate and the nature of the massive analytical processing that sometimes occurs in the ODS.

The first factor affecting the ODS workload is that of the rate of entry of the activities from the system of record systems. When many small transactions are being entered, where those small transactions are causing inserts or other space management activities, the workload is very sensitive to the resources being consumed. If only a few transactions are being entered, and if those transactions are causing only minimal space management activities, then the effect on the workload is minimal. Of course, since update is occurring, the entry of these transactions is magnified. If the transactions can be batched and summarized before arriving at the ODS, for example, the performance impact is mini-

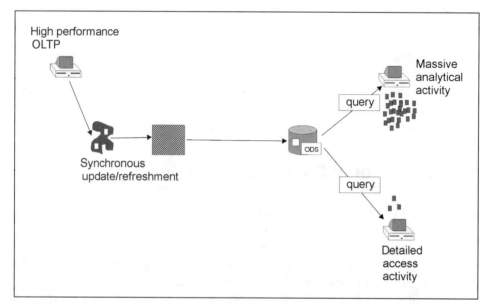

**Figure 4.12** A typical workload profile for an ODS that does synchronous processing.

mal. But batching and summarizing are normally not the nature of class I transactions.

The second workload factor is the access of the ODS data by the analytical community once the data has arrived. There are essentially two kinds of analysis that occur here: very fast, detailed analysis where many transactions are entered, each transaction accessing only a small amount of data, and a few very large transactions where a massive amount of ODS data is analyzed.

The first kind of transaction usually causes the most concern because it is expected that the small transaction will enjoy fast response time—two to three seconds—in the ODS environment. As long as all workload factors can be managed, it is indeed possible to provide consistent two- to three-second response times in the ODS (something that should never even be attempted in the data warehouse environment!). The workload manager has to worry about two aspects of this type of query: What is the rate of arrival and what kind of resources does each of these transactions consume? It is understood that update is not done by these small, fast-running transactions in the ODS environment. As long as there is some degree of predictability to these small, fast-running transactions then the workload can be sized and the proper platform can be selected.

The second class of end-user transaction that is run in the ODS environment is that of the large "lunking" transaction. The resources consumed by these large transactions can be minimized by doing two things: limiting the number of them to be run, and limiting the time of day they can be run. Usually these limitations are not too restrictive to the end user. But if they are too restrictive, then the end-user requirements should be considered carefully and the operational data store should be designed to accommodate the end-users' needs. An alternative, of course, is to move the processing to the data warehouse or even an exploration warehouse. However, the nature of these requests is such that they are defined heuristically so that it is very difficult for the end user to know what is needed until he or she discovers what is possible. For this reason, heuristic, massive analysis of the ODS is best relegated to the wee hours of the morning when the machine has spare cycles and no one is impacted by one transaction sucking up huge amounts of resources.

## Segmenting the Operational Data Store Day

Because there is a need to balance the resource utilization in the ODS environment between predictable high-performance processing and heuristic analytical processing, the ODS day is typically broken into different "time zones" of operation. Figure 4.13 illustrates what those typical time zones might look like, showing that early in the morning the platform and the data that reside in the ODS are dedicated to mass loads of data from the legacy system environment.

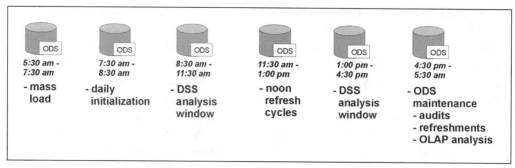

**Figure 4.13** Sectioning off parts of the day for different activities for the loading and use of the ODS.

This is true of even class I ODS where more than one source feeds the ODS environment. Later in the day (but still early!) the daily initializations and other utilities are run. Once the day starts only DSS analysis is done, and if the ODS is a class I environment, transactions are accepted from the source systems. At noon, end-user access drops off and the spare machine cycles are used to run small utility and batch analysis jobs. After lunch, end-user utilization picks up again and the system is dedicated to end-user analysis. At the end of the day, as direct transactional end-user access plummets, the heavy-duty sequential DSS analysis starts. Later in the evening, ODS maintenance and batch processing commence until the early hours of the morning, at which point the cycle begins anew. The use of time zones allows the ODS to be used for multiple purposes without undue interruption or disturbance to any one community.

## Managing Resources

In light of the fact that resources are a precious commodity in the ODS environment (especially the class I ODS environment), there are several micro-strategies that can be employed to improve the general profile of resource consumption. Figure 4.14 outlines some of the more important design and development practices that can be employed. For the massive heuristic queries (the "lunkers"), the following is good practice:

**Checkpoint the transaction frequently.** This means that if restart is needed, massive amounts of work will not have to be repeated. In addition, frequent checkpointing has the effect of freeing up internal resources to the database management system and operating system that may be needed by other programs and transactions.

**Run at off-peak periods,** such as at 2:00 A.M. or on Sundays. Moving these programs to off-peak processing flattens the pattern of resource utilization

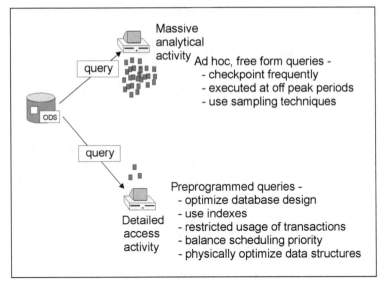

**Figure 4.14** The different kinds of queries/access to the ODS.

over the life of the platform and extends the range of the platform and database management system technology that houses the ODS.

**Use sampling techniques,** especially where heuristic analysis is being done. Instead of discovering what the parameters of success are for an analysis by initially operating on massive amounts of data, start the heuristic process by operating on only a small amount of data, until the final heuristic analysis is ready to be run.

Optimizing the performance of the high-performance, transaction end-user analysis can be done in the following way:

**Optimize database design** so that the normal request for data can be accommodated with a very small amount of I/O. Normally this entails creating a database design at the physical level so that different kinds of data are mixed together and are optimally located for speedy access.

**Make sure indexes exist and that they are used properly.** Using indexes (or hashing) properly ensures that the primary access of data is done efficiently.

**Restrict transaction processing during peak period times of day,** if necessary. For example, a department may be told that they can run transaction types $A$, $B$, and $C$ during the morning and transaction types $A$, $D$, and *E* during the afternoon. Such restrictions are not popular but can greatly extend the life of a platform.

**Balance scheduling priority.** At the system level certain transactions can be given priority over other transactions when they enter the system. Those with low priority do not enjoy this scheme, but such a ploy can create overall system performance at the expense of only a few users.

**Physically optimize the structure of the data.** Employ techniques of denormalization that have the effect of optimizing performance of data. Of course, to successfully employ this technique you have to know what transactions will be enhanced and what transactions will be deoptimized. Deoptimizing the wrong set of transactions can be a hazardous thing (to the career of the system designer!).

From a strategic perspective, the single most effective thing that can be done to improve performance in the ODS environment is to move the ODS from a class I environment to a class II or class III environment. Figure 4.15 illustrates the difference that changing classes makes.

Where there is online general-purpose update of data, the system and the database management system run under a tremendous amount of overhead. Where the general-purpose update is restricted to a load process rather than an update process, and especially where the load process can be run after hours, performance can be enhanced.

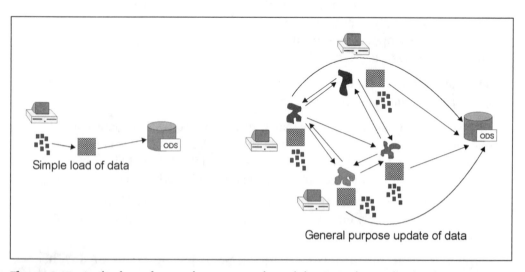

**Figure 4.15** In the face of general-purpose update of the ODS, the application becomes more complex than if asynchronous update of data is done.

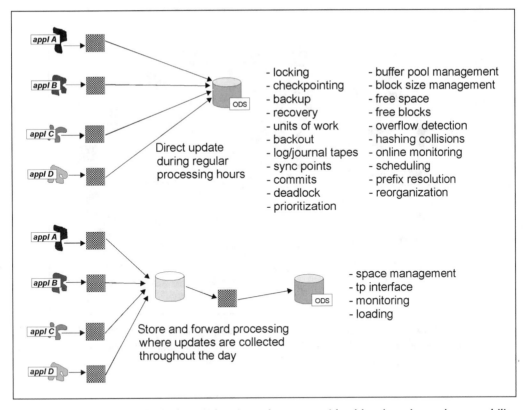

**Figure 4.16**  The technological considerations change considerably when the update capability during normal processing hours is added to the ODS.

The dramatic effect of the enhancement is shown in Figure 4.16, where, from a systems perspective, one can see the difference that is made by not doing general-purpose update during the online day. There are many reasons why performance suffers when there is an insistence on doing peak-period online update. The end result is that when update is done synchronously in the ODS and where there is much access of data, there is the very real possibility that the ODS and its platform will become a tremendous performance bottleneck. Figure 4.17 shows this possibility.

One technique that can help alleviate the ODS from becoming a performance bottleneck is that of understanding where it is being accessed during its peak period. By understanding where the ODS is being accessed, the systems designer can spread data out and/or add indexes where appropriate to enhance performance. Figure 4.18 shows the monitoring of the ODS to determine the location of the performance bottleneck.

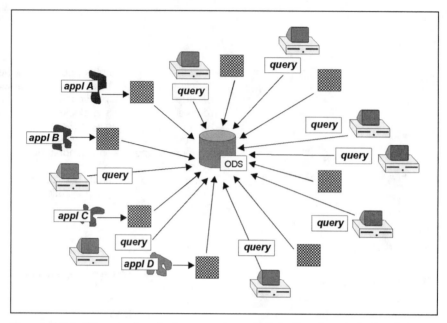

**Figure 4.17**   When update is done synchronously in the ODS and where there is much simultaneous access of the data, there is the very real possibility that the ODS will become a performance bottleneck.

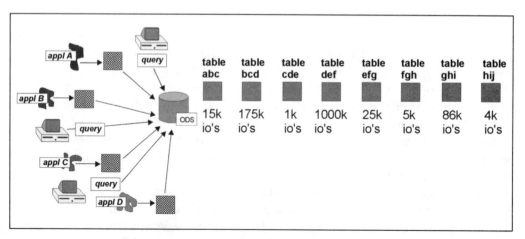

**Figure 4.18**   Monitoring ODS operations tells where tuning should be done, where data is best moved to the data warehouse, where indexes should be added, and where summarization ought to be done.

# Metadata and the Operational Data Store

Metadata in the ODS environment plays as important a role as it does in the data warehouse environment. Figure 4.19 symbolically illustrates the role of metadata in the ODS environment.

The primary reason why metadata plays the role that it does in the ODS environment is that is where informational processing occurs. Informational processing begins with the discovery process. In the discovery process, the end user begins to formulate what is required. The discovery process begins with a survey of what the possibilities for analysis are, and it is in this capacity that metadata plays a vital role. Metadata allows the end user to understand what data is available for analysis. In addition, the ODS metadata allows the end user to make distinctions between different types of data found there. The end user can find out not only what data is available, but what is the *best* data available for analysis. The end user can look at such things as

- What was the source of the data in the ODS?

- What was the integration/transformation processing that occurred as the data passed into the operational data store?

- When did the data pass into the ODS?

- How much of the data is there in the ODS?

- How does one unit of data in the ODS relate to another unit of data in the ODS?

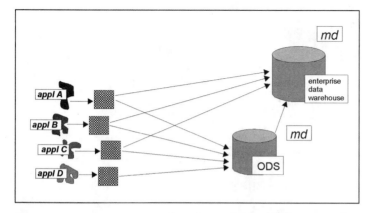

**Figure 4.19** Because metadata is used for informational processing, metadata is as important in the ODS environment as it is in the data warehouse.

- Where does the data go after it leaves the ODS?

- What business names does the data in the ODS have?

Metadata, then, is a great enabler for the benefit of effective analysis of data in the ODS. As time passes and the contents of the ODS become more varied and voluminous, the role of metadata increases. Indeed, as long as the ODS contains only a modest amount of data, the role of metadata is not obvious.

# Executive Information Systems and the Operational Data Store

Executive information systems (EISs) have an important role to play in the larger picture of DSS. An EIS is the executive's window into the operation of the corporation. The role of the EIS in the data warehouse has long been recognized and discussed. What remains largely unexplored is the role of the EIS in the ODS environment. The EIS, in fact, has an important role to play with regard to the ODS, however different that role is from the role that the EIS plays in the world of data warehousing. Figure 4.20 identifies the role of the EIS in the ODS environment.

The EIS in the ODS environment plays an executive-level operational role. The decisions that are looked at through the EIS in the ODS environment are

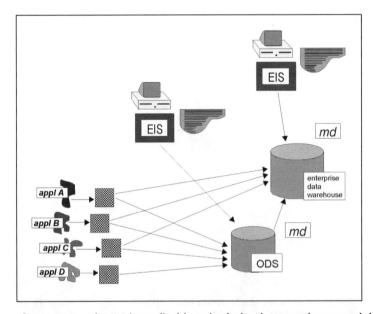

**Figure 4.20** The EIS is applicable to both the data warehouse and the ODS environment. But the implementation and usage of EIS in both environments is very different.

up-to-the second, summary-level, corporate decisions. Contrast these decisions with the ones made through the EIS in the data warehouse environment. In the data warehouse environment the executive information systems assisted in making long-term, strategic decisions. There was little or no immediacy of decision in the data warehouse EIS environment. However, in the ODS EIS environment, there is a very real immediacy of decision. The following are some examples of corporate, executive-level immediate decisions:

- At what rate should we loan money to a large multinational customer?
- Should we place a group order for a new product line right now, based on how well the products are selling across our chain of stores?
- How should we react to a competing airline's lowering of fares in order to keep the most market share and at the same time lose the least amount of revenue?
- What lines of products are selling well in this Christmas season and which ones should be put on sale?
- What insurance policies will be affected by a hurricane off the Florida coast?

These are the kinds of considerations that are both immediate and at the executive level. The ODS coupled with executive information systems form a foundation appropriate to the answering and analysis of these temporal business conditions.

It is noteworthy that the ODS forms a very solid foundation for EIS. Trying to do EIS processing without the data that resides in the ODS is an exercise in futility. There simply is no way that legacy data can be organized, transformed, and analyzed quickly enough to support the fast-changing needs of top management. The ODS allows the EIS to do what it does best, analyze and present information without having to worry about the underlying foundation of data.

# The Operational Data Store and Parallel Technology

There is an excellent fit between the needs of ODS processing and parallel technology. The parallel architecture of data and processing (sometimes called an "mpp"—massively parallel processing—approach) is one that is able (among other things) to

- Manage large amounts of data
- Break processing up into units that can be operated on independently
- Provide scalable processing

- Provide good response time across massive amounts of data
- Allow individual units of data to be accessed very quickly and randomly

In truth, there are some other interesting properties of parallel processing that make it attractive for other kinds of processing. But for the purposes of ODS processing, the characteristics listed above are the ones that are of greatest interest to the ODS architect.

The ODS typically has a fair amount of data stored in it. Parallel architecture is good at managing lots of data. The ODS environment often has massive requests that scan lots of data. Breaking a request up into independent units allows even very large requests to be handled efficiently. Programs and transactions that are written for one level of data work as well at another level of data in the ODS environment. The ODS requires good response time, and parallel processing can be made to realize speed of access and processing. And the ODS requires that massive amounts of data be accessible in one or two I/Os. Again, parallel processing arranges units of data so that any one unit is a few short I/Os away. For these reasons, then, there is a very comfortable technological fit between parallel processing and the ODS.

## Operational Data Store and Database Management System Software

While hardware platforms and architectures are very important, there are other technological considerations for the ODS. One of those major considerations is that of the basic database management system technology in which the ODS runs. Figure 4.21 makes some important points about the basic database management system technology that underlies the ODS.

If the ODS that is built is class I, then the underlying database management system, of necessity, needs to be a full-function, general-purpose, record-level update database management system. But if the ODS that is being built is class II, III, or IV, then a more niche-oriented database management system can be chosen. There is no need to do online, general-purpose update in this case, so a

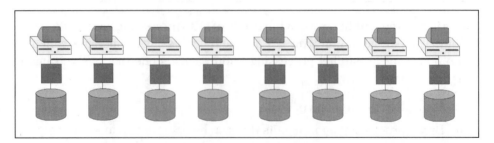

**Figure 4.21**   The functionality of the ODS has a big impact on the type of database management system software that is chosen.

much more efficient database management system can be considered. Indeed, in this case the database management system that is selected may look like the one that serves the data warehouse world. Of course, a database management system that is load-and-access oriented will operate much more efficiently than one that is dragged down by the need for data and transaction update integrity.

## Backflow of Data

Nearly all data (approximately 99 percent) flows from the ODS to the data warehouse. However, there is an occasional backflow of data from the data warehouse to the ODS that is just as important, as illustrated in Figure 4.22.

Even though this backflow makes up only 1 percent of the volume of moving data, the business importance of this data is disproportionately high. The backflow of data occurs when analysis is done in the data warehouse and the results of that analysis are passed back to the ODS, usually in a concise form. Some examples of this type of backflow are

- Interest rate changes by a bank are calculated based on detailed activity found in the data warehouse. Once those rates are recalculated they are passed to the ODS for the purpose of making business decisions.

- Production schedules by a manufacturer are calculated based on the detailed activity found in the data warehouse. Once the quotas and schedule are calculated, they are passed to the ODS for the purpose of making day-to-day business decisions.

- Premium rates by an insurer are calculated based on the detailed activity found in the data warehouse. Once the rates for different policy types are calculated, they are passed to the ODS for the purpose of making day-to-day business decisions.

Given these situations, it is clear that the backflow of information from the data warehouse to the ODS is a very important aspect of the corporate information factory.

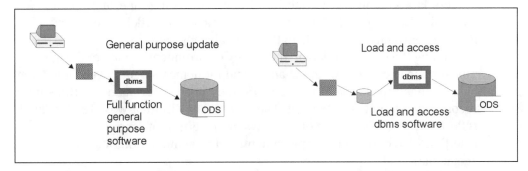

**Figure 4.22** There is a backflow of data from the enterprise data warehouse to the ODS.

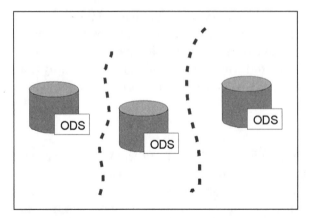

**Figure 4.23**   Multiple ODS are possible as long as there is no overlap among them.

## Multiple ODSs

Although it is not normal, the possibility exists that a corporation might have multiple ODS, as shown in Figure 4.23. If there is overlap among the ODS, there is the possibility of a design flaw. If a significant overlap is comprised of redundant data, then there is cause for concern. However, if the multiple ODS are designed from the same data model and there is no significant overlap of data, then there most likely is no problem.

## Summary

The ODS is an optional feature in the corporate information factory. Some companies have business conditions that demand it; other businesses do not. There are three classes of ODS—class I is where online update is done synchronously, class II is where refreshment of the ODS occurs in a store-and-forward mode, and class III is where the ODS is refreshed asynchronously. The refreshment process is accomplished by means of accessing a log tape or trapping calls within the database management system. Occasionally a delta file is used. Even less frequently, access is made to the actual legacy data.

Defining the source of data in the legacy environment is a major design step. This is done iteratively, where changes and refinements occur over time. When changes need to be made to the ODS, they need to be made at the source record, not within the ODS itself. There are many different ways legacy data is reflected in the ODS. Some of the ways are insertion of records, replacement/insertion of records, field replacement, field accumulation, and record-level accumulation.

Normally the ODS operating day is divided into "time zones." These time zones free up the ODS platform allowing it to become optimal for the different types of processing that occur throughout the day. Collectively the time zones provide all the windows needed for the different ODS activities.

# Operational Data Store Design: High-Level Design

Operational data store development is essentially a compromise in design. The ODS has online characteristics and DSS characteristics. This means that ODS design attempts to serve two masters at the same time. Unfortunately the two masters that must be served are in conflict with each other. On the one hand the ODS must provide online high-performance response time. This requires that transactions be optimized for performance and that data be juxtaposed so that it is efficient to access. On the other hand, the ODS must support DSS processing. This entails organizing data for flexible access. The design can be built one way or the other, but not both ways at the same time.

Because of this dichotomy, every ODS design is a compromise. Unfortunately designers like to have a hard set of rules that spell out how something is to be done. ODS design requires judgement and compromise, something that designers often feel uncomfortable with. When developing your methodology for the ODS, you begin with general project planning, including the sizing and phasing of the project, project evaluation, and ODS maintenance. Next, steps need to be taken to set up the technical environment and determine its capacity, as well as estimating the data and applications requirements. The next step is to develop the operational processing of the ODS. The ODS database should then be created by creating various diagrams and data models. Next, the ODS applications and database should be tested, and finally, the end users' decision support environment and repository should be created. For details about all of these important steps in the planning methodology for the ODS, please consult

Appendix A for a thorough overview of all the steps involved, the time estimates, and the special considerations involved.

## Structuring the Operational Data Store

The structure of the contents of the ODS are shaped around the major subject areas ("entities") of the corporation. The major subject areas of the corporation are defined in the corporate data model. Figure 5.1 shows a simple corporate data model with its entities. The major subject areas of the corporation are usually at a high level of abstraction and typically include customer, product, order, shipment, and payment.

It is normal for an ODS data model to be created from the corporate data model. The ODS data model starts with the corporate data model as a point of departure. But there are some notable differences between the corporate data model and the ODS data model. While the corporate data model is inclusive of all the data the corporation needs for its information, the ODS data model includes only the data that is needed for operational online integrated processing. Traditionally the amount of data needed for online integrated processing is less than the entirety of corporate data.

The exclusion of nonoperational, nonintegrated, nononline data usually means the removal from the corporate data model of such information as historical information, summary information, management browsing information, and information not directly related to the requirements of the processing at hand. In short, anything not directly related to the integrated online processing

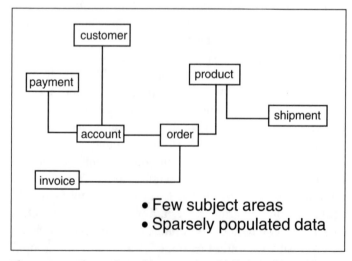

**Figure 5.1**   The major subject areas typically found in an ODS.

that is not supported by the ODS is jettisoned from the corporate data model as the ODS model is built. The result of these modifications to the corporate data model is that the ODS data model is "sparsely populated," or "minimalist." Only the data elements needed for ODS processing are carried in the ODS data model.

The first foundation for database design for the ODS environment is the normalized model that flows from classical ER modeling. The only difference between classical ER modeling and ODS modeling is that the ODS model is minimal. However, there is another set of needs for database design for the ODS and those needs occur for the parts of the ODS that are regularly and heavily used. In other words, some parts of the ODS are lightly and randomly used and other parts of the ODS are heavily used. A different approach to modeling and database design is needed for that portion of the ODS.

# The Operational Data Store and the Data Model

Looking at the ODS data model as the basis for the design of the ODS often gives a warped and misleading perspective. The data model perspective of the structure of the data in the ODS is one that is flat, where each entity appears to be equal to every other entity and where all attributes are on an equal footing. However, such is not the case as the ODS architect heads for implementation. Figure 5.2 presents a different perspective of the structure of data found in the ODS.

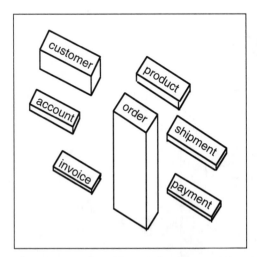

**Figure 5.2**  All entities are hardly created equal—in terms of volume, some entities tower above the others, and it is in these massive entities that the most interesting information hides.

The data in Figure 5.2 is seen to be distributed very unevenly over the different subject areas. Some subjects in the ODS areas have very little data in them while other subject areas are heavily populated. It is common for the subject areas that contain the most occurrences of data to be those that relate to transactions or other important details. In the case of retailing, the majority of the occurrences of data in the ODS relate to stocked items or sales. In a marketing and sales firm, the bulk of the occurrences in the ODS relate to customers, and so forth. Each business has its one or two most populous entities. And it is these "most populous entities" that often have the most potential in providing a real business advantage in the ODS online operational environment.

## Star Joins

The most populous and heavily used entities often represent data that is at the heart of the business. Because of their great importance in the ODS environment, these most populous entities are designed to be in a construct unique to data warehouses and the ODS—that of a "star join." Figure 5.3 illustrates a simple star join.

The notion of a star join in a DSS context was pioneered by Ralph Kimball in his work with large-scale data mart systems. The star join fits the data mart as handily as it does the ODS. The star join data construct is one in which the primary data is held and stored in the one or two large tables of the ODS (which usually represent transactions). Foreign key relationships are included with the

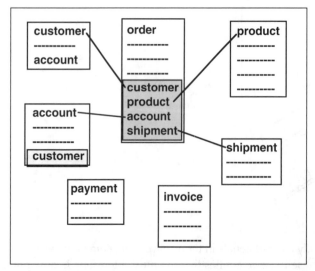

**Figure 5.3**   A typical structuring of ODS data, sometimes called a "star join."

primary data to reference smaller tables, which occasionally need to be accessed after having accessed the large, primary table. These smaller tables are said to be prejoined to the larger, primary table. The incidental, secondary tables in the ODS—when drawn around the large primary table—*join* to form a starlike structure, hence the name.

One of the interesting features of a star join is the simplicity of its structure and the data contained in it. Given the volumes of data that are being contemplated, there is simply no place for complex, slow-to-traverse structures in an ODS. The star join, then, becomes the most fundamental description of the design of the most populous data found in the ODS.

With the star join, data relationships can be explored quickly. In addition, whole sets of data can be identified and ferreted out in the primary grouping of data. The ability to easily and efficiently identify subsets of data using a star join greatly facilitates the ability of the DSS community to use the ODS effectively.

Thus there are two design approaches to the design of the data found in the ODS. For lightly used data, where there are a minimal number of occurrences of data, a classical normalized design is optimal. For the other parts of the ODS, where there is data that is heavily used with a pattern of regularity and where there are a large number of occurrences of data, a denormalized star join approach to the design of the ODS is in order.

There is no problem in mixing these two types of structures in an ODS. A star join fits comfortably with normalized structures in the same architectural structure.

# Data Relationships in the Operational Data Store

One of the important features of the data found in the ODS is the data relationships that are contained therein. As in all other database forms, data relationships are vital in the ODS. However, data relationships in an ODS are implemented in a structure known as an "artifact" of a relationship. (Note: Artifacts of relationships are found in the data warehouse as well as the ODS. Refer to the Tech Topic by Prism Solutions, vol. 1, no. 5, on data relationships for an in-depth discussion of artifacts of relationships.)

Standard data relationships that are commonly found in a database management system, such as referential integrity or logical relationships, are applicable to operational systems. In a world of DSS analysis and integrated, online processing, many data relationships take on a new meaning. Most relationships that are found in the ODS environment are the result of a transaction that has transpired. As a result, the only relationship that is accurate and relevant is the relationship that was in force at the time of the transaction. A "snapshot" is made at the moment of the transaction and the relationships relevant to the transaction at that instant are captured. Figure 5.4 shows an example of an artifact of a relationship in the ODS environment.

The creation of a relationship is started by some "event" occurring. An event can be a discrete happening, such as the placement of an order, the completion of a sale, or the payment of an invoice, or an event can be the marking of the regular passage of time, such as the end of the day, the end of the week, the end of the month, and so forth. An event signals that a snapshot of some primary unit of data is to be taken. The snapshot focuses on something such as the placement of an order or the completion of a transaction. Once the snapshot of the order or the transaction is taken, other incidental relationship information that is relevant to the order or transaction at the instant the snapshot is captured.

This incidental relationship information that is captured as part of the snapshot process is the relationship artifact information. Suppose a snapshot is made of an order. Other incidental information that might be captured with the order might include

- The identification of the clerk who handled the order
- The product unit of measurement being ordered
- The priority of shipment
- The type of shipment requested
- The credit rating of the customer as of the moment of the order

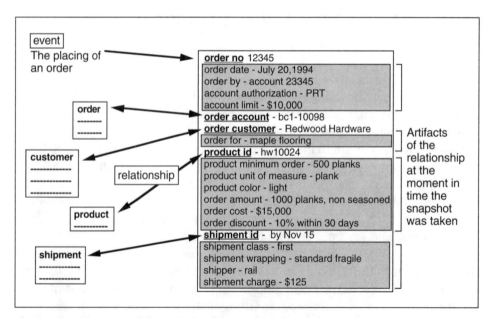

**Figure 5.4** Elements of data relationships in the ODS environment.

The incidental information stored along with the order is called *relationship artifact information*, and is accurate only as of the moment the snapshot was taken. Any inference of the relationship before or after the moment of the snapshot is purely coincidental and random.

Creating relationships in the ODS by means of snapshots makes the ODS a structurally streamlined environment. There are no cumbersome ties of data from one table to the next. There is no concern about changing business rules, or about having to synchronize the purge date of different tables in the ODS because of relationships.

# Summary Data and the Operational Data Store

Summary data can be created from the detailed values found in the ODS, but summary data is seldom if ever stored within the ODS itself. In order to understand the unusual role of summary data in the ODS, consider how summary data is created, as illustrated in Figure 5.5.

The creation and calculation of summary data in the ODS environment is simple. Detailed ODS data is accessed and refined, then a calculated value is created. At first glance, there is nothing unusual occurring here. But summary data created from detailed ODS data has a curious property. When a summarization is created in the ODS, it is accurate *only* as of the instant it is created; in the very next instant the summary data may well be inaccurate.

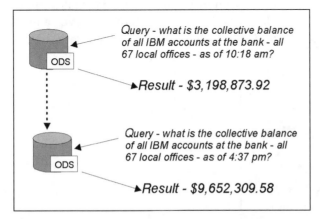

**Figure 5.5** Summary data can be calculated from the ODS, but the value that is calculated is accurate only as of the instant the data is calculated. Furthermore, a recalculation of the same data at a later point may yield different results.

For example, suppose a bank officer uses the ODS to calculate the corporate balance for a large multinational corporation. Suppose the calculation is made at 10:35 A.M. At 10:40 A.M. the calculation is rerun and a different summarized result is achieved. Does this mean that the value calculated as of 10:35 A.M. was incorrect? Not at all; detailed ODS data is constantly changing (especially class I ODS data). The value that was calculated at 10:35 A.M. was accurate at the instant it was calculated. At 10:40 A.M. another value was calculated (that in turn was accurate only as of that instant in time). The difference between the values obtained at 10:35 A.M. and 10:40 A.M. says nothing about the accuracy of the results.

When summarization is done on constantly changing details, the summary data that is created can be called *dynamic* summary data. Although dynamic summary can be very useful for many different kinds of business decisions, it is not appropriate for every kind of business decision. Dynamic summary data has several properties:

- Dynamic summary data is accurate only as of the instant of calculation, therefore storing dynamic summary data usually does not make sense. Indeed, storing dynamic summary data and using the data for a decision at a later point in time may prove to be the cause of erroneous decisions.

- Dynamic summary data is almost impossible to audit. In order to audit dynamic summary data, the details that go into the calculation have to be returned to a set of values as of the instant in time when the summary was made. Resetting massive numbers of variables back to an instant in time is usually very difficult if not impossible to do.

For these reasons then, dynamic summary data is not stored in the ODS.

Contrast the dynamic summary data that is found in the ODS with the type of summary data that is found in the data warehouse (Figure 5.6). There is a whole host of summary data found in the data warehouse. In fact, there is even a hierarchy of summary data that is found there—lightly summarized data, highly

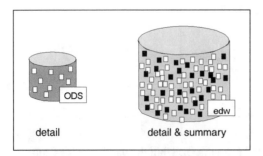

**Figure 5.6**   The ODS contains only detailed data; the enterprise data warehouse contains a mixture of summarized and detailed data.

summarized data, and so forth. But the summary data found in the data warehouse is very different from that which can be created in the ODS.

Data warehouse summary data is static summary data. Static summary data is data that can be created and stored. Static summary data can be recalculated at any point in time in the future and the result will always be the same. For example, suppose at the end of the month a corporation's revenues are calculated. If the corporation should desire to go back and recalculate those revenues later (say, at the behest of the IRS), the calculation would come out the same. In addition, if there is a need to audit a calculation in the data warehouse, it could easily be audited. There is, then, a fundamental difference between the dynamic summary data found in the ODS and the static summary data found in the data warehouse.

# Broadly Defined Keys

One of the issues faced in the structuring of ODS data is that of the scope of the key. Each table in the ODS has a primary key. Some primary keys are intuitively and easily defined; other keys are not. As an example of a key that is open to interpretation, consider CUSTOMER, as seen in Figure 5.7. Who is a customer? Is a customer someone who currently is a customer? someone who once was a customer? someone who might be a customer? Is a company that has both a local office and an international office a customer? Is the local office a customer in the same way that an international office is a customer?

The architect of the ODS can struggle with these issues and attempt to rationally sort through the problems and predetermine the best answer. The prob-

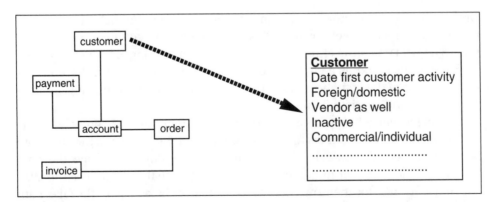

**Figure 5.7** Attributes that serve to discriminate one type of customer from another are added to the data found in the ODS, leading to what can be called the "broadly interpreted key."

lem is that whatever interpretation the architect puts on the definition of the data in the ODS, it will be wrong! Inevitably the ODS architect will exclude one or more classes of data that rightfully belong in it.

There is a technique for organizing and defining data that addresses many of the problems of the ODS architect. That technique entails making use of a "broadly interpreted key." A broadly interpreted key is one that encompasses as many possibilities as is feasible. The definition of the key the ODS architect uses is one that encompasses as many subsets as can be reasonably encompassed. The data is loaded into the ODS so that many subsets of the data are included. Attributes of data are included to allow one subset to be separated from another subset. Then the usage of the ODS data is up to the DSS analyst. Upon accessing the ODS data, the DSS analyst specifies discerning criteria to distinguish one subset of data from another.

As an example of the selectivity possible with a broadly interpreted key, consider the data shown in Figure 5.7. Using the attributes to qualify what data was required, a DSS analyst could look at all customers who:

- Were currently active
- Were foreign, inactive commercial
- Were active customers who were vendors as well
- Were individual, inactive, domestic customers

The use of the broadly interpreted key gives the DSS analyst all possible flexibility, freeing the ODS architect from prejudging the use of the ODS.

# The Operational Data Store—Centralized or Distributed?

One of the major structural and architectural decisions that must be made by the ODS architect is whether the ODS should be distributed or centralized. Figure 5.8 depicts this basic choice. Unless there are mitigating circumstances, the ODS functions better as a centralized structure than as a decentralized one. A large amount of data will be in the ODS and it will have to serve many communities with a wide variety of interests.

Creating a centralized ODS allows the maximum number of people with the maximum number of agendas to access the same ODS data. When the ODS data is decentralized, the data is divided into different domains. Once the data becomes separated over multiple domains, the DSS analysts who use the ODS data must arrange for their own access to the many places where the ODS data is distributed. Such a distributed access may not be a simple matter.

The only natural way that the ODS can be easily distributed is to break it up into separate functional arenas and distribute the functions. In such a man-

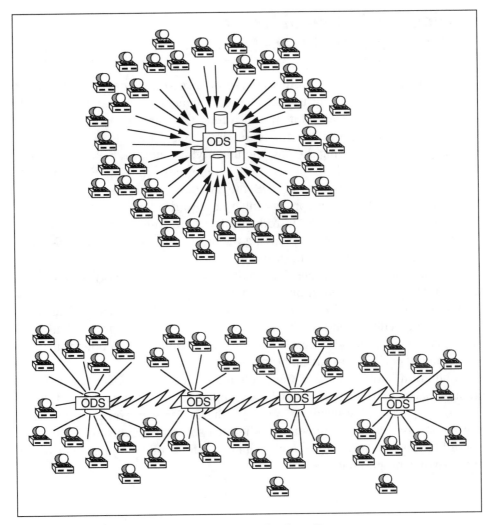

**Figure 5.8** Should the ODS be centralized or distributed?

ner, ODS data and processing can be distributed. A problem arises with this structure when data from one unit of ODS data needs to be mixed with data from another ODS unit. Crossing the boundary from one distributed ODS node to another, if any significant amount of crossing is to be done, is not an enticing prospect. In addition, when the ODS is designed and managed centrally, there is the possibility of a much tighter degree of control over design and content. Once ODS data becomes distributed, all thoughts of control vanish.

# Moving the System of Record to the Operational Data Store

There is the notion that over time the system of record for data will shift from the application environment to the ODS environment. Such a shift is possible (Figure 5.9), but is not without its ramifications. One ramification (discussed in Chapter 7) is the implications for technology. When the ODS is a load-and-access environment during the day, the underlying database management system technology needed to service it is simple and efficient. But when the system of record is shifted to the ODS, the database management system technology underlying the update processing is necessarily complex and inefficient. Because of the inefficiencies introduced by the advent of general-purpose, record-level update processing, moving the system of record to the ODS calls for a serious consideration of performance.

There are other implications for moving the system of record to the ODS. One is that much application processing must be moved there. When the system of record (or part of it) is moved to the ODS, the ODS takes responsibility for capturing, editing, and application execution, which heretofore had been done in the legacy applications. The movement of application code to the ODS environment complicates the environment.

In addition, moving part of the application data to the ODS and keeping another part of the data back in the legacy applications may not be desirable. So moving only part of the system of record to the ODS may not be an option. Having an *all-or-nothing* circumstance when it comes to moving the system of record to the ODS probably is not optimal for the application designer or the maintenance programmer.

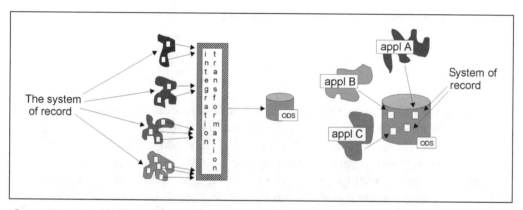

**Figure 5.9**  Moving the system of record to the ODS entails moving an entire infrastructure of application code to the ODS.

# The Operational Data Store and Object-Oriented Technology

There is a very comfortable fit between object-oriented technology and the ODS, at least at a high level of conceptualization. Figure 5.10 illustrates the relationship between object orientation and the ODS.

The basic orientation and design of the ODS is around the major subjects of the corporation. The major subjects of the corporation form the basis for organizing data into objects. Code surrounds the ODS in two ways:

The integration and transformation layer that shields the ODS from the legacy production applications.

The application code that the DSS analyst uses in order to access and analyze the ODS data. The basis of the integration and transformation algorithms is derived from the business rules of the organization.

There is, then, a very close fit between the notions of object orientation and the implementation of ODS.

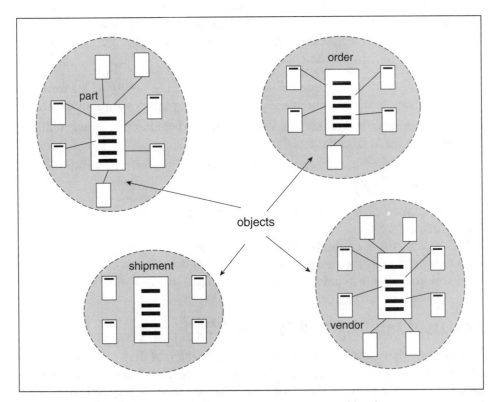

**Figure 5.10**    The ODS and object orientation at the conceptual level.

# How Big Should the Operational Data Store Be?

The size of the ODS—the volume of data to be found within it—is one of the most important design and implementation issues facing the ODS architect, and there are several issues that relate to the size of the ODS. The ODS is rarely even close to the size of the data warehouse. The ODS does not contain a great amount of historical data, and does not contain summary data, at least, no static summary data. For these reasons, the ODS is smaller than the data warehouse.

However, the ODS can still end up containing a huge amount of data. Given that the technology housing it is expensive, that it entails update, and that update implies a complex underlying technological infrastructure, the volume of data managed in the ODS becomes an issue. One reason is that every unit of data in an ODS is one or two I/Os away from direct access. There is a significant cost associated with keeping massive amounts of detailed data immediately accessible and updatable. For this reason alone, the ODS volume of data should be scrutinized carefully.

As a rule, an ODS should contain only data that is needed on hand for collective integration. There will be many details that are important to the corporation but that will never find their way into the ODS. The ODS will contain three types of values:

- Back reference data that allows the end user the ability to go from the ODS back to the system of record in the legacy applications environment
- Discriminator data that allows the end user to distinguish between different classes of ODS data
- Up-to-the-second collective integrated values needed for corporate-integrated decisions

Any other types of data should be scrutinized carefully as to whether they belong in the ODS.

The structure and contents of the ODS can best be described as a minimalist structure. In at least the first few iterations of the development of the ODS, the ODS architect should avoid the temptation to place in it alot of unjustified data.

## Design of the ODS and Type of ODS

Interestingly there is a correlation between the design of the ODS and the class of the ODS. Given that data passes through the integration and transformation programs that are built for class I ODS very rapidly, there is very little if any fundamental conversion or reformatting that the programs can do. Therefore the data model that best represents a class I ODS is one that looks very much like the operational systems that feed the ODS. However, for class II, III, and IV ODS, there is the chance in the integration and transformation programs to fundamentally reshape the data found in the ODS. Because of this opportunity, the data model that represents class II, III, and IV ODS data models looks very much like the corporate data model, which reflects the corporate need for data. This is yet another reason why class I ODSs are rare structures.

# Sizing Up the ODS

Many variables affect the sizing of the ODS. Because some of the ODS is DSS in nature, its requirements are not known until the first iteration is built. However, some rough parameters can be used to size the ODS. These parameters are

**Number of ODS users in an online mode.** Once this number is established, determine how many transactions a day a user will be submitting, on average. If there is a peak period—hourly, daily, weekly, monthly, etc.—when is that peak and how bunched will the transactions be? This calculation is made to determine the processing capacity of the ODS.

**Number of units of data.** In order to do this calculation, a data model must be constructed. From the data model, determine how many entities will exist. For each entity, determine how many occurrences there will be per entity. For example, if the ODS is to encompass customers, how many customer records will be contained in the ODS?

Once the number of records is estimated, the next step is to estimate the size of each record. The final step is to carefully determine how much history the ODS will contain. This is always a specious calculation because it is normal for an ODS to start its life with the intention of containing a limited amount of history, but as time passes and the ODS matures, the amount of history placed in the ODS grows. This is especially true when the ODS is built before the data warehouse. In this case, there is often a very clear point where ODS history ends and data warehouse history begins.

In any case, at some point the ODS designer has an estimate of the history that will belong in the ODS. The ODS designer is now ready to make a stab at the volume of data that will reside in the ODS:

Entity × Number of occurrences for the entity × Record size for the entity
× Amount of history = Estimated raw data size for the ODS

After the designer has calculated the raw data size for the ODS, the designer must then factor in other normal system space, such as

- Index space
- Overflow space
- Block size "fit" space
- Buffer space
- Spooling space
- Sort/merge space
- Join space
- Other work space
- Other system space

Now the actual amount of space required for the ODS is calculated.

## Summary

The foundation of the design of the ODS is the corporate data model, where major subjects (entities) are identified. The entities are not equal in terms of volume of data. Some major subjects will have many occurrences of data, other entities will contain relatively few occurrences of data.

Some data is organized around the "star join" structure. The star join structure allows the very large tables in the ODS to participate in a prejoined foreign key relationship with the smaller tables. The star join contains a simple amount of minimalist data.

Summary data in the ODS is different from most other data because the values of summary data are accurate only at the instant they are calculated. This type of summary data is called "dynamic summary data." Because dynamic summary data is accurate only as of one moment in time, it is not stored in the ODS.

Data architects in the ODS environment employ the design technique referred to as the "broadly interpreted key." This allows the DSS analyst using the ODS to specify whatever subset of data is desired for analysis. One of the most important strategic decisions the data architect must make is whether the ODS is to be centralized or decentralized. As a rule, the ODS should be built and operated in a centralized mode.

CHAPTER

6

# Operational Data Store Design: Low-Level Design

The classical system development life cycle (SDLC), pioneered by Ed Yourdon, Tom DeMarco, Chris Ganes, and Trish Sarson (among others) in the late 1960s and early 1970s, begins with the gathering of end-user requirements. Requirements are analyzed, synthesized, and shaped into a system design. The system design is then translated into a series of programs, which are written, tested, and debugged. Once the programs reach a state of reliability and stability, they are implemented.

The classical SDLC applies to operational application systems where clerical activities are being done at a detailed level, where collection/edit/update is occurring, and where the same activities are repeated throughout the day. Figure 6.1 depicts the steps of the SDLC at a high level.

The SDLC serves the world of operational processing well, but there is another legitimate system development life cycle that is the antithesis of the SDLC —the CLDS (so named because in most ways it is the opposite of the SDLC). The CLDS applies to DSS analysis where the end user discovers—as the last step in the process—what the requirements for processing are through a heuristic development process. The CLDS begins with the ability to get some data that has been implemented (usually detailed transaction data). Once the implemented data becomes available, a certain amount of probing and testing is done to the old transaction data to determine exactly what data is available and the status of that data. After the initial probes and tests of the implemented data are done, some exploratory programs are developed.

```
SDLC                                    CLDS

• Gather requirements.                  • Start with implemented data, usually transaction.
• Analyze, synthesize.                  • Probe, test to see what is available.
• Design system.                        • Develop exploratory programs.
• Program system.                       • Based on results of exploratory programs, create a design.
• Test, debug.                          • Take results of design, analyze and synthesize.
• Implement system.                     • Understand requirements.

Classical application                   DSS discovery-driven development
requirements-driven
development
```

clerical community/ repetitive processing

analytical community/ heuristic, analytical processing

**Figure 6.1**   Some approaches to system development.

These exploratory programs access and analyze the implemented data. The programs are developed iteratively, where each successive step of development refines and builds on the results attained in the previous step. After the heuristic programs have been built and patterns of data and processing start to emerge, a more formal design is done and more programs are written based on the design. Results are obtained and analyzed. Finally, the requirements to satisfy the needs of the DSS analyst are isolated and understood.

The CLDS best applies to DSS where there is very little repetitiveness of processing and much analysis. The CLDS applies to a very different audience than does the SDLC. The CLDS applies to an analytical-oriented management community, where long-term decisions are being made.

## A Spectrum of Development Life Cycles

The SDLC and CLDS are both perfectly valid development life cycles and can be considered to be at opposite ends of a spectrum of development approaches. As with any spectrum, there are many gradations and variations between the extremities. ODS development involves some of *both* SDLC and CLDS development. In fact, if we depict the SDLC and CLDS spectrum, ODS development falls in the middle, as seen in Figure 6.2.

There are positive elements of both the SDLC and CLDS in the development of the ODS. On the one hand, the repetitive requirements of the end user shape the ODS insofar as repeated access to data is concerned. On the other hand, the ODS needs to be able to accommodate the changing heuristic needs of the DSS analyst who uses it for informational processing.

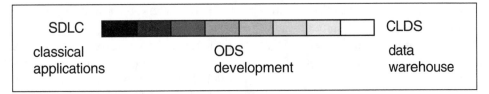

**Figure 6.2**   Where ODS development fits on the development scale.

## The Data Model/The Process Model

Another way to view the spectrum of development is not through the perspective of SDLC and CLDS development but through the relationship of the development life cycle to the data and process models. The data model consists of identifying and organizing the entities, keys, definitions, and attributes of information of the corporation. The process model consists of identifying and organizing the functions and processes of the corporation. Figure 6.3 shows how the data model and the process model can be arranged in a spectrum in order to reflect the different needs of development.

As in the case of the SDLC and CLDS, ODS development is a mixture of both data modeling and process modeling, sitting somewhere in the middle of the spectrum. There is an equal measure of influence from the process model and the data model in the development of the ODS. The ODS must accommodate repetitive processing and, as such, must make use of the process model. The

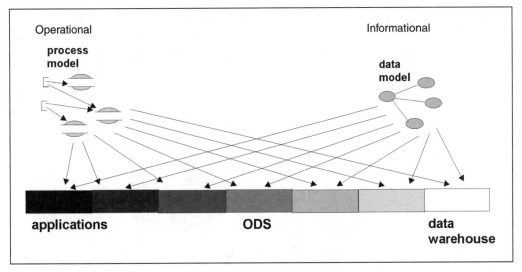

**Figure 6.3**   The different forms of processing—applications, ODS, and data warehouse—each have their own relationship to process modeling and data modeling.

same operational transaction is run repetitively by the end-user analyst throughout the day, so the ODS must reflect those needs.

By the same token, the DSS analyst uses the ODS in an iterative fashion, as a vehicle for discovery. Because of the need to use the ODS for informational processing, the data model needs to be included. The interests of these two very different communities and their very different patterns of usage dictate that the design and development of the ODS be influenced in equal measure by the process model and the data model.

Using both the data and process models in equal measure, the ODS is developed iteratively. Developing the ODS under the "big bang" theory is a very poor idea. Under almost *no* conditions should the ODS be built on a one-time only, all-at-once basis. Instead, it should be built in a series of fast "pulses," where tangible results are achieved and modified quickly. Figure 6.4 illustrates the iterative nature of ODS development.

Initially the ODS is designed and populated with a subset of the data that will eventually reside in it. The data that is initially loaded into it is explored and, inevitably, some adjustments need to be made. The iterative adjustments are made to both the ODS and the code that surrounds and shapes it. Adjustments are quickly made and another iteration of a small amount of data is added to the ODS. More adjustments are quickly made and the iterative development process continues.

## Physical Tables and Logical Entities

Each of the major subject areas—or entities—found in the corporate data model turns into a physical table in the ODS. Figure 6.5 shows the relationship of the corporate data model to the physical tables found in the ODS. The major subject areas found in the corporate data model form the foundation of design for the tables of the ODS. The key structure of the entities in the data model

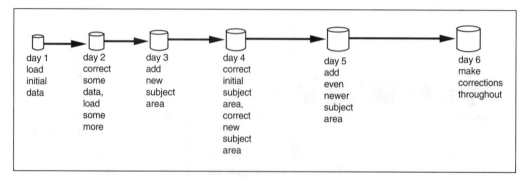

**Figure 6.4** The iterative nature of ODS development.

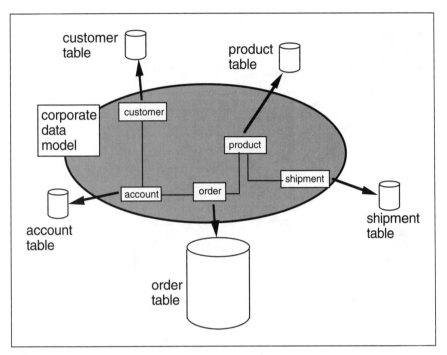

**Figure 6.5** Each of the entities in the ODS data model produces a physical table that is part of the ODS.

becomes the key structure of the tables found in the ODS. The attributes identified in the data model become the basis for the attributes that go into the ODS. The corporate data model attributes are "filtered" so that only those attributes that are appropriate to the ODS are brought forward into it.

For large tables (i.e., tables that contain a massive number of occurrences), the data model entity can be implemented in the ODS as a series of related tables. There is no need to have a single physical ODS table correspond to a single entity. Figure 6.6 shows such an example, where the data model has specified ORDER as an entity. But there will be many orders that will populate the ODS, so the entity ORDER is implemented as multiple physical ODS tables—foreign orders, back orders, current orders, and precious goods orders. Implementing several physical ODS tables in the case of large and/or complex major subject areas has several effects:

- Breaking large amounts of data into a series of smaller amounts
- Creating environments where the uniqueness of tables can be accommodated
- Breaking the work load into separate streams, where each stream is oriented to different styles and kinds of processing

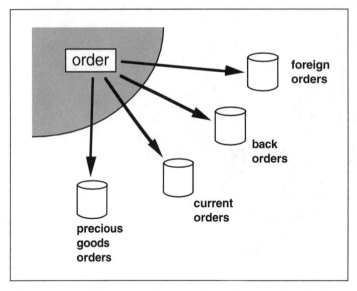

**Figure 6.6**   Entities that are large and complex are often broken into more than one physical table.

Of course, the different physical ODS tables that are created can be related through common keys and through data values. While the same *type* of data may appear across multiple related tables, the same *occurrence* of data will not appear across multiple physical tables in the ODS.

## The Operational Data Store and the Process Model

The ODS is shaped by the process model in the same way it is shaped by the data model. Figure 6.7 shows the relationship of the ODS to the process model. Different processes and activities are identified in the process model. These processes become the basis for the design of the programs and transactions that are found in the ODS operating environment. The process model is useful for identifying such things as

- Input/output to the process
- Sequence of execution of the process
- Algorithmic content of the process
- Transformations/conversions made during the process
- Conditions relevant to the process
- Flow of the process

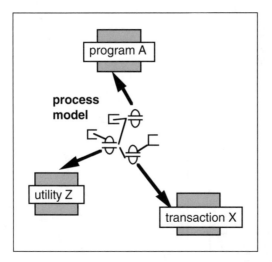

**Figure 6.7** The process model shapes the programs and transactions that will be written to access the ODS.

From the process model comes the identification of the programs that will execute in the ODS operating environment. (Note: Those programs that will execute repetitively are identified and analyzed here. Of course, the heuristic processes that will be run are not part of the process model that is built for the ODS.) Once the programs are identified, how they will operate on the tables that are to be part of the ODS is specified, as seen in Figure 6.8, which shows that the interaction of the programs in the ODS operating environment is scrutinized very carefully. ODS program-to-data interactions that are analyzed include

- How many times a day the program will execute
- How many resources will be used during an execution
- The arrival rate of the programs
- The time of day when peak interaction will occur
- The sequence of programs' execution
- Whether update will occur
- The expected response time
- The impact of a system outage on execution
- The need to periodically restructure/reorganize data

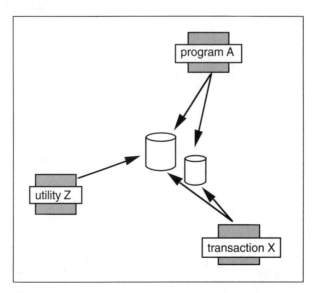

**Figure 6.8**  The programs and transactions that constitute the processing that will be done against the ODS shape its content and structure.

Based on the profile of execution of the programs that have been identified, the ODS architect can predict which parts of the system will be performance sensitive and can adjust the design of the ODS environment accordingly.

The process model for the ODS environment is constrained along the same lines as the data model. Figure 6.9 shows that the ODS process model is, like the ODS data model, a minimalist one. The ODS process model contains only the bare-bones requirements for ODS usage. Because general purpose applications are not normally built in the ODS, the process model is small (compared with a general purpose, applications process model).

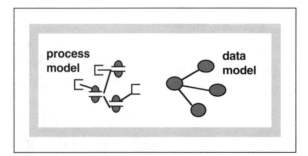

**Figure 6.9**  Both the process model and data model are constrained by the analytical activities that will occur within the ODS—they are not general purpose at all.

# CASE and Operational Data Store Process Model Development

CASE tools make a very good foundation on which to house and build the ODS process model. Figure 6.10 shows the relation of CASE tools to the ODS. In an ODS environment, CASE tools are good for procedures such as:

- Collection and organization of requirements
- Specification of different levels of process
- Sequencing of process

CASE technology is also good for gathering the requirements for the transformation and integration of data as it flows into the ODS. Of course, CASE tools are not appropriate for the gathering and synthesizing of heuristic requirements.

## Mixing the Requirements

Once the program requirements are specified, they are used as input in the design process for the actual physical data structures of the ODS. While the requirements of each process must be considered, processes are not equal participants. Some sets of requirements are much more important than others. Figure 6.11 shows the blending of the requirements based on different levels of participation and priorities of different programs. Some transactions run much more frequently than others. In addition, some transactions have a much higher priority than others. The design of the ODS is weighted to accommodate those

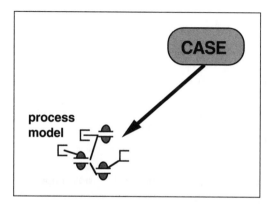

**Figure 6.10**   CASE technology is quite appropriate to the building of the process model.

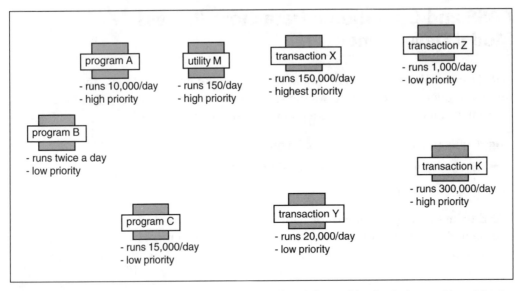

**Figure 6.11** All of the processing that goes into the daily workload mix is considered in the design of the ODS.

frequently executed, high-priority programs and transactions. In every database system ever written, design trade-offs have been made. In the case of the ODS, the trade-offs are made in favor of the most important activities (Figure 6.12).

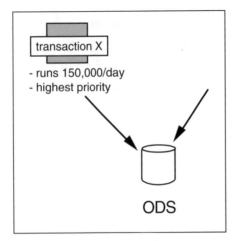

**Figure 6.12** The ODS is designed to optimize the performance of the most important activities.

# Accommodating the Most Important Processes

The accommodation of the most important processes begins with the consideration of the input/output operations (I/O) used by the most important transactions. I/O is the center of attention because it is the largest performance bottleneck in a fast-response, transaction-oriented environment. I/O refers to the act of placing data onto and retrieving data from a disk device. Data that resides on a disk device is stored and accessed in terms of mechanical speeds. Inside the computer, the code executes at electronic speeds; electronic speeds are typically three to four orders of magnitude faster than mechanical speeds. For that reason, when a programmer issues a simple READ$\ldots$ statement and the READ$\ldots$ statement needs data residing outside the computer, there is a severe slowdown in the execution of the program.

The job of the ODS architect is to minimize the total system I/O required to run the ODS environment. In minimizing the total system I/O, there will be an overall performance gain. The way I/O is minimized across the system is by looking at the most important, most frequently run transactions and minimizing the I/O required for their execution.

# Design Techniques: Minimizing Input/Output

Several design techniques can help minimize the amount of I/O used. Most of these design techniques fall into the category of physical denormalization of data. The subject of physical denormalization has been discussed at length in the trade press and in books and presentations. See the reference section at the back of the book for in-depth discussions of denormalization.

In order to optimize the access of data and minimize the use of I/O, first the transactions and programs must be organized according to their importance and frequency of execution. The most important and most frequently executed programs and transactions are then selected and the way they access data is analyzed. Figure 6.13 shows the identification of the pattern of access of these transactions and programs.

When the process of physical optimization of the placement of data commences, the tables of data that will reside in the ODS are generally highly normalized. Because of this, they do not contain redundant data, they are structured so that there are no repeating groups of data, and each unit of data stands on its own merit, independent of any other group of data. In addition, there is no summarized data and data is connected logically by means of foreign keys.

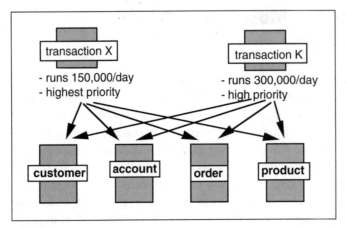

**Figure 6.13**   Optimizing the design begins with looking at the most important transactions and determining how they access data.

The access patterns of the most important programs and transactions are gathered and analyzed to determine whether there is a repeating pattern of access. In most cases, there is a predominant pattern of access of data that is repeated by many programs and transactions. The predominant pattern or patterns of access are identified and the data is physically rearranged in order to accommodate them. In doing so, the programs accomplish exactly the same functions they were designed to, but they use less total I/O in order to perform those functions. Some of the techniques of physically rearranging data will be discussed in the following section.

## Physically Merging Tables

The most powerful design technique to enhance the reduction of the total amount of I/O used is that of merging two or more tables together. Figure 6.14 shows an example of this technique, where customer data, account data, and product data have been merged with basic order data. Fortunately this technique fits very nicely with the notion of star joins. By merging the data into a single location, the end user can conveniently and efficiently access data without having to go to different physical tables. The merging of data into a common physical location greatly reduces I/O. In addition, when this technique is employed properly, the data can be arranged so that the end user sees the data "naturally," as he or she is used to seeing the data

The design trade-off of the technique of merging tables is that redundancy of data will creep into the design. In addition, while this technique makes access and processing efficient for some programs and transactions, it is inefficient for others. That is why the first question that must be asked is: What are the most important programs and transactions?

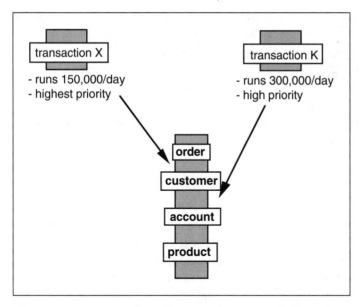

**Figure 6.14**   Merging data allows it to be accessed efficiently.

## Indexing Data

A very simple way to reduce the total amount of I/O is to judiciously employ indexes. Figure 6.15 shows the introduction and usage of indexes. An index is an independent collection of data that contains at least two essential pieces of data—the key value (or other identifier) of an occurrence of data and the phys-

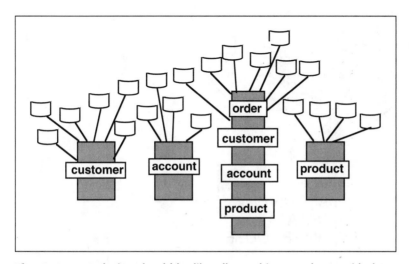

**Figure 6.15**   Indexing should be liberally used in accordance with the use of the data in both sparse and fully populated mode.

ical address of the data. The index is arranged according to the sequence of the key and is very efficiently accessed. Once the index is searched, it is simple to go directly to the location where the data is. When it comes to searching for data, the index can be a great saver of I/O; in many cases, the alternative would be a full scan of the table, which entails many, many I/Os.

The pattern of access of data is the best indicator as to how indexes should be created. Indexes should be built to accommodate the most frequently used patterns of access.

## Purge Criteria

An important facet of operational data store design is that of the specification of its purge criteria. Figure 6.16 shows this specification. The operational data store holds data that is very fresh—it is usual for it to hold data for about three or four days—up to one month in some cases. If an ODS holds detailed data for much longer, the volume of data starts to mount and other system complexities start to emerge, such as in performance and management of overflow of data. Therefore, it is important that data be purged from the operational data store environment before it starts to become stale.

There are several strategies for purging data from the ODS. Some of the more common ones are

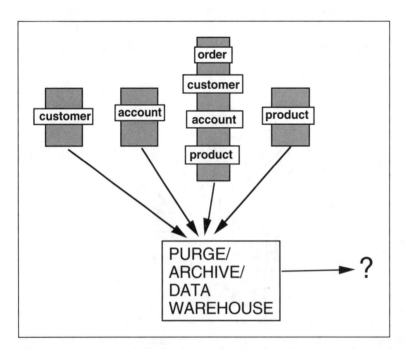

**Figure 6.16** Purge criteria for data in the ODS is an important design decision.

- Removal and destruction of data

- Movement of data from the ODS to the data warehouse

- Movement of detailed data to an archival medium

- Creation of rolling summaries of data where data is rolled up into successively higher levels of detail in the data warehouse as it ages

There are as many alternate strategies for purging data from the ODS as there are types of data; they can be employed in any combination. Whatever the strategy employed, allowing detailed data to remain in the ODS for any length of time is an architectural mistake. See Figure 6.16.

## Turning Off the Log Tape

If, in fact, detailed data is to be stored at the ODS level and performance is an issue, then under certain circumstances it is possible to turn off the log tape while the ODS is being updated. In doing so, the database management system operates much more efficiently. Figure 6.17 shows this option.

Turning off the log tape during update processing is a dangerous approach that is applicable only under abnormal conditions. On occasion, the disappearance of one or two updates makes little or no difference to the ODS end user. In some cases, the transactions that are stored in the ODS can be easily retransacted if need be. In other cases, the transactions themselves are stored in the ODS after having been performed in the legacy application environment. In this situation it may not be necessary to have each transaction executed in the ODS in a high-integrity fashion. If any or all of these circumstances apply, it may be

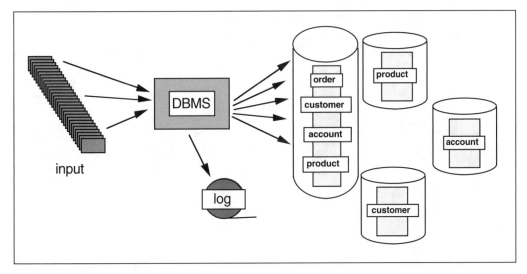

**Figure 6.17**  Efficiency may be enhanced by turning off the log tape during online update.

feasible to turn off the log tape during ODS processing and save considerable overhead.

## Preprocessing Detailed Transactions

In some cases, it may be possible to enhance ODS performance by doing a significant amount of preprocessing of detailed transactions before they are allowed to enter the ODS environment. By preprocessing transactions prior to entry to the ODS, the ODS environment is spared the consumption of unnecessary resources, and performance is enhanced accordingly. This alternative of design is illustrated in Figure 6.18, which shows that transactions can be preprocessed by an application before the transactions pass into the ODS. Typical processing might include

- Heavy editing and verification of the transaction
- Combining of like transactions into a single composite transaction
- Selection of unique transactions (such as the last transaction of the day) and rejection of other transactions

By carefully editing and manipulating the detailed transactions prior to entering the transactions into the ODS job stream, much processing can be saved in the performance-sensitive ODS environment.

## Space Management for the Operational Data Store Environment

The issues of performance extend down to as low a level as basic space management. Because update is done in the ODS environment, some amount of free space must be left in the physical block where ODS data is stored to avoid conflicts during update. Figure 6.19 shows free space being left in the physical

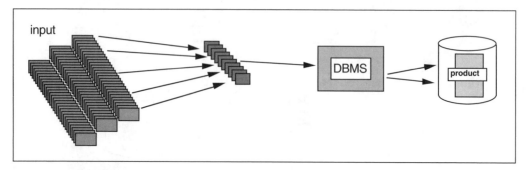

**Figure 6.18**   Preprocess bulk input data off-line before entering it into the ODS environment (for class II and class III ODSs).

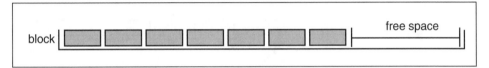

**Figure 6.19**   At initial load, some amount of space must be left for future expansion.

block. The exact percentage of free space that is left is entirely dependent on exactly how much update will occur, whether inserts will be allowed, whether variable-length records will be updated, and so forth. Note that the philosophy for the management of free space in the ODS environment is the opposite of the philosophy for free space management in the data warehouse environment, where there is no free space allocated upon loading a table. Figure 6.20 illustrates the common kinds of updates that can be done and their effect on free space management in the ODS.

In addition to the basic issues of free space management that go hand in hand with ODS updates, there is the issue of managing space in the indexes that point into the ODS. Figure 6.21 shows the need for the management of space at the index level as well as at the data level.

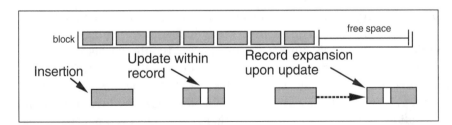

**Figure 6.20**   The type of update being done has a large impact on the amount of free space that is required.

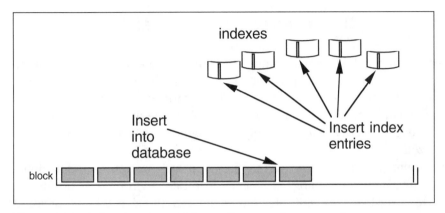

**Figure 6.21**   Index management is a performance issue as well.

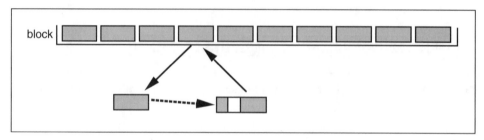

**Figure 6.22**   Variable-length data can present its own performance considerations.

Every time an insert is made to an ODS table, multiple indexes have to have an entry made to them. And when an indexed field is altered, two index entries must be modified—the index entry that points to a now-defunct value must be disabled, and a new index entry must be made for the newly defined value. All of the index activities contribute to a performance drag on the ODS environment.

Variable-length records offer their own peculiar space management problems in the face of ODS update. The problem of variable-length space management is shown in Figure 6.22. Variable-length data is packed tightly into its block upon being loaded, then at a later point in time it is retrieved and an update is made to the variable-length record. Unfortunately this update causes the length of the variable-length record to grow. When the variable-length record is returned to its original location, it will no longer fit. At this point, space management can become a nightmare. The specification and management of variable-length records presents its own challenges in the face of ODS updating.

## Minimizing I/O at the Hardware Level

Another way in which I/O can be minimized is through the parallelization of the hardware environment. In the parallel environment, different units of data are managed by different processors. When a request for I/O is issued, the request can be satisfied by machines running in parallel. There does not have to be a sequential execution of the I/O. In doing so, the amount of time required for I/O is minimized.

There are many considerations as to the way parallelization should be done. In some environments memory is shared. In other environments nothing is shared. However I/O is done, if it is done in parallel, the elapsed time required for execution is greatly minimized, thereby enhancing performance.

# Design Review in the Operational Data Store Environment

Design review is the practice of carefully reviewing the design of an application before the first line of code is struck. The motivation for design review began with the first online system that had to be rewritten because of poor design. The idea behind design review is that the system being managed would have been built quite differently had the right questions been asked at the right times. Design review attempts to ask the right questions at the right times, *before the system is built,* thereby potentially saving huge amounts of rework in design and development.

Design review has always been especially relevant to online, high-performance systems, and in that regard the ODS environment qualifies admirably. Indeed, the diversity of processing that occurs in the ODS environment makes it a prime candidate for the ongoing practice of design review as new parts are added to it. It is in the best interest of the ODS administrator to make design review a regular and normal part of ODS administration.

Design review is best done early in the ODS development process. As soon as the new development in the ODS environment is formalized, it is time to do design review. Design review is almost always best conducted by an outsider—someone who is not connected with the ODS development effort. If it is conducted by an insider, the review process can turn into an exercise in politics and personal criticism. The more political and personal a design review becomes, the less effective it is. Having an outsider conduct a design review is the best way to ensure that the review process is apolitical and impersonal.

Preparation for the ODS design review process is minimal. The designer simply takes what design documents have been created and uses them as the basis for review. If a massive preparation effort is done on behalf of a design review, then the review is being conducted improperly.

The ODS design review typically takes two or three days, depending on the size and complexity of the development being reviewed. If it takes fewer than two or three days, then the review is probably superficial. If a review takes longer than two or three days, then it becomes tedious and loses much of its value.

The actual ODS design review is conducted from a standard checklist, such as that suggested by Figure 6.23. All the participants in the ODS design review are allowed to view in advance the questions and issues that will be discussed. The participants in the review include anyone who has a stake in the success of ODS development and operation. Typically these participants include

- The ODS developer
- The data modeler
- The end user

- The DSS analyst
- System programmers
- Database administrators
- Programmers
- Auditors
- Management

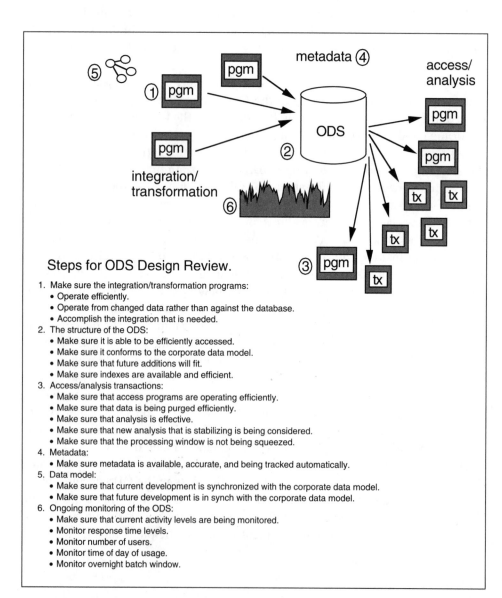

Steps for ODS Design Review.

1. Make sure the integration/transformation programs:
   - Operate efficiently.
   - Operate from changed data rather than against the database.
   - Accomplish the integration that is needed.
2. The structure of the ODS:
   - Make sure it is able to be efficiently accessed.
   - Make sure it conforms to the corporate data model.
   - Make sure that future additions will fit.
   - Make sure indexes are available and efficient.
3. Access/analysis transactions:
   - Make sure that access programs are operating efficiently.
   - Make sure that data is being purged efficiently.
   - Make sure that analysis is effective.
   - Make sure that new analysis that is stabilizing is being considered.
   - Make sure that the processing window is not being squeezed.
4. Metadata:
   - Make sure metadata is available, accurate, and being tracked automatically.
5. Data model:
   - Make sure that current development is synchronized with the corporate data model.
   - Make sure that future development is in synch with the corporate data model.
6. Ongoing monitoring of the ODS:
   - Make sure that current activity levels are being monitored.
   - Monitor response time levels.
   - Monitor number of users.
   - Monitor time of day of usage.
   - Monitor overnight batch window.

**Figure 6.23**    Design review in the ODS environment.

Of the participants, the end user and the DSS analyst are easily the most important; their input is invaluable.

In many cases, having the end user and the DSS analyst in the same room as the developers inspires direct communication that otherwise would not occur. This direct conversation can be an extremely important in a design review. The topics of conversation should include any topics relevant to the success of ODS development. The more controversial the topic, the more appropriate it is for discussion.

As the ODS design review is occurring, notes are taken. At the end of the review the notes are reviewed and form the basis for the formal findings of the review. Generally speaking, the notes are divided into several categories: general observations, action items, and red flags. But the bottom line of design review is to make sure expectations are met with no untoward surprises.

## Summary

The SDLC and CLDS are the ends of the development process spectrum. The ODS fits midway between these two ends. Another development spectrum can be created by the extremes of the data model and the process model. Again, the ODS fits between these two extremes. In any case, the ODS is best built in an iterative manner, where small, fast steps of design define it.

Each entity in the data model corresponds to a physical table in the ODS. In the case of a large number of occurrences of data, an entity may be represented by multiple physical tables in the ODS. The process model shapes the ODS in the same way that the data model does. The functions and activities defined in the process model result in programs and transactions in the ODS environment.

Once the programs and transactions are identified, they are analyzed with regard to frequency and priority of execution. The most important programs and transactions are identified and the system is physically designed to optimize their performance. Popular design techniques that can enhance system performance include

- Merging of tables
- Proper indexing of data
- Proper purging of old data to keep from cluttering up the ODS environment
- Turning off the log tape (when circumstances warrant)
- Preprocessing of transactions prior to their entry into the ODS environment
- Proper space management

# Hardware and Software Requirements

Technology required to support the ODS falls into a number of categories. Since an ODS (like a data warehouse) is a solution made up of numerous components, each component should be looked at separately. An overall picture of the ODS looks something like Figure 7.1. Notice that the major components required are transformation software, the hardware and software platform that will support the ODS, and the middleware that will be used to access it.

## Transformation Software

The first component of the ODS that will be examined is the transformation software. It is here that data is transformed, scrubbed, and propagated from the legacy environment into the ODS. Transformation software has three components. The first handles selection and extraction of the data in the application environment. Note that not every application record needs to be read and not all data needs to be selected. The second component of the transformation program handles conversion or integration. Input data needs to be transformed into the structure and content needed for output. This conversion process is easily the most difficult and time-consuming process. The third component handles loading the data into the ODS. This loading needs to be handled efficiently.

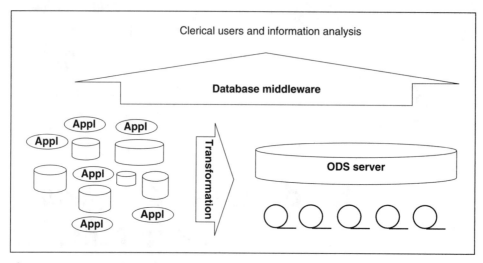

Clerical users and information analysis

Database middleware

Appl
Appl
Appl
Appl
Appl
Appl

Transformation

ODS server

**Figure 7.1** An ODS is made up of three core technologies: middleware, transformation software, and the ODS server environment.

Various tools are available in the market that support these functions either directly or by generating the necessary code to implement these functions. This type of support often proves to be critical to the success of an ODS (or a data warehouse), since it permits the flexibility required to iteratively implement a solution.

In this discussion, transformation is considered to be a logical layer that extends from the legacy data to the point of insertion into the ODS. Various components of this software may exist on the source platform or on the target ODS platform. Indeed, transformation software often runs on a third platform, such as a workstation, and generates the functions needed onto the source and target platform, as shown in Figure 7.2. This discussion does not differentiate between these approaches.

## Support for Numerous Source and Target Platforms

An obvious requirement of a transformation tool is that it can deal with the format and structure of the system of record data stores that will be used to populate the ODS. This includes an understanding of the data types and the conversions necessary to populate the ODS platform. Conversely, the transformation tool should target a wide variety of ODS platforms, with the flexibility to add new ones as they become available. The transformation tool is the first line of defense against vendor lock-in within the ODS, since it can provide portability to new technologies as they become available.

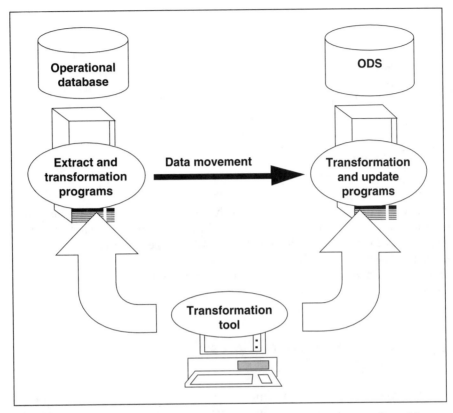

**Figure 7.2** Some tools that automate the transformation layer actually reside on a third platform and generate the code necessary to do transformations.

## Ability to Capture Change

The key to maintaining synchronization in the ODS is the ability to quickly and efficiently capture change in the operational environment. Facilities that automatically capture change can dramatically impact the complexity of an ODS project by negating the need to modify decades of legacy code in order to write application exits for capturing change. As mentioned earlier, reading journal tapes is an effective way to implement a class III ODS, since it allows for the processing of tapes away from the production environment. It requires that the tool perform the complex task of understanding the images on the tape and relating them to the database design. The downside is that near-synchronous propagation of data is not possible since tapes must be filled and dismounted. In certain environments, such as when data is time sensitive (a class I ODS) or when the ODS is being used as a platform for reengineering, this may not be sufficient. In those cases it may be necessary to capture transactions as they happen and feed them directly to the transformation logic, as shown in Figure 7.3.

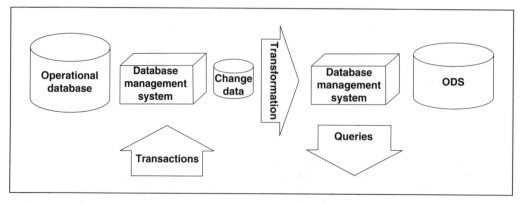

**Figure 7.3**   In cases where data is very time sensitive or the ODS will be used as a basis for reengineering, near-synchronous propagation may be required. This is often done by having the database management system in the legacy environment (DB2, IMS, etc.) generate a record of changes made to the operational database. This change is often in the form of log tapes that are then read by the transformation layer and applied by the database management system in the query environment to the ODS.

## Ability to Support Multiple Types of Transformations

An important technological requirement is that the tools being used support most of the transformations needed in the ODS. These transformations are similar to the types of things that would be done in a data warehouse, since they include integration, decoding, aggregation, and so on. The difference is that the tools must update data that is in place and may be required to trickle information in a near-synchronous manner. If this is the case, the tools must be able to receive data from the change capture facility and pass it directly into the target ODS. In addition, a tool must be able to integrate custom transformation logic written by the enterprise to support unique requirements.

## Ability to Quickly and Easily Adapt to Design Changes

In an ODS, as in a data warehouse, change is the order of the day. Because ODSs are built in an iterative fashion, it is often necessary to change the design and therefore the transformation layer. Clearly one of the benefits of transformation tools is a reduction of effort required to modify and add new transformations by automating this process. Transformation tools often generate software to do the transformations or use a rules engine to allow changes to be made. The ease of use of this tool in modifying the transformation layer is extremely important.

## Ability to Ensure Delivery of Data

It is important that the transformation layer ensure the delivery of data to the ODS. If the ODS is unavailable for any reason, change must be applied to it when it comes back online, otherwise the data in it will be inconsistent with the operational environment. This means that some method of store and forward should be present for ODS outages. Likewise, the transformation layer must have the ability to ensure proper completion of the updates and inserts to be applied against the target ODS. This implies that the transformation layer must have control over transaction boundaries such that it can ensure the completion of inserts, updates, and deletes from the ODS. It is desirable for performance and locking reasons to be able to vary the size of the groups of changes that are committed together. In some cases, it is advantageous to have the ability to group changes based on their business implication such that a consistent view of the business is presented. In Figure 7.4, the implication is that users will tolerate an inconsistent view of item sales across stores but not within a store.

## Metadata Support

The transformation layer of the ODS environment has a great deal of responsibility in the maintenance of the metadata in an ODS. The transformation layer is where knowledge of the current state of the ODS and the rules used to create

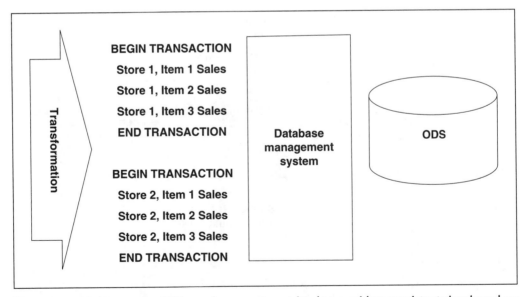

**Figure 7.4** Updates to the ODS may be group committed to provide a consistent view based on the users' requirements. In this example, all updates relevant to a particular store are committed by the database management system as a single transaction.

it reside. This information is invaluable to the users of the ODS because it provides a sense of the timeliness and origin of the data being used. The transformation tool should store metadata in an open and accessible way for users.

## The Operational Data Store Platform

The hardware and software platform that supports the ODS has a number of requirements placed on it. These requirements vary depending on the class of ODS implemented. The most demanding is a class I ODS, since this requires a combination of the characteristics of an online transaction processor (OLTP) system and a high-performance query system. Specifically, the platform must be at a unique intersection of systems that have the ability to manage large volumes of data, perform transactional updates, perform large-scale query, and manage large populations of clerical users, as shown in Figure 7.5. The following are the key areas of interest for implementing a class I ODS. Many will carry over into class II, III, and IV implementations.

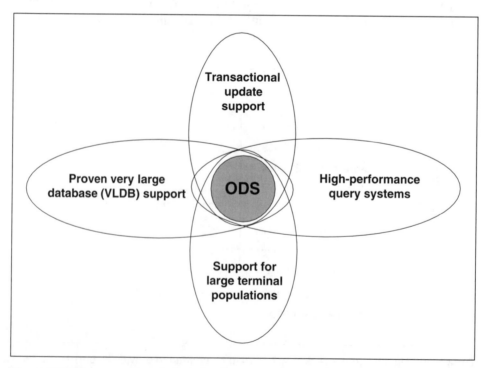

**Figure 7.5** The computing platform used to support an ODS lies at the intersection of four diverse requirements.

# Scalability

The ODS platform must be capable of cost-effective, incremental growth. This allows the platform to support a small initial implementation and to grow seamlessly as subject areas and users are added over time. In addition, the range of scalability must be extreme in order to support a potentially demanding implementation. One approach to this is to build the ODS on a software environment that will allow it to be ported over a wide range of computer systems. If the ODS outgrows the platform that supports it, the platform can be replaced with a more powerful one. Many database management system environments today are capable of running on multiple computer platforms that allow the entire ODS to be ported if needed. The downside of this is that a "box swap" is required rather than growing the existing investment; there is, as well, the potential to become tied to the vendor who sells the portable environment.

Another approach is to provide scalability through the use of parallel processing. In this scenario, individual tasks are spread over multiple processors and disk and I/O devices to enable growth through addition. Parallel processing has only reached maturity with a few vendors, but in those cases it has demonstrated the ability to handle large volumes of data and complex query loads. It also has the advantage of allowing incremental scalability in small units of growth as workloads increase.

# A Word about Parallel Processing

Some of the discussion in this book refers to parallel processing. While this is not a requirement for support of an ODS, there are a number of reasons why it is a useful technology. Two commercial flavors of parallel processing computers are used today: symmetrical multiprocessing (SMP) and massively parallel processing (MPP). This is shown in Figure 7.6.

SMP systems are characterized by multiple processors having access to a common pool of memory. This is the most popular method because of its relative ease of implementation. One copy of the operating system and database software resides in memory as it would in monolithic systems and it has been taught to schedule multiple threads of execution across all of the processors. This approach will provide scalability until memory becomes a bottleneck for communications and then will exhibit a decrease in processing speed for each processor that is added.

MPP systems are characterized by nonshared memory. The concept is similar to a distributed network of computers, each with its own operating and database management systems. The difference is that in an MPP system, these "computers" are aware of each other and can work on a common task. Because of the speed of the interconnect and the peer-to-peer nature of the system software, the distinction between processors is blurred in an MPP, resulting in what

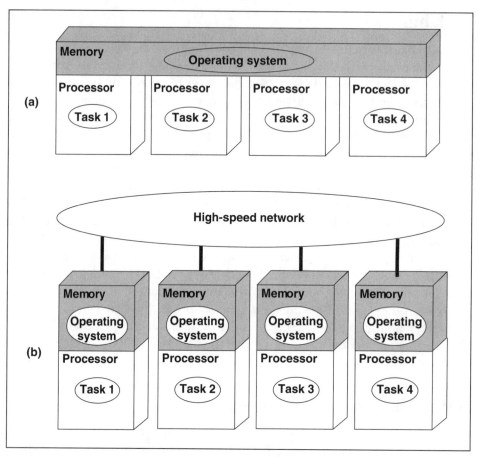

**Figure 7.6** (a) Shared memory implementations such as SMP have a single instance of the operating system, which schedules work across many processing resources. (b) Shared nothing implementations, known as MPP, have an instance of the operating system in every processor, which must work together to present a single system image.

appears to be a single large computer. An MPP system is relatively difficult for a vendor to build, since it requires multiple copies of the operating and database management systems working so closely together that they appear to be one. The advantage is that there are no shared components to produce bottlenecks or failures.

It is possible to build a system that is much more scalable and available than SMP systems. A side effect of parallel processing is that because of the use of multiple, parallel components, each having its own mean time between failure, system availability can decrease as system size increases. This must be addressed by designing into the system such availability features as the ability to continue execution when components have failed. The continuity of execution is a natural thing to do in a parallel environment because work can be spread to the remaining portions of the system.

What is important to note is that parallel hardware for an ODS is not difficult to build. It is the software that is key to making the parallel environment work and that is still an evolving market. There are only a handful of commercial database management systems that were designed from the start to work in an SMP environment, and even fewer can deal with MPP. Compaq Computers' NonStop SQL is an example of a database management system designed for an MPP environment, which explains why it has demonstrated the ability to scale into the terabyte databases. Database management systems need to be able to support interquery parallelism (concurrent queries) as well as intraquery parallelism (the ability to execute a single query in parallel). While early attempts at parallel query would simply decompose a query into subqueries for each processor to handle, newer designs are allowing the entire query to be optimized in a parallel fashion, as shown in Figure 7.7. This can dramatically enhance performance.

In addition, all of the system utilities used should be able to work in parallel. If a computer has 100 processors and any job or utility cannot be run in parallel, the job will operate in 1/100th of the system, which may be less than optimal. This applies to loading, inserting, index creation and maintenance, data

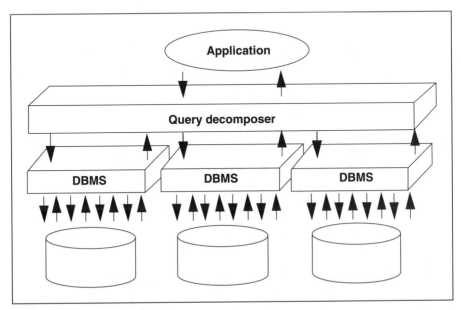

**Figure 7.7** Simple parallel query can be achieved by external parallelization, which allows a large query to be broken into subqueries that are executed separately. Newer implementations use internal parallelization for better efficiency.

reorganization, sorting, scanning, joining, and so on. It is important to remember that scalability, the implied benefit of parallel processing, can be mitigated by the inability to manage large, commercial databases if unproven technology is applied.

## Support for Large, Diverse, and Demanding Networking

An ODS has two sets of networking requirements: one that puts data into the system and one that allows it to be taken out. On the inbound side, high bandwidth communications are required to allow data to be moved into the ODS. The need is often for legacy interoperability using proprietary mainframe protocols, but more and more can be achieved using open communications protocols such as asynchronous transfer mode (ATM) and fiber distributed data interface (FDDI). Because cost rises exponentially with bandwidth, it is important that the ability to parallelize this type of communication over numerous low-cost lines be available (Figure 7.8).

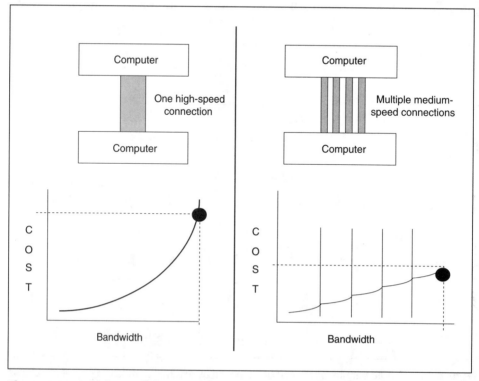

**Figure 7.8**   Multiple parallel connections between systems provide a more cost-effective solution for moving data, but the system software must make this transparent.

On the outbound side of an ODS it is necessary to support both legacy connections, to allow terminal environments to access the ODS and high-speed open connections for local area networks (LANs) and wide area networks (WANs). Because of the potential for a large clerical user population using prebuilt query applications, support for legacy system access will prove useful. In order to allow access to the widest variety of workstation tools, mainstream LAN and WAN connectivity, such as TCP/IP and Xerox Network System (XNS), are needed. In addition, communication facilities capable of high-speed data transfers might be needed if the ODS must snapshot data into a data warehouse residing on a separate physical platform.

## High Availability

It is often assumed that because DSSs are query only, they can fail with minimal impact. This is not always true. Both data warehouses and ODSs can have a major impact on the enterprise when they become unavailable because they service many important decision makers. The owners of the world's largest DSS in retail, telecommunications, and transportation will typically list system availability as one of the biggest challenges they face. In an ODS this is paramount, since the data is often very timely and since it supports tactical, short-term decision making by senior management and large numbers of clerical workers. If an ODS supports 400 operators in a call center, for instance, an hour of unavailability could cause havoc (as well as a great deal of career planning for the IS department).

The platform supporting the ODS should have the ability to survive component outages wherever possible without interruption of service to the users. This should include disk, processor, and software failures. Availability goes well beyond component failures. Operations (backup, reorganization, restructuring, etc.) that are performed on a regular basis should be able to run in an online fashion with full user access. With many companies moving to international operations, it is increasingly difficult to dedicate batch windows for system unavailability.

## Ability to Perform High-Performance Inserts, Updates, and Deletes

Central to the concept of an ODS is the fact that it is not appending new snapshots of data like a data warehouse. It is a moving snapshot of the operational systems and as such requires insert, update, and delete capabilities. Contrary to popular belief, these added capabilities do not inherently cause a database management system to perform more slowly on queries (query path length does not grow because a database management system can perform audited updates), but they do generally increase the cost of the product. One reason for the increased cost is that full-function database management systems generally have to support mission-critical environments. These database management systems must be built to rigorous standards with heavy quality assurance. This is a curse or a blessing depending on the degree of cost consciousness versus risk aversion that is required.

In an ODS it is imperative that inserts, updates, and deletes can be applied to the database. In a class I ODS, this activity must be performed with absolute integrity. Otherwise the ODS can fall out of synch with the operational systems. As will be mentioned later, the availability of a well-hosted transaction processing monitor can improve the performance, integrity, and manageability of this function. The database management system must be able to deal with random as well as sequential changes to the database. This requires an efficient lock management system, which should include row-level locking and the ability to detect a deadly embrace (two transactions locking each other out of completion). In addition, it is important that the system can either read through locks or provide a consistent image of changing data, depending on the users' requirements. Designs that provide a before snapshot of changing data may be preferable unless update volume is large, in which case the before images can overrun the system.

In order to handle random and sequential insertions as well as the deletion of aged records and update of variable-length fields, the ODS platform must have an efficient way of dealing with block splits. Block splits occur when records are deleted from and inserted to a sequentially organized data structure, causing fragmentation of the blocks. If block splits are not minimized or make inefficient use of space, database fragmentation will cause performance to be reduced due to the data losing its sequential nature. Failing to minimize block splits can cause the database to need frequent physical reorganization.

## Transaction Processor Monitor Functionality

A transaction processor (TP) monitor is loosely defined as containing process management, link management, and transaction management, as shown in Figure 7.9. Some of these functions are now being provided by database management system vendors. These capabilities are often more important in the ODS than in a data warehouse. The reason is because a data warehouse might have a profile of 50 users running queries with a relative difficulty of 10, while an ODS might have 500 users running queries with a relative difficulty of 1 and 30 users with a relative difficulty of 10. Because of the larger user population and shorter query profile, the ability to provide multithreaded access to the database can dramatically reduce memory requirements in an ODS. Traditional TP monitors provide such features as load balancing and recoverability, which make the implementation much easier to manage. In addition, a well-imple-

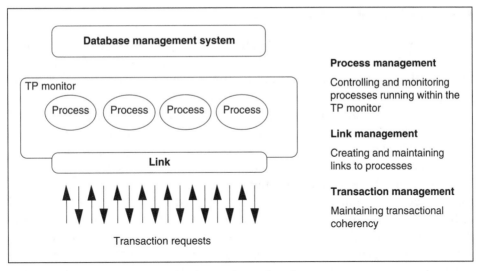

**Figure 7.9**    A TP monitor provides three primary functions.

mented TP monitor can actually increase performance for updating and inserting by performing such techniques as deferred writes and group commits. Prioritization capabilities provided by a well-implemented TP monitor will often prove invaluable for the task of mixing workloads as needed by an ODS.

## Availability of a Performance Monitoring/Tuning Infrastructure

It is critical in an ODS as well as a data warehouse that the supporting platform be instrumented for performance monitoring and tuning. Otherwise, management can become overwhelming due to the mixed workload and complexity of the ODS. This means that the major subsystems are instrumented in such a way that they provide meaningful information on system performance, CPU utilization, cache utilization, data access patterns, and query optimization. It is important to be able to capture this information and relate it to users and user groups in order to understand usage patterns. A common complaint among people who have implemented these systems is that the system is running at capacity but no visibility exists into who or what is using it. Unlike a data warehouse, an ODS does not readily allow summaries to be added to enhance performance; it is susceptible to traditional OLTP tuning, such as alternate indexes and physical data reorganization and redistribution. All of this must be tempered with the knowledge that some users are going to be doing truly ad hoc queries that defy most OLTP tuning tricks.

## Online, Granular Manageability

In order to manage large volatile databases such as an ODS, two key capabilities are needed. First, users should be able to access the database while operating database utilities. If this is not possible, users must be taken off of the system for maintenance. Database management systems exist today that allow activities such as index creation, backup, repartitioning, redistribution, and reorganization to be performed while users have full read, write, and update capability. The last of these—reorganization—is particularly important because data is being inserted and updated, causing block splits to occur.

Second, in addition to being online, database operations should be performed at a very granular level. This is to say that work should be performed only on the piece of the database that is to be affected without impacting the rest of the system. If, for instance, a reorganization needs to be performed, it should be targeted at a specific segment of a specific table and run at a low priority while online operations are performed to that partition at a high priority. Reorganization should be able to be throttled, paused, and restarted.

## Database Administration/System Programmer and System-Controlled Placement of Data

Placement of data in a query processing system is very important. As shown in Figure 7.10, sometimes it is beneficial to have data spread randomly over many disk volumes and sometimes it is best to have data in sequential order. Many DSS queries, for instance, have an element of time in them (how many widgets were shipped last Tuesday) that might imply a range of sequential data. It might be beneficial for the data to be placed in contiguous disk space. In other circumstances, it might be best to have contiguous data spread over many disk volumes to reduce hot spots or areas of high activity.

It is important for the database administrator (DBA) to have control over the placement of data, including tables and indexes, such that he or she can select a method of data distribution that is optimal for the environment. Ideally, data which is very active could be specifically placed by range in certain locations. This is especially important in some parallel processing environments, since data placement can affect allocation of processing power. In other situations, uniformly spreading data using hashing or striping is very useful. Methods such as these attempt to spread data evenly over a large group of disks automatically. System-managed storage is of value as long as it is open to operator intervention. In fact, for managing temporary space, such as sort space and temporary or intermediate tables, it is almost mandatory.

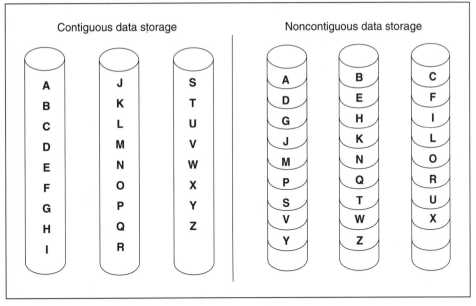

**Figure 7.10**   Much of the query processing is range based; thus sequential storage of data is helpful while other workloads benefit from a random distribution of data.

## Ability to Perform Massive Queries

One aspect of an ODS that makes it very difficult to support with current technology is the multiple personalities that a platform is required to support. While there is technology on the market that is good at transaction processing, complex query processing, or capable of supporting large amounts of data, the intersection of these three capabilities is fairly limited. In particular, high-performance query processing presents a few challenges. One example is retrieving the data from disk. Assuming that the data cannot be accessed via an index, it must be scanned, which is very costly.

Once the data has been retrieved, it must be joined with other data, which often implies sorts. Since sorting is a logarithmic function, time to complete grows exponentially with sort size, making traditional sort/merge techniques costly for large databases. One clever approach to solving this is heavy use of indexing. Technology exists that allows a table to be heavily indexed with minimal storage overhead, thus reducing scans and sorts. However, the creation and maintenance of indexes is costly from a CPU standpoint. The trade-off between indexes and insert/update performance is shown in Figure 7.11. It is for these reasons that high-performance parallel processing is currently a leading technology for ODS implementation, with a proven ability to deal with high-

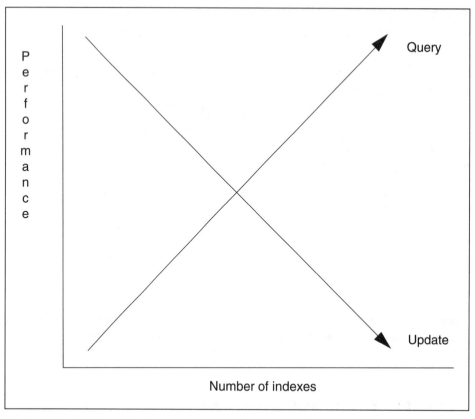

**Figure 7.11**    While adding indexes can benefit query performance, it has a negative impact on update workloads typical of an ODS.

performance scanning. A few implementations have a track record for supporting large amounts of data in a high-performance query environment.

The platform supporting the ODS must therefore be able to perform extremely high-speed scans of data for environments where analysis requires access without indexes. The platform must be able to perform large joins, unions, and aggregations. More advanced database management systems have implemented hashing techniques for joining and aggregation, which scale far better than traditional methods due to their elimination of sorting. The platform must still be able to sort large amounts of data. Although these hashing techniques can eliminate most sorting done in queries (a requirement to eliminate the logarithmic effect mentioned earlier), sort utilities will still be needed for normal operation and management of the system.

## Ability to Perform Mixed Workloads

Multiple types of workloads are present in an ODS:

**Short queries** designed to support the clerical community and the EIS users. These are often simple selections of data with the need to find next/find previous within a sequence of data.

**Long and complex queries** designed to support the analytical community. These often involve reading millions if not billions of records and performing large joins and aggregations of tables.

**Inserts, updates, and deletes** involved in keeping the ODS in synch with the operational systems. In a class I ODS, these can be extremely demanding.

It is important that the ODS platform be able to mix these workloads, otherwise the users would have to be relegated to certain times of the day and the near-synchronous updating of a class I ODS would not be possible. Long-running queries need to run at a lower priority and be interruptable by shorter high-priority queries and updates, as seen in Figure 7.12. The system should also be able to schedule queries such that large non-time-critical queries can be scheduled for overnight execution. Some query environments today can deal with this issue and even detect large queries prior to execution, suggesting to the user that they be deferred. It is also important that these types of rules be defined at the user and/or user-group level.

## Efficient Index Support

Based on the trade-off mentioned earlier, it is important to have as efficient an indexing mechanism as possible. Since an ODS is built in an iterative fashion, one of the things that may become necessary is to add alternate indexes to the database for performance reasons. Assuming that the management infrastructure mentioned earlier is available, the DBA will begin to see patterns of use appear primarily from the clerical and EIS users because of the repetitive nature of their activity. When this happens, alternate indexes must be built quickly and maintained by the database management system using minimal storage. If it is a parallel processing environment, the creation, deletion, and maintenance of the indexes must be done in parallel to provide minimal impact on daily operations. In addition, the database management system should be able to perform index-only scans when the data requested is contained entirely within an index.

## Single-Image Distribution of Data

One way to mitigate the decision of centralization versus distribution is to base the ODS on a technology that provides transparent distribution of data. There are two challenges here: transparency and bandwidth. Transparent dis-

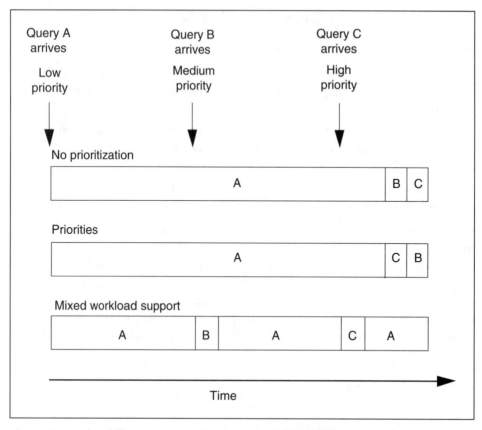

**Figure 7.12**   The ability to support mixed workloads effectively allows large queries to be interrupted by high-priority clerical users.

tribution has been evolving into database management system technology for some time. Some database management systems today allow multiple physical sites to appear as a single database. The best implementations allow a single table to be partitioned across multiple sites. In this case, the optimizer will recognize queries that can be satisfied from local ranges of data and will not impact remote locations. If queries are launched that encompass the entire database, the multiple sites return their result sets to the user as a single answer.

The drawback to this is in the area of bandwidth. If a database management system is asked to join two 100GB tables across a traditional Ethernet, the query might outlive the user. For this reason, the question of centralization versus distribution is based on the requirement for internode queries and the profile they may have. This is not true in some parallel processing environments, however, because users can own sections of the computer and yet it can operate as a whole for enterprise questions.

## Logging and Journaling

Transaction logging is a key function for a platform to support an ODS. How well and how fast the platform provides this function can define the limit to growth and timeliness of an ODS implementation. Specifically, high-performance locking should be available and is characterized by the ability to do group commits and deferred writes, and support multiple, configurable logs. Group commits allow transactions to be written to the log in batches, which increases performance due to the boxcar effect. The *boxcar effect* is the ability to improve performance by taking many units of work and performing them in an organized sequence, such as grouping transactions and committing them in a sequential pass of the heads over a disk. By lining up the commits like cars of a train and committing them sequentially, performance can actually improve as the system comes under load. Deferred writes allow the transactions to be logged but not immediately written to the base tables and indexes. In this way, the system can write a large number of changes to the database in a single pass over the disk yet maintain transaction integrity. Having multiple parallel logs is important in dealing with the potentially large number of changes that might be applied to an ODS as it is refreshed. In the interest of reducing log space, audit compression should be supported, which allows change to be logged at the field level rather than the row level. This is important in an ODS because fields are often modified within an otherwise unchanged row. It is also important that logging can be configured for individual tables and indexes.

## Middleware

The network middleware is an important part of an ODS. Middleware provides the glue between users' applications and the data contained in the ODS, as well as in the data warehouse and operational systems, as seen in Figure 7.13. In some cases it is valuable to relate information in the ODS to information in a data warehouse. If, for instance, the requirement is to isolate a group of customers who are candidates for a new sales program, it might be beneficial to determine their historical buying habits as well as their current account status. In these situations it is the middleware that can provide a common access method for numerous data stores (given that the data stores are not already within a common distributed database management system). It is also the middleware that often determines which platforms, tools, and network protocols are available for use. Following is a discussion of important considerations for middleware in an ODS implementation.

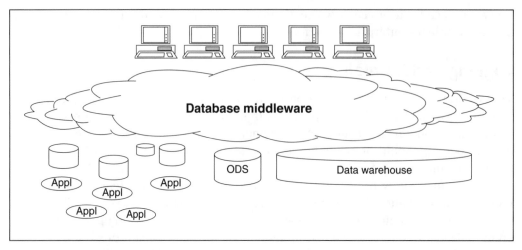

**Figure 7.13**    Database middleware provides the glue between users and the various sources of data in the enterprise.

## Support for a Wide Variety of Client Interfaces

Clearly the middleware used in an ODS needs to be versatile in its support of tools and applications. This is best achieved by supporting multiple-client machines and multiple programming interfaces. The most common clients are PCs and Macintoshes, but others need to be considered. In the implementation of three-tiered client-server systems it is common for the ODS to be accessed by midtier servers running a flavor of UNIX. This allows relatively small PC clients to be used by offloading analytical processing to a midtier server. It is also important in an ODS to consider the large number of clerical users who may still be attached via terminal to legacy systems. In this case, the current operational platform acts as a client to the ODS and must be supported. All require support for common data-access programming interfaces. The interfaces described are manifested in the form of formats and protocols (FAPs), application programming interfaces (APIs), and dialects, as shown in Figure 7.14. All are important because the most robust middleware product would be of little value if it required a massive investment to replace thousands of terminals or a large network environment.

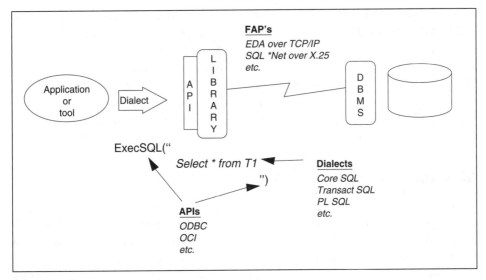

**Figure 7.14**    The difference between FAPs, APIs, and dialects.

## Compatibility with Many Relational and Nonrelational Database Management Systems

Since middleware is the glue that connects users to data, it is equally important that a middleware product connect to a variety of data management systems. Since data may be contained in a legacy environment with mere pointers in the ODS, it is important that the middleware be able to access the production systems as well as the ODS. This is not to say that one could use middleware to negate the need for a data warehouse or ODS, since most of the benefits of data rearchitecturing would be lost. Used together, middleware and an ODS make a powerful combination. This implies that the middleware must understand and deal with modern relational structures as well as older flat file or network databases, and perhaps over time, object data stores as well.

## Distributed Schema Awareness and Routing

One of the more valuable things that middleware can provide to an ODS is an overall awareness of the schemas of the various data sources. If the middleware is intelligent enough to work at the schema level, it then has the ability to present a single integrated catalog to the user's application that masks the physical location of the data. This implies that the middleware is capable of decomposing a query that might access multiple physical platforms, allowing each to retrieve a partial result set that is returned to the user in an integrated fashion. Database integration is typically done by requiring that the various platforms return data sorted in the same order and then merging this data, as shown in Figure 7.15. It is not easy to do this well, since it implies that much of the intelligence of a database management system should reside in the middleware.

## Monitoring and Statistics Gathering

Because the middleware is the common software through which all query activity will pass, it is in a unique position to assist in the administration of the ODS environment. If the middleware gathers enough meaningful data about usage of the ODS environment, a foundation is provided for understanding the entire decision-making environment in a way that the ODS platform cannot. Middle-

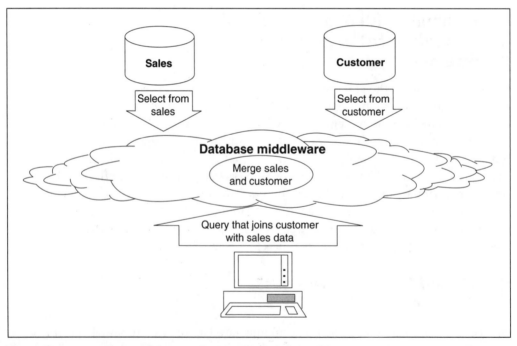

**Figure 7.15**   Database middleware decomposing a query to be executed on two databases and merging the results for the user. These databases could reside in different database management systems or even on different physical computer systems.

ware will have a view of which users launched queries, at what times, and what data elements they touched. If, for instance, it was clear that ODS users were repetitively retrieving data from the operational system, the DBA might decide that it would be advantageous to propagate that data to the ODS periodically. If a data warehouse is present, the middleware can provide valuable information about the need for certain summary views, which would enhance performance.

## Queuing and Scheduling

One of the often-overlooked benefits of middleware is in the task of overall query management. A user might want to issue a query or report that runs every Monday morning at 8:00 A.M. Middleware exists today that allows the user to insert this query into a schedule for regular execution. Likewise, this type of middleware can precost the query and, if over a certain threshold, suggest or even mandate to the user that it be run at off-peak hours. Since most query platforms see diminishing returns as the number of concurrent queries rises (due to thrashing for memory or disk contention), some middleware can track the number of submitted queries and queue them if need be for delayed execution. If the middleware is to provide deferred or batch execution of queries, it is implied that it must be able to store and forward the results. The ability to store and forward is particularly valuable if the client is not always available, as is the case for a retail buyer who works on the road with a portable computer.

## Summary

Technology to support an ODS can be complex. Technology is required to support functions that are not often found on a common platform. Compared with a class I ODS, implementing a class II or III ODS is technologically less demanding. The technology required to support an ODS falls into three areas: transformation software, the ODS platform, and middleware. The transformation software must be able to effectively link legacy environments to the ODS, potentially in a near-synchronous mode. Using vendor-supplied transformation software as a base can accelerate the deployment of the ODS by reducing the effort needed to build this layer from scratch.

The ODS platform may require a great deal of the functionality needed to support OLTP, such as logging, updating, and online manageability, as well as the high-performance query associated with some query-only environments. Parallel processing is a suitable technology for the ODS and is currently maturing in the market. The middleware used in an ODS is responsible for interfacing the various user populations to the ODS as well as allowing them to retrieve data from the operational systems.

CHAPTER

8

# Implementing the ODS: Case Studies

The implementation of an ODS is an evolutionary process, however it is accomplished. This chapter describes the development and implementation of five ODSs. The first case study is based on observations that were made over a number of years of the development of a real ODS for a telephone company. One of the most interesting aspects of this implementation of an ODS is that the ODS was not built deliberately. Instead, it was built as the result of the interaction of several strong forces within the organization, both business and technical. This unplanned, spontaneous nature of an ODS implementation is very typical. Four shorter case studies follow this extended ODS example. Each illustrates a different implementation scenario.

## Interacting Forces

In the telephone company case, the corporate forces that interacted with each other to produce the ODS were

**Business forces.** There was a strong business incentive for an ODS. The telephone company had a need to directly interact with its customer base in a very knowledgeable manner, and to do so interactively. At the same time the telephone company needed to base direct customer interaction on the analysis of a customer's historical and demographic information. The driving force behind the ODS then was a business need to capture and maintain market share.

The business requirements did not appear magically or all at once. Instead they evolved from a basic set of needs that grew in sophistication each day. The business requirements were as much influenced by what was possible as anything else. There was more than one occasion when the business analyst asked, That's an interesting thing to do, but does it have business impact? Is there a marketplace need for that capability? How can we make money on that information?

**Technical forces.** There was a need to perform online transaction processing and to operate on the results of the analysis of historical data at the same time. Neither a DSS structure nor an OLTP structure alone would suffice. There simply was no technology designed specifically for the business problem at hand. Complicating the technical solution were the volumes of data maintained by the telephone company. On the one hand there was a significant amount of data. On the other hand, in order to be useful, the data had to be kept at a very detailed level. Because detailed, historical data was needed, the volumes of data that were necessary were very large and hence the technological factors were daunting, especially in light of the business requirements.

# A Nontraditional Development Effort

The ODS implementation process that is described here is nontraditional in that what will be described happened in an almost offhand fashion. (It is of course possible that no ODS is ever built in a classical manner.) The good news is that the results of this evolutionary development process were very successful. The bad news is that apparently much of the success was an act of randomness, and was certainly unplanned.

## Parallel Development Efforts

The development of the ODS proceeded down two parallel paths: development of the data warehouse that ultimately supported a class IV ODS, and development of the ODS itself. The ODS began life in the simplest and most humble of ways. But the merger between the ODS and the data warehouse produced rather spectacular results. What will be described then is two parallel development efforts that ultimately merged or intersected into a class IV ODS.

# The Customer Data Warehouse

The data warehouse that ultimately led to the ODS was a customer data warehouse. There were several nascent efforts at data warehousing that preceded the first data warehouse, resulting in data being captured and elegantly displayed for management decisions. These efforts were called a data warehouse, but in fact they were very small DSS efforts with limited capability. To call the early efforts a data warehouse required a real stretch of the imagination.

But these early efforts at data warehousing served a very useful purpose. They sold management on the idea of building more than online transaction processing systems. The early versions of the warehouse convinced the organization to take affirmative steps toward building a real data warehouse.

Once the organization made up its mind to build a real data warehouse, it did so with resolve. The first data warehouse was to center around a customer. Figure 8.1 shows some of the simple feeds that went into the first iteration of the data warehouse. A single subject area—customer—was chosen and the designers and developers set out to build the warehouse. A data model was built and served as a basis for the design of the customer warehouse. In fact, the corporation had built a number of data models previously. The data warehouse data model represented an amalgamation of several of the earlier data models. Because the data warehouse data model did not have to be built from scratch, the modeling process was completed quickly.

Very early on the designers and developers recognized that the issue of granularity was significant. Because the design was for a telephone company, the size of the warehouse posed a real problem. Even though the first iteration of the warehouse was based on customer, it was recognized that future iterations

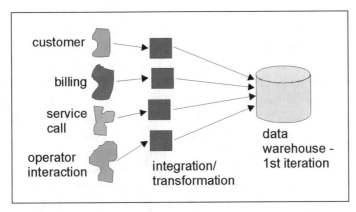

**Figure 8.1**   The first iteration of the data warehouse.

would have to include telephone usage data. Although a telephone company has many customers records, it has many more usage records (every time a customer picks up the phone and makes a call, a usage record is created). So if the first iteration of the warehouse was to be large, future iterations of the warehouse would be even larger. Much larger.

If the detailed usage data could be condensed—by aggregation, by summarization, and so forth—the total volume of the data for the data warehouse could be reduced significantly. But every time the data was condensed, detail was lost, meaning that less analysis could ultimately be done on the data. Therefore, the data modeling discussions led to discussions of granularity, which in turn led to discussions of functionality which then led to discussions of capacity, which in turn led to discussions of the technology required to support the data warehouse. Each topic was tightly and importantly linked with the others. No resolution or decision could be made without consideration of other factors affected by the decision.

Not only were these early discussions complex, but the decision-making process was hampered by the fact that different departments participated in the discussions and each department had its own agenda. In order to be successful, all departmental agendas needed to be satisfied. While there was consensus of opinion that customer should be the focus of the first iteration of the warehouse, there was little consensus about anything else. Making matters worse was the fact that organizational personnel were constantly changing.

Finally, it was decided that if the organization really wanted a data warehouse, one group would have to make the final decisions. A "warehouse group" was created whose responsibility it was to build the data warehouse and to make final decisions. The warehouse group was responsible for gathering and satisfying all agendas as best as they could. Trying to design and create a data warehouse by committee was deemed to be unworkable. The warehouse group then went about collecting all the known requirements for the data warehouse.

The warehouse group first set out to benchmark both hardware and software. There was one good piece of news: there were very few hardware and software vendors to choose from. Complicating matters was the fact that certain pieces of software would run on more than one hardware platform. Even though there were not many technology choices to be made, the technologies needed to be considered in combination with each other.

The technological considerations were more architectural than tactical. In other words, the emphasis was not so much on how much data the technology could swallow in the immediate future, but how much could the technology swallow in the long term. The scalability and the cost of scalability of the infrastructure became the focus of investigation. In order to achieve the scalability that was needed, a technological approach using some form of parallelism was mandated.

Of interest, there were some very real differences in the database management systems that were considered. The database vendors that did not have technology that could take advantage of parallelism tried to mask their deficiencies. Given that testing or simulation on a fully loaded production machine was not a technological or economically viable option, the vendors that had inferior parallel technology cleverly tried to hide their weaknesses. However, careful analysis succeeded in sorting out the differences.

The differences between the database management systems centered around the degree and the type of parallelism supported by the technology. Some database management systems were designed to support a form of parallelism centering around an SMP architecture. While an SMP architecture has many desirable features, it has an upper limit after which it cannot gracefully and economically handle large volumes of data. The alternative to the SMP architecture was an architecture known as an MPP architecture. Figure 8.2 shows that a parallel approach was the only viable long-term architecture.

The MPP architecture is a bit more expensive and a bit more "brittle" than the SMP architecture, but the MPP architecture has no technological upper limit on how much data it can handle. (There is an upper limit of MPP technology, but generally speaking, that upper limit is economic rather than technological.) Therefore an MPP solution appeared to be the best chance for managing the volumes of data that were anticipated for the phone company. After many observations and benchmarks, the hardware and software platforms were chosen.

The next decision of the warehouse group was that of selecting an automated tool for creation of the interface between the legacy environment and the data warehouse. (Previous attempts at building a data warehouse had all been done using manual coding to move the data out of the legacy application environ-

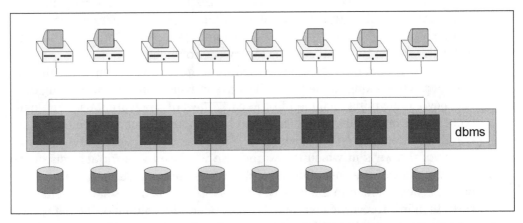

**Figure 8.2**  In order to accommodate future growth, a hardware platform and a database management system platform that were optimal for a parallel environment were selected.

ment into the data warehouse.) At that time there were not that many tools to choose from. The differences between tools were in the robustness of transformation offered by the tool. The more robust tool was very difficult to set up and use; the less robust tool was much easier to use. The trade-off then was between completeness of transformation capability and ease of use. The telephone company chose productivity and selected the less robust tool.

It was felt that most transformations could be handled by the tool selected. The transformations that could not be handled could be coded by hand. In adopting this strategy, the telephone company got the advantages of an automation tool that was very easy to use and at the same time they were able to accommodate the occasional very difficult transformation.

At this point the data modeling was done, the infrastructure selected, and the automation tool chosen; now work on the warehouse commenced. The first subject area chosen was customer. There were about sixty-five different sources that needed to be integrated in order to feed customer data. The data was selected and converted using the automation tool. The warehouse was populated in about three months time.

The tools of access and analysis were already being used by the telephone company when the data warehouse first came up, so there was no question which end-user tools were going to be selected. Instead the focus became how the end user and analysis tools could get access to data in the data warehouse. There were two basic ways that data in the warehouse was accessed: data was accessed directly, and data was moved off into a data mart where it was then accessed directly. Multiple access and analysis tools had to be accommodated because each user community had its own favorite tool and seldom did any two user communities agree.

After the data warehouse was first put out for general use, it was discovered that there was bad data in the warehouse. Actually there was not that much bad data, but the data that was bad became glaringly obvious. A fair amount of correction was done by going back to the originating source and adjusting how the data was brought forward from the legacy environment.

After a period of time the data "settled" into the data warehouse and the end users started flocking to the data. The ways in which the data was being used was beyond anything imagined in the early days of the warehouse. The existence and the availability of the data warehouse spurred people to think in ways that they had never before imagined.

One of the ways in which the warehouse was used was for analysis of the demographics of the customer base. While this analysis was being done, new data was being added to the data warehouse. Usage data was added—first gingerly, then in a torrent. As usage data was added, the volume of the data warehouse grew rapidly. But with the addition of usage data came the opportunity to extend the types of analyses that could be done. Figure 8.3 illustrates the early smallness of the data warehouse.

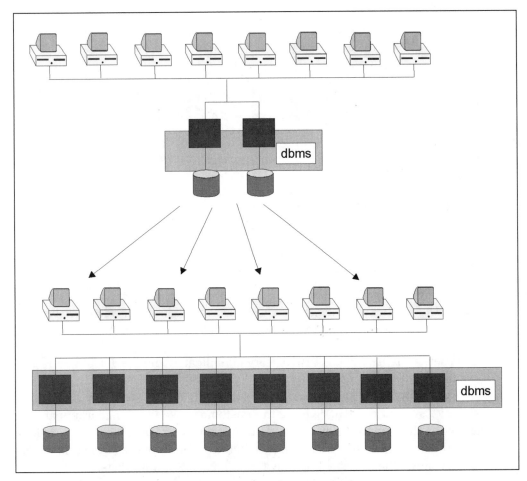

**Figure 8.3**   The data warehouse started out small but quickly grew.

It was the addition of call-level detail which caused the warehouse growth to explode, as seen in Figure 8.4. But call-level detail was not the only factor contributing to the rapid growth of the warehouse. The second factor contributing to growth was that of the collection of historical data. Figure 8.5 shows that historical data was collected over time into the data warehouse. The net effect of call-level detail, historical data, and customer data was a very dramatic increase in the volumes of data found in the data warehouse. Figure 8.6 depicts this growth.

As the data first appeared, the end-user community approached the data warehouse rather timidly. The first queries were simple, as seen in Figure 8.7. But soon the queries grew in sophistication. The end users discovered that with integrated data very interesting queries could be formulated. In short order the

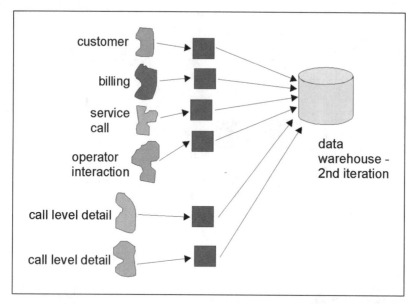

**Figure 8.4** For the second iteration, call-level detail was added to the data warehouse.

end users were asking all sorts of very complicated and insightful queries, as seen in Figure 8.8.

One of the first analytical activities was to divide the customer base into a series of submarkets. By dividing the customer base into submarkets and by analyzing the activity of the submarket, the end user at long last began to get a feel for how the customer base really reacted to forces in the marketplace. Figure 8.9 shows the division of the customer base into submarkets.

But for all of the analysis being done—and for the first time the telephone company was beginning to understand who its customers really were—there

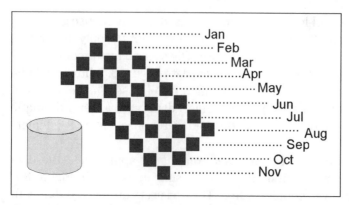

**Figure 8.5** Soon history began to collect in the data warehouse.

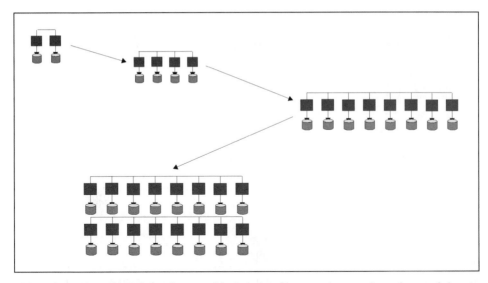

**Figure 8.6** As call-level detail was added to the data warehouse, the volume of data in the data warehouse increased dramatically and at a very fast rate.

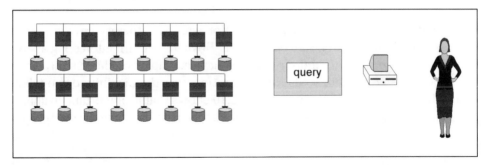

**Figure 8.7** When the DSS analysis community first discovered the data warehouse, the queries were simple.

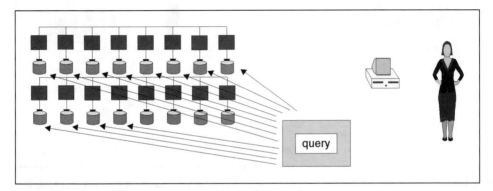

**Figure 8.8** Soon the queries grew in sophistication, examining more data and looking at detailed relationships.

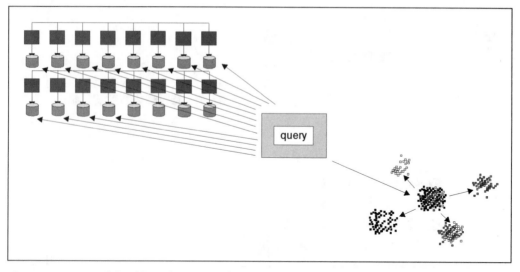

**Figure 8.9**   One of the things the DSS analysts did was to hone in on the different markets of the telephone company. Once the aggregate markets were identified, then the submarkets were sorted out.

developed a vague frustration. That frustration was, Now that we have analyzed our customer base, what can we do about it? How do you turn interesting analysis into proactive products and services that have an impact on the marketplace? As the analysis continued, so did the frustration over the inability to capitalize on newly discovered information. Figure 8.10 shows that as important as analysis is, turning analysis into marketplace advantage is another matter entirely.

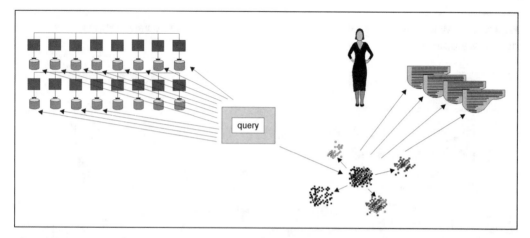

**Figure 8.10**   From the analysis created by looking at the different submarkets of customers, the DSS analysis community discovered some very interesting information. However, using that information at the point of customer contact proved very difficult.

# The ODS

In a completely different part of the telephone company an ODS grew in parallel to the development of the data warehouse. The ODS was not known as an ODS when it was first conceived, but it was an ODS nevertheless. The ODS was born out of the frustration of having many applications that were unintegrated. Application programmers gave up on the idea of trying to go into the legacy environment and make significant changes to the old applications. When application programmers realized that major rewrites of old applications were not going to happen, there was a realization that there was still a need for integration of operational transaction processing systems.

The first step toward the ODS was simple. An application designer looked at several customer applications and decided that if she could bring data into a common operational transaction processing application there was a chance for real operational integration. Figure 8.11 shows this first attempt at an ODS.

The ODS in its nascent format was very simple. All that the business wanted to do was to create a single place where operators could go in order to handle customer inquiries and requests. All that was contained in the first version of the ODS was basic integrated customer information. Figure 8.12 shows that the first attempt at an ODS was to manage direct customer contact. The ODS was more of a response to the need for integration than anything else. Since integration was not going to be achieved in the legacy environment, then it had to be achieved in another structure.

The infrastructure that was chosen was optimal for transaction processing. While there was a significant amount of data found in the ODS, there was nowhere near the amount of data found in the data warehouse. There was no

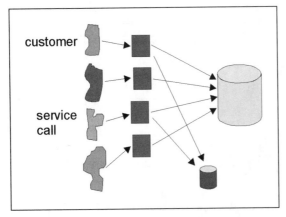

**Figure 8.11**  A very simple ODS is created from legacy customer databases and service call databases.

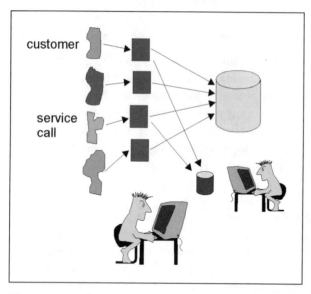

**Figure 8.12**   The ODS was used in its simplest form for direct customer contact.

usage data or historical data found in the ODS. Figure 8.13 shows that the initial thrust of the ODS was very simple customer relationship management.

The organization that built the ODS was politically separate from the organization building and using the data warehouse. One of the ironies was that many of the sources that fed the ODS also fed the data warehouse. Unlike the data warehouse, relatively little thought went into the selection of the technology required to support the ODS. The ODS as originally designed had a very application-oriented flavor to it.

**Figure 8.13**   The simple ODS is used interactively, but has limited usage due to the simplicity of data.

One day a manager asked, "Why can't the data analyzed in the data warehouse be included in the ODS?" Figure 8.14 shows this insight. At first there was resistance to the idea:

- There was political resistance because the organizations that built the environments were not the same.
- There were technological objections because the technologies housing the two systems were different.
- There were design objections because the systems were never conceived to have a connection.

However, each of the objections was overcome. There was no political reason why the ODS could not contain data that had been analyzed and amalgamated from the data warehouse. And there was no technological reason why data from the data warehouse could not be used in the ODS.

The structure of loading data into the ODS from the data warehouse is shown in Figure 8.15. One of the aspects of the loading of data that may not be apparent in Figure 8.15 is that some of the analytical processing that is the source of the load is done periodically—monthly—while other analytical processing is done sporadically—on no time schedule at all.

The sort of analysis loaded into the ODS is information such as

- Is the customer an upscale customer?
- Is the customer a very frequent caller?
- Is the customer a chronic complainer?
- Is the customer profitable?

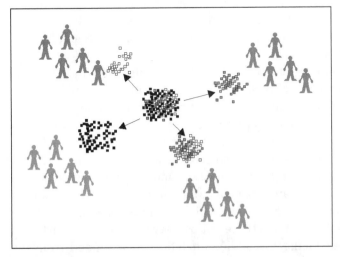

**Figure 8.14** Someone noticed that the analysis done by the DSS community could be used to group customers into different categories based on various types of information.

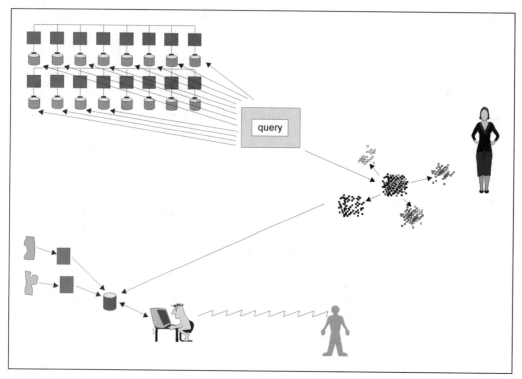

**Figure 8.15**   The data from the DSS analysis is periodically off-loaded into the ODS, creating a class IV ODS.

Some of the information is calculated in a rote manner. Other information is calculated in a heuristic manner that tends to change over time. In any case, however the information gets there, the information is in the ODS and is available at the moment of first customer contact.

With the information at hand, the operator who is in direct contact with the customer has the advantage of knowing a great deal of information about the customer. The information is precalculated and is available the instant a customer contact is initiated. There is no performance problem because the information comes with every customer record. Also note that this class IV ODS constantly improved its information. As more data was loaded into the data warehouse and as the end-user analyst became more sophisticated in the retrieval and analysis of data warehouse data, the information fed to the ODS likewise became more sophisticated. The ODS started out as a simple online customer interaction facility and was turned into a very sophisticated customer relationship management facility by adding analytical data refined from the data warehouse.

# Additional Case Studies

The following case studies demonstrate the various uses of the operational data store. There are four different scenarios that depict suggested purposes for the ODS. These case studies show how the operational data store can:

- Facilitate completeness of operational data
- Foster data synergy due to the integration of operational data
- Improve accessibility of critical operational data
- Shorten the path of data warehouse construction

The cases demonstrating these uses are given in order and are combinations of several different companies' experiences in building the operational data store. They do not represent any one specific corporation.

## Case 1: Facilitation of Completeness

The customer is a major domestic bank that consists of many branches serving multiple sites. The bank services both commercial and personal checking or savings accounts in addition to other services, such as savings clubs, car and home loans, and safe deposit boxes. However, its most important product and biggest risks are the large commercial loans it makes and processes for various corporations.

### The Challenge

Loan officers are responsible for determining the loan amounts and interest rates on their large commercial loans offered. The amounts and rates are very sensitive to the financial track records of the corporations applying for the loans. The loan officers want to include in their analyses the applying corporation's track record for all of its banking activities occurring in the various bank branches.

Because the bank bought many other banks, merged with others, was not consistent in the development of its own systems, and so on, it has myriad platforms, software, and applications that make integrating the bank's information very difficult to do.

In order to determine the overall activities of their customers in all branches, they would have to examine many systems on a variety of technologies, each one containing some part of the overall customer information. The analysis would take weeks and, in some cases, months to perform. This time frame makes it useless for the loan officers.

## The Solution

The solution is to build an operational data store. A logical data model of the Customer and Account subject areas is created and the operational data store data model is then created from the logical model. Only relevant customer and account transaction data is used in the operational data store model, for example, customer name and addresses; type of bank accounts and their activity; loan information, such as loan amount, interest rates, and payment schedules; and the activity for those loans. The metadata defining the operational data store data and its relationships is kept in a metadata repository easily accessed by ODS users.

Because of the volatility of corporations and their financial situations, the bank determined that extracts of the customer records should be generated from the various systems every hour for their commercial customers. These extracts are integrated into a common customer identifier and combined into one set of records per customer. At that point, various transformations take place, including the following dynamic summarizations or derivations:

- Total outstanding loan amounts
- Total bank account amounts
- Total daily banking transactions

The individual transactions occurring during the day are also integrated and stored in a uniform format in the operational data store.

Through the operational data store, loan officers may now view a corporation's total activity with the bank or, if they wish, look at the individual transactions occurring enterprisewide for a specific customer. The ability to determine proper loan amounts and the appropriate interest rate for those loans has been vastly improved. An additional benefit is the improved ability to determine the risk of loans already made. By tracking all activities made by a specific corporation, the bank is able to project where and when specific loans may be in jeopardy in the near future.

## Technological Overview

| | |
|---|---|
| Volumes of Data: | 400+ gigabytes |
| Hardware Configuration: | Massively parallel processing |
| DBMS: | Informix |
| End User: | Bank Loan Officers and Analysts |
| Rate of Flow: | One-hour refreshes |
| Expected Response Time (average): | Less than 20 seconds |
| Number of Users (average): | 50+ |

# Case 2: Fostering Data Synergy

A multi-billion-dollar oil and gas company produces crude oil and natural gas from hundreds of wells in the south central and southeastern United States. From these raw materials, several petroleum-based products are produced, such as Styrofoam, automobile gasoline, and asphalt.

## The Challenge

The majority of the wells operated by the company are partially owned by the company or leased from another party. The tracking of royalty and lease payments on these wells is central to the maintenance of these agreements. These payments are based on the production of gas and oil from the various wells involved. Therefore, the ability to track the specific production transactions from each well is critical to the payments made on the royalties and leases.

The company does not have an easy way to map well production to specific lease or royalty because the production data is kept in several disparate systems, as is the lease and royalty information. The reconciliation of well production to royalty and lease payments takes several weeks of analysts' time and is fraught with potential errors due to the manual effort involved.

## The Solution

The company decided to build an operational data store to integrate the well production data and subsequent royalty and lease payments. They used a data model of the Well and Contract subject areas. In addition, they defined all the metadata for the transformations as well as the attributes and entities contained in the model. This metadata resides in the same database as the operational data store and is accessed by the same data access tool.

The well-production data is gathered from the different systems, integrated into a uniform format, and loaded into the operational data store. Then, the lease and royalty information (e.g., who the partners are in each well, their addresses, interest percentages, etc.) is extracted, transformed to an integrated format, and loaded into the operational data store.

This information along with the metadata is used to generate appropriate payments for each partner or lease agreement for each well. The company is not only able to generate these payments much more quickly but they are able to issue one check for each recipient rather than issuing multiple checks as was required by the previous situation.

Not only is the timeliness of payments improved but the audit trail generated for these payments is greatly enhanced. The company is able to determine at a glance how payments were calculated and to whom these payments were made.

## Technological Overview

| | |
|---|---|
| Volumes of Data: | 100 gigabytes |
| Hardware Configuration: | IBM Mainframe |
| DBMS: | Oracle |
| End User: | Accounts Payable Clerks and Financial Analysts |
| Rate of Flow: | Daily (24-hour) refreshes |
| Expected Response Time (average): | Less than 1 minute |
| Number of Users (average): | 15 |

# Case 3: Improving Data Accessibility

A high-technology company manufactures and sells satellite communications equipment to government agencies and private enterprises. The company either buys or manufactures the parts that go into the construction of satellites.

### The Challenge

Because the communications equipment is very expensive and must perform under harsh conditions for a long period of time, the company must track with great vigor the manufacture and performance of the individual parts making up the satellites.

These parts also have a definite shelf life and must be used within a specified time frame or be retired. Therefore, a great deal of time and effort is spent monitoring and tracking the progression of these parts as they are constructed into bigger and bigger components until they are finally sold to the customer.

Because the information exists in old tapes from systems no longer used and in newer databases from systems that are not integrated, the process of tracking specific parts over time is labor intensive and difficult to perform. Regulations are demanding that better monitoring be performed.

### The Solution

The company developed a data model for the Inventory subject area, specifically the entities and attributes concerned with the equipment construction. The metadata defining the source of the data and transformations performed on the data as it moved into the operational data store is kept in the same database and may be easily accessed by the end user.

Data was extracted once from the old legacy tapes, and transformed, integrated, and loaded into the operational data store. The data is now in a uniform format agreed upon by the company and interested parties and is accessible using a simple end-user access tool.

The data residing in the current systems is extracted on a daily basis. The extracted data is transformed using the same algorithms used for the legacy data. Once transformed, the data is loaded into the operational data store in the same common format and is accessible using the same access mechanism. The metadata for the current data is defined in exactly the same manner as the legacy data where feasible and any differences between the two sources are noted.

End users are now able to track a particular part from its receipt into inventory throughout its productive life as a component of a satellite. In addition, they are able to determine how much of their inventory is assigned to a particular project, how much is scrapped or unaccounted for, how much requires maintenance, and so forth.

An additional benefit due to the improved tracking of components and their parts is the ability to determine more accurately the mean time before failure of specific types of parts. This information, along with the total number of parts that are scrapped, enables the company to look more closely at parts having suspected design flaws.

### Technological Overview

| | |
|---|---|
| Volumes of Data: | 30–40 gigabytes |
| Hardware Configuration: | RISC Workstations |
| DBMS: | Sybase |
| End User: | Inventory Analysts and Managers |
| Rate of Flow: | Daily (24-hour) refreshes |
| Expected Response Time (average): | Less than one minute |
| Number of Users (average): | 35 |

## Case 4: Shortening the Path to Data Warehouse Construction

A company manufactures and sells computers and computer peripherals both domestically and internationally. They have retail stores and distribution centers worldwide. Individual customers may purchase their products from any of the retail stores, and distributor customers may buy in bulk from any of the company's distribution centers.

## The Challenge

The Sales and Marketing department has determined that it must become more customer oriented. One way to become more customer focused is to have detailed sales history immediately available when dealing with a customer.

Armed with this information, the Customer Service Representatives servicing the customers could view recent purchases made by specific customers when they call, and therefore offer more personal service for the customers' requests. In addition, the Marketing and Sales department would like the opportunity to offer other products to that customer based on the customer's particular buying profile.

Because the company has grown rapidly and left much of the technological decisions up to the individual distribution centers and retail stores, they are faced with a difficult situation in which none of their systems interfaces with the others.

In addition, because it is an international company, there is no standard "batch window" when the data can be downloaded and examined.

## The Solution

The company decided to solve the problem in a two-pronged approach. First it decided to implement a client-server environment in which each sales area has its own "node" or client. Day-to-day operations are entered into the existing application within a sales area.

A corporate node is set up as a central repository for all operational data store data. Here, data for the operational data store is collected from the various operational systems used in the service areas. A timetable is set up to accommodate each system's working hours and four-hour extracts of customer activities are performed during an appropriate time frame.

These extracts are sent to the central node for processing, that is, the data is integrated, transformed, and merged with the data already existing in the operational data store. An ODS data model of the Customer, Order, and Product subject areas acts as the road map for the data transformations.

After processing, the data and metadata are segregated or packaged based upon service area requirements. The integrated ODS is returned to the local service areas using the client-server technology. The central node maintains the corporatewide view of customer activity.

The local ODS data allows the customer service representatives (CSR) in each sales area to respond more quickly to customer requests and problems with products by permitting the CSRs to view immediately the specific products the customer recently purchased. The customer does not need to keep product information (model number, serial number, etc.) on hand because it is readily available to the CSR. Specials for peripherals for those products may also be mentioned to the customer as well as enhancements to the existing products already purchased.

The second approach the company used is to build a data warehouse, which would draw its data from the central node's operational data store. The data integration and transformation occurring for the operational data store database makes the implementation of a data warehouse quite simple. The data from the operational data store is summarized, derived, given a time stamp, and so on; it is then loaded into the data warehouse and made available for decision-support analysis.

The data in the data warehouse tracks customer buying habits over long periods, demonstrating the trends in customer purchases. In addition, demographic customer data was brought into the data warehouse to analyze and compare with their customer database. The metadata for the data warehouse is based on the metadata describing the operational data store, but includes any new summarization or derivation algorithms needed for the warehouse.

The data warehouse allows the corporate decision makers to examine the success or failure of specific products in each of the regional sales areas. By using the demographic data, the decision makers are able to come up with lists of products that are likely to be bought by specific customers. This information gives the analysts the ability to determine where and when certain promotions or sales should occur and for what types of customers these activities should be targeted.

Now the CSRs receive information about specific customers' product buying habits on their screens, thus allowing them to suggest additional products to a particular customer when he or she calls. These suggestions are based on the predictive models generated from the demographic data in the data warehouse that has been matched to the specific customer identifier. The list of potential product purchases by specific customers that is generated by the data warehouse is displayed on the CSR screen as soon as the customer calls in.

## Technological Overview

| | |
|---|---|
| Volumes of Data: | ODS—50–100 gigabytes<br>Data Warehouse—150–200 gigabytes |
| Hardware Configuration: | Client-server |
| DBMS: | Oracle |
| End User: | Customer Service Representatives and Marketing Analysts |
| Rate of Flow: | Four-hour refreshes |
| Expected Response<br>  Time (average): | ODS—subsecond;<br>Data Warehouse—one to five minutes |
| Number of Users (average): | 150–200 |

# Summary

The road to the building of an ODS may not be straightforward and as described in the text book. There are probably as many paths to a successful ODS as there are ODS. In the case discussed, the ODS was built in parallel to the data warehouse. Only after a period of time did the merger of the ODS and the data warehouse interests become apparent. Because the ODS and the data warehouse had already been built, the biggest obstacles to success were political and organizational obstacles.

The ODS that was built was a very successful class IV warehouse. Ironically, the initial design of the ODS was unaware of either ODS as an architectural structure or class IV ODS in particular. The development process described was full of iterative development. There were wrong turns at every place thoughout the development process.

The telephone company had a fixation on the underlying technology that would be in support of the data warehouse and ultimately the ODS.

# Managing the Operational Data Store Environment

The ODS environment presents an administrative challenge like no other because it contains so many types of processing. The ODS environment contains high-performance transaction processing, heuristic DSS processing, batch loads, and a host of other processes. In order to successfully run the ODS environment, all of these disparate types of processing must be accommodated. In many cases, design and operational practices that are optimal for one type of processing are not at all optimal for other types. The result is that the ongoing administration of the ODS environment is no simple matter.

## Monitoring System Utilization

There are many facets to the ongoing administration of the ODS environment. Perhaps the most important activity of ODS administration is the continual monitoring of its hardware and software activities. The ODS environment requires constant monitoring because it is like a finely tuned car; it can easily get out of balance.

The system environment of the ODS is constantly changing. Data is being added, more users start to run programs, the system of record needs to be altered, and so forth. Each change in the ODS environment requires that some adjustment be made. Only through careful and consistent monitoring will the ODS architect be aware of the changes that are occurring and be able to respond.

One of the telltale measurements that the ODS administrator needs to look at is the profile of hardware utilization that is created by monitoring hardware activity, as seen in Figure 9.1. The pattern of hardware utilization usage reveals many things:

- When the hardware is starting to become overwhelmed
- When the hardware is not tuned properly
- When the usage patterns of the end user are changing
- Where spare machine resources are
- At what rate usage is growing

The pattern of hardware utilization is one of the most important measurements that can be captured by the ODS architect.

## Contrasting Utilization Profiles

Continuously monitoring hardware utilization is a resource intensive activity. Turning the hardware monitor on requires its own significant set of resources. Because resources are required for measuring hardware utilization, most organizations turn on the hardware monitor only sporadically. A common practice is to monitor hardware utilization at selected periods or intervals. Those intervals are collected and compiled to form a profile of "average" utilization. Then when the ODS environment experiences performance difficulties, the profile of hardware utilization during the period of difficulty is compared with the profile representing average utilization. Figure 9.2 illustrates the practice of contrasting patterns of hardware utilization.

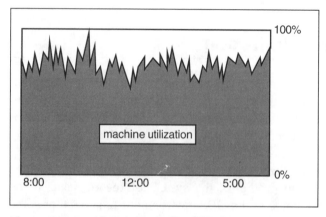

**Figure 9.1**  Looking at the profile of hardware utilization periodically can enhance system performance.

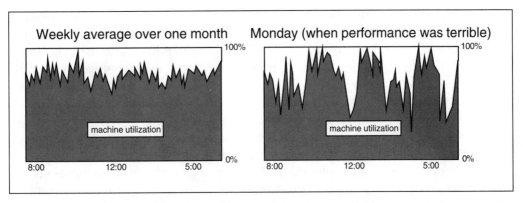

**Figure 9.2** Comparing problem days with normal days is a good way to spot performance difficulties.

There can be several causes for poor performance in the ODS environment. There may be an anomaly occurring in system utilization. If there are 200 end users it is possible that 195 of them hit the ENTER key at precisely the same moment. There may be a system problem: buffers may have overflowed, or an update function may have neglected to take checkpoints periodically. There may be a design problem resulting in one table suddenly becoming a bottleneck. Whatever the problem is, the contrast between the pattern of hardware utilization when things are running properly versus when things are not running properly tips off the ODS administrator as to how to solve the problem.

Another important ongoing measurement that the ODS administrator needs to track is the growth in the number of users and their rate of system utilization and activity. Figure 9.3 shows a simple graph that tracks the number of end users of the ODS. There are several important reasons why the number of end

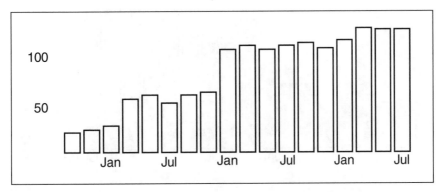

**Figure 9.3** Measuring the growth of the number of users over time.

users should be monitored. The most obvious reason is that the growth of hardware can be tracked along with growth in utilization. But there is another important reason why the number of end users should be tracked. Occasionally the ODS administrator is called upon to justify the expenditures made on its behalf. Having the exact number of end users and a profile of their activity is a first line of defense in justifying resource expenditures for the ODS.

Another important parameter that should be measured over time is that of the growth of storage within the ODS environment, as suggested by Figure 9.4. Like the data warehouse, the ODS has a tendency to accumulate volumes of data over time. These volumes of data, if unmanaged, can clog things up and cause all sorts of system and application problems. Therefore it is important for the ODS administrator to keep a close watch on the growth of data within the ODS to ensure that it is anticipated and managed properly.

In fact, managing the growth of data is so important that managing growth at a wholesale level is probably not adequate. The ODS administrator should be advised that managing growth by individual table is probably in order. Figure 9.4 shows growth being tracked on an individual table basis. When growth is tracked by tables, the ODS administrator develops a feel for what data is being used the most and where the advances in the volumes of data are coming from. When it comes time to make decisions about purging data from the ODS environment and moving the data off to archival and data warehouse environments, the administrator knows exactly where to consider pruning.

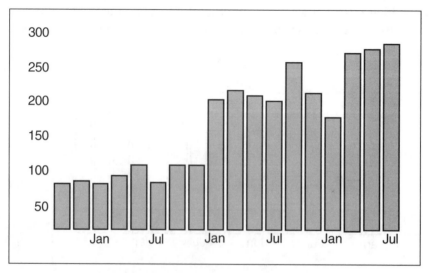

**Figure 9.4**   Measuring the growth of storage in gigabytes over time.

# A Look at the Daily ODS Workload

When viewed from the perspective of the daily workload, the differences between ODS operational processing and ODS decision support processing become obvious. Figure 9.5 shows that difference. The ODS workload depicted in Figure 9.5 is one where very different kinds of activity flow through the ODS computing environment during different periods of the day. Many activities flow through the ODS. Some are single-row searches for limited amounts of data, some are large queries of many rows of data, and some are updates of data inside the ODS.

During the daylight hours the ODS experiences much online transaction activity. The online transactions are executing in a manner where a two- to three-second response time is the norm, and the amount of resources used by any given online transaction is small during this time frame. The arrival rate of the transactions determines the system load. Because there are so many small transactions executing at any moment in time in the daylight hours ODS, the overall profile of execution is very ragged, with many small peaks and valleys. The left-hand side of Figure 9.5 illustrates this erose pattern of activity. The percentage use of the computer changes very rapidly as the transaction arrival rate rises and falls.

The workload *after* daylight hours processing for the ODS is markedly different than the daylight hours processing profile. The after-hours ODS processing profile is for decision support processing and is almost flat. The percent of computer utilization being used inside the ODS computing environment varies at an almost leisurely pace. There are indeed increases and decreases in the utilization of the computer during these hours, but these are very gentle. The kinds

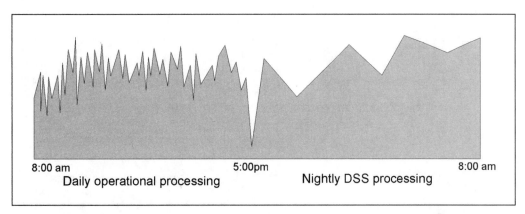

| 8:00 am | 5:00pm | 8:00 am |
| Daily operational processing | Nightly DSS processing | |

**Figure 9.5**  There is a clear difference between the types of processing that are done throughout the ODS operating day and night.

of processes that are executing during these hours are very few transactions, but they are transactions that consume huge amounts of processing power.

Because of the fundamental differences in utilization profiles and the profile of the underlying transactions, it should come as no surprise that the parameters of management success of the different ODS environments are very different, as outlined in Figure 9.6.

## Parameters of Success

The primary parameter of success in the daylight hours processing of the ODS is online transaction response time. The primary parameter of success for the night-time processing of the ODS is the management of the volumes of data that start to aggregate in the ODS. The challenge of the DBA charged with managing the ODS environment is in satisfying *both* sets of parameters. Satisfying one set of objectives and not the other is not acceptable for the ODS environment. Unfortunately, in many cases a design practice that is optimal for daytime processing is not optimal for nighttime processing, and vice versa.

For example, the more details of data that an online transaction has immediately available, the greater the chance for very good response time. Therefore the online system designer of the ODS will specify much detailed data in the database of the ODS in order to keep good response time. But the more data there is—especially detailed data—the larger the ODS grows. From the perspective of the decision support analyst using the ODS, these volumes of data

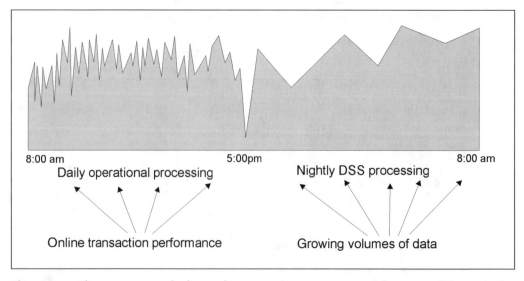

**Figure 9.6**  The parameters of what makes an environment successful are very different in the ODS environment.

need to be kept to a minimum. Therefore it is in the best interest of the decision support analyst to minimize the amount of data in the ODS database design.

## Online Performance in the ODS

In order to achieve optimal system performance during the daytime in the ODS, the system manager must keep the flow of transactions through the ODS system queues even and steady. Figure 9.7 shows two queues where transactions are flowing through the ODS system. The queue on the left of the figure shows that the transactions running through it are small and uniform in size. In this case, the system manager can expect an optimal flow through the system as well as an optimal transaction response time.

The queue on the right of the figure shows that large transactions are freely mixed with small transactions. The net result is a very uneven flow of transactions through the system. Consequently there will be poor response times for all transactions. It is obvious that there will be poor response times for the large transactions as they go into execution. What is not obvious is that there will also be poor response times for the smaller transactions that are queued behind the large transactions as they wait for them to get through the system. There is a fundamental conflict in transactions and their resource utilization that results in poor performance when large transactions are mixed with small transactions. The system manager of the ODS understands the profound effect of mixing transaction types in the queue when it comes time to optimize system performance and keep transaction performance in the ODS at an acceptable level.

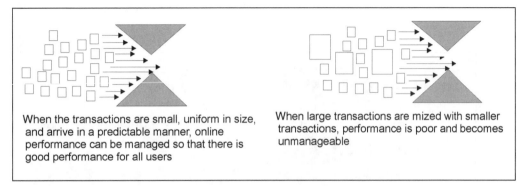

When the transactions are small, uniform in size, and arrive in a predictable manner, online performance can be managed so that there is good performance for all users

When large transactions are mized with smaller transactions, performance is poor and becomes unmanageable

**Figure 9.7** Good online performance is achieved by carefully creating and managing the transaction workload that passes through the ODS environment.

## Flattening Out the Workload

When it comes to daylight management of the ODS, the system manager attempts to even out the workload. Figure 9.8 shows that the ODS system manager has three options:

- Remove large transactions from the queue
- Delay large transactions and let them run after hours
- Break large transactions up into a series of smaller transactions

Given the nature of the ODS workload during daylight hours, moving large transactions to after hours is a very normal and easy thing to do since most of the daylight transactions are from the clerical community and of a very limited nature. The problem is in determining the size of a transaction before it goes into execution. What the system manager for the ODS needs is a tool that lets him or her understand the fundamental nature of transactions. Such tools examine a query before it is submitted and estimate how many resources the query will be using.

## Managing the ODS After Daylight Hours

Managing the ODS after daylight hours is very different from managing the ODS during daylight hours, and the parameters of success are very, very different. In after-hours processing, the ODS is doing decision support processing, not online transaction processing. When managing the ODS for after daylight hours, the ODS system manager must concentrate on the growing volumes of data that are found in the ODS. Even though the ODS contains limited amounts of historical data, there is still a tendency for the ODS to grow to large proportions. Some of the reasons for the growth of the ODS are

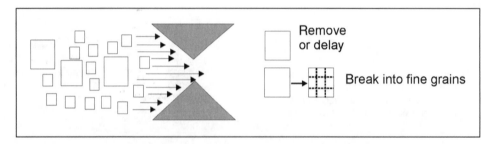

**Figure 9.8**    There are options when large transactions are mixed with much smaller transactions in a jobstream that needs to be optimized on operating efficiency.

**The granularity of data found in the ODS.** Because there is a very low level of granularity of data found in the ODS, the volumes of data quickly mount.

**The usage of the ODS expands beyond anyone's imagination.** Many organizations find that the ODS represents the first truly integrated data that has ever existed in the corporation. Once the ODS data is made available, the organization finds many uses for it that were never imagined when the ODS was first built.

**The history in the ODS creeps into longer and longer periods.**

For these reasons and more, the volume of data that resides in the ODS is significant and grows over time. Large volumes of data are detrimental to doing DSS processing in the ODS for two reasons: large volumes of data both hurt performance and cost a lot. Performance is hurt because indexes grow larger, load times grow larger, data that is being sought starts to "hide" behind other data, and so forth. Costs go up because more disk storage is required and more processors are necessary. For all these reasons it is in the best interest of the system manager to minimize the amount of data found in the ODS when doing decision support processing.

## Dormant Data

Whenever there is rapid and significant growth of data, a phenomenon called *dormant data* is created. Dormant data is data that enters the system, sits there, and is never used, so there is no return on investment for it. Figure 9.9 shows dormant data as it grows into a large system environment.

When there is only a small amount of data, there is no problem with dormant data. However, as time passes and as the volume of data grows, more and more of the system turns into dormant data. One day the system manager for the ODS wakes up and finds that a significant part of the ODS is dormant. Not only does this dormancy entail significant expense, it hurts performance.

There are several reasons for the growth of dormant data in the ODS:

**Requirements change.** The ODS is designed for one set of requirements and ends up being used for another set of requirements. However, the data needed to support the original set of requirements is never changed or deleted.

**Data starts to age.** Even though the ODS contains a limited amount of historical data, end users find that for most of their processing they are interested in only the most current data.

**Summarization occurs inside the ODS.** A summarization table is created and established as a permanent part of the ODS, however, the purpose of

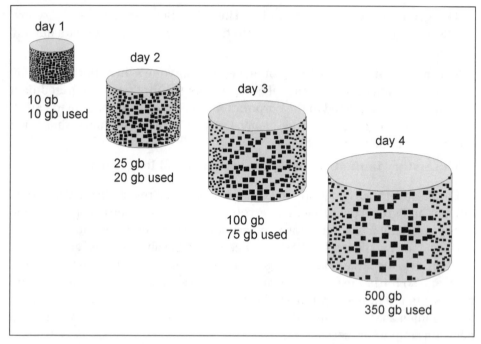

day 1

10 gb
10 gb used

day 2

25 gb
20 gb used

day 3

100 gb
75 gb used

day 4

500 gb
350 gb used

**Figure 9.9** Dormant data is the expected phenomenon in the DSS environment.

the summarization table is forgotten. Now the summary data just sits there with no one using it. Computer operations are afraid to delete the table because they do not know what decisions might be made from the table. So the table sits in the ODS with no users.

As time goes on, the volume of data and the dormancy of the data become big issues for the ODS system manager.

Ultimately the ODS system manager needs to move to a variation of the classical architecture for the ODS which mandates that data be placed on disk storage. As long as there is only a modicum of data, this strategy works fine. But at some point, as the ODS grows larger, the system manager must consider placing some of the data in the ODS onto alternate storage forms.

## Alternate Storage Forms

Figure 9.10 illustrates the possibility of near-line storage for the ODS environment and shows that the data that resides in the ODS is divided into three categories:

- Data that is very actively used
- Data that is used only some of the time
- Data that is used very infrequently

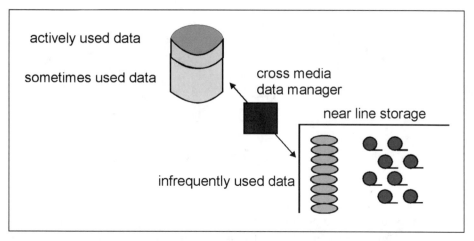

**Figure 9.10**  The architecture that minimizes the expenses of the ODS and optimizes the performance of the ODS.

The data that is used actively is placed onto disk storage. Data that is less frequently used is placed in the disk storage portion of the ODS as well. But data that is used very infrequently is placed in the near-line component of the ODS. By making this division of data based on the probability of usage of data, the system manager for the ODS has simultaneously reduced the cost of the ODS and increased the performance of the environment.

But in order to make such a division of data, the system manager for the ODS environment must know what data is and is not being used. For the data that is not being used, he or she must be able to determine where there is a high probability of usage even when there is no past indicator that would otherwise verify this.

## Monitors

During daylight hours processing, the system manager for the ODS must know what activity is going on inside the system and what the transaction mix is like. In order to manage the decision support component, the system manager must understand what data is and is not being used. In order to gather the necessary information to manage these environments in a comprehensive manner, the system manager needs to have monitors. Figure 9.11 shows the two types of monitors that the system manager needs.

An *activity monitor* tells what the response time and transaction profile look like. Such a monitor can also be called a *performance monitor*. The other kind of monitor is an activity monitor that examines the types of activities that are flowing through an ODS and infers what data is and is not being used by the

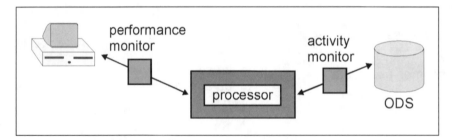

**Figure 9.11**    Monitoring the data and the activity in the ODS environment.

users of the system. An activity monitor and a performance monitor complement each other because both are required in order to provide the ODS manager with the information necessary to manage the ODS environment. Keeping an ODS up, running, and operating efficiently requires making constant trade-offs. Figure 9.12 shows the constant balancing act that the ODS system manager must perform.

## Using the Results of Monitoring

There are many uses of the monitors that look at ODS activity. The most obvious is to use the monitor to tell what is going on inside the system. When the system manager for the ODS gets a phone call from an irate user, the system manager turns to the activity monitor to see if anything unusual is going on with the user. If something undesirable is occurring, such as an explorer query unexpectedly entering the system that requires a huge amount of resources, the systems manager directs his or her attention to fixing the problem at hand. If nothing unusual appears to be happening, the system manager calls the user back for a more detailed explanation of the concern.

Monitoring is also used to determine long-term trends. It is impossible to detect incremental changes from one week to the next when the changes are small. The best way to understand trends is to track numerous measurements

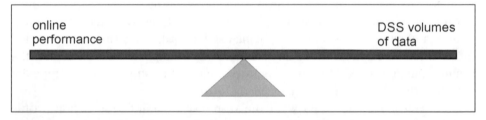

**Figure 9.12**    The optimization of the ODS environment requires that the opposing forces of online transaction performance be balanced with the management of the volumes of data that aggregate around the decision support use of the ODS.

over time. The monitor is used to capture the time-stamped measurements of system activity which are then charted over time. In doing so, the system manager is able to operate on a basis of predictability rather than operate in a react mode.

Yet a third use of the monitors found in the ODS environment is in comparing current activity against average activity. To understand why this might be useful, consider a system manager who is faced with answering the question, "How is system utilization and response time today?" Unless the system manager has something to compare the current activity to, there is really no intelligent answer that the system manager can give. A good approach to answering this question is to create an *average* profile which can span a day, week, or month of processing. The averages are created by factoring in information gathered from monitors over a lengthy period of time. With the average profiles in hand, the system manager is able to make a comparison between current activity and utilization and the average.

There are many other ways that activity monitors provide a basis for managing the ODS environment. The techniques suggested here are merely the most basic ways that monitor results can be used.

### Monitoring Overhead

Every monitor has its overhead, and in the daylight ODS environment resources may be so precious that the system manager may want to use the monitor sparingly. There are several ways to reduce the impact of monitoring:

**Use the monitor only on a part-time basis.** In such a manner, the results can be extrapolated from the moments when the monitor has been turned on.

**Use a monitor that does not require processing cycles.** For example, many "sniffing" monitors do not use mainline processing cycles.

**Monitor only selected activities.** Not all activities need to be monitored.

# Capacity Planning in the Operational Data Store Environment

In addition to the design review, described in Chapter 5, the ODS architect should institute the ongoing practice of capacity planning for ODS administration. Figure 9.13 shows some of the activities of ODS measurement and monitoring in which the ODS architect engages. In addition to other measurements, the ODS architect has an ongoing interest in the growth of hardware (CPU, memory), DASD and other forms of storage, and end-user activity.

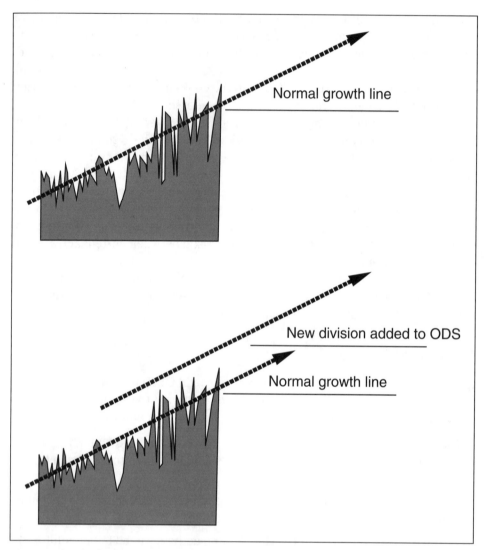

**Figure 9.13**   Capacity planning in the ODS environment.

Once the ODS architect starts to develop the measurements that reflect current system activity, he or she can then start to project those measurements to predict future growth. There are two simple ways that growth is projected:

- Current growth is linearly extrapolated.
- Known future expansion not yet factored into current growth is added to the extrapolation.

The net of these two considerations is an expectation of how much capacity will be needed in the future and when.

# Verifying the System of Record

Although the ODS designer tries very hard to identify and properly use the system of record at the outset of the design effort for the ODS environment, the system of record has a habit of changing over time. One of the ongoing activities of the ODS administrator is to periodically review the system of record to see if changes need to be made. There are many reasons why the system of record may change, for instance:

- The nature of the business has changed
- Legacy systems have changed
- The DSS analyst has pointed out a new opportunity

The changes that need to be made to the ODS environment show up in the modification of the system of record itself, the transformation and integration interface into the ODS, and the actual definition and content of the ODS itself.

Figure 9.14 shows the system of record periodically being reviewed. The ODS administrator looks for such things as the following:

- Has the application underlying the system of record changed?
- Has a new application been added that will make a better system of record?

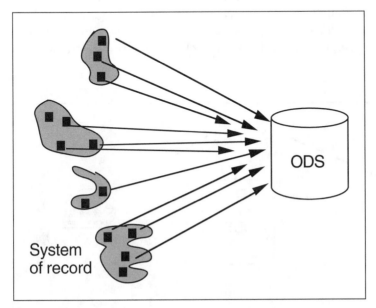

**Figure 9.14** Alignment of the ODS and the system of record needs to be periodically checked.

- Has the interpretation of the ODS data changed so that under today's conditions there is a better system of record?

- Has the end user or the DSS analyst requested a change?

The ODS administrator must not assume that the system of record will remain permanently cast as originally defined once the ODS is built and has been populated.

# The Metadata Infrastructure

As with the system of record, the metadata structure of the ODS also undergoes change. Figure 9.15 illustrates the metadata infrastructure of the ODS environment. The metadata infrastructure in the ODS environment encompasses four venues:

- Definition of the system of record
- Transformation of the system of record into the ODS
- Contents of the ODS
- Availability of the metadata to the end user

New requirements and changes to existing requirements for the ODS environment are usually generated in one of two places, as seen in Figure 9.16. Changes in requirements will occur in the integration and transformation of the legacy data to the ODS environment. Typically the requirements generated here are part of the iterative development process in which the DSS part of the ODS participates. On occasion, there is the need to change the transformation and

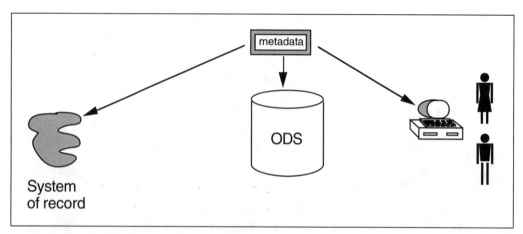

**Figure 9.15**   Periodically reviewing the metadata infrastructure.

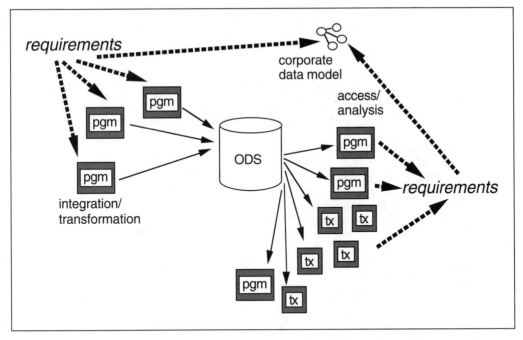

**Figure 9.16** Integrating external requirements into the ODS and internally generating new requirements.

integration programs because of the changes in the legacy environment itself. The size and complexity of the transformation and integration programs are a natural target for changes in requirements.

The other type of changes that often occur in the ODS environment are those that are picked up as end-user feedback at the access and analysis level. These changes are often a reflection of new opportunities and discoveries made by the end user and DSS analyst. Changes here are a sign of the success and usage of the ODS environment. Regardless of the nature of the change, it is the job of the ODS administrator to constantly monitor the feedback generated by the end user and DSS analyst.

## Service-Level Agreements

Because there is an important online component of the ODS environment, service-level agreements are a standard part of the ODS environment. A service-level agreement is a statement of the expected (quantified) level of service to be provided by a system. Typically the service-level agreement specifies levels of performance and hours of availability, although in truth a service-level agreement can specify almost anything. The service-level agreement for the ODS is

Service-level agreements:

Performance:
Mon – Fri — 8:00 am to 5:00 pm
   class A transaction - 3-second response time
   class B transaction - 30-second response time
   class C transaction - 5-minute response time
   90% of the time

Availability:
Mon – Fri — 8:00 am to 5:00 pm
system available 95% of the time
no more than 2 outages a week
outage to last no longer than 10 minutes

**Figure 9.17**    First establish and then manage within the confines of a service-level agreement.

agreed upon and published before the system is executed. As such, the service-level agreement provides measurable parameters of success for the ODS developer. A sample service-level agreement is shown in Figure 9.17.

The service-level agreement for the ODS is in effect a contract between the end user and DSS analyst and computer operations. Computer operations agree to provide a specified level of service throughout the life of the system. The end user knows what that level of service is before the ODS environment is built. If the service level is not high enough, the end user is free to raise the level of service as long as the end user is willing to pay for the enhanced service.

Periodically, ODS service is measured and benchmarked against the published service-level agreement. Because of the quantified nature of the service-level agreement, there is never any doubt as to whether the service-level objectives are being met.

## Listening to the End User/DSS Analyst

Above everything else the ODS administrator does, he or she must listen carefully to feedback generated by end users and DSS analysts. The ODS administrator should filter the requests made by this community. Figure 9.18 illustrates this ongoing task.

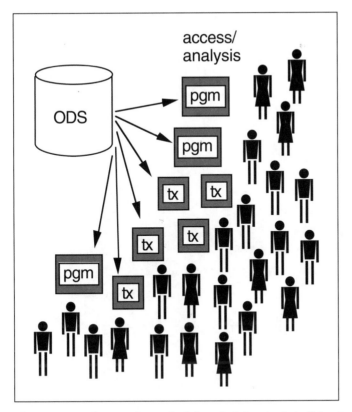

**Figure 9.18**   The ongoing task of the administrator is to listen to the end user/DSS analyst community—on any subject relevant to the success of the ODS.

## Summary

The administration of the ODS environment begins with the ongoing monitoring of system activities, such as hardware utilization, end-user growth, and growth in the volume of data. Both "average" and "problem" utilization profiles are created. The difference between these two types of profiles creates a basis for solving performance problems.

Design review is the process of carefully interrogating an ODS design before the design is coded. Design review is especially important for the high-performance portion of the ODS environment. Reviewing a system properly can save huge amounts in redevelopment costs.

Capacity planning is another ongoing activity of the ODS environment. Both normal growth and planned expansion should be taken into consideration.

The system of record and the metadata infrastructure must be periodically reviewed. Service-level agreements need to be specified before the ODS environment is established.

# Managing the ODS: An Organizational Perspective

Managing an ODS is a challenge. The first issue facing all organizations is that the ODS is a new structure that does not conveniently fit into previously defined organizational boundaries. It is a hybrid, part operational and part DSS data warehousing. The hybrid nature of the ODS is illustrated in Figure 10.1.

Both the operational environment and the data warehouse are challenging to manage in their own right. The operational manager is concerned with issues such as transaction response time and maintenance. The decision support manager must contend with increasing volumes of data and ever-changing DSS requirements. Adding an ODS presents the organization with an entirely new layer of complexity.

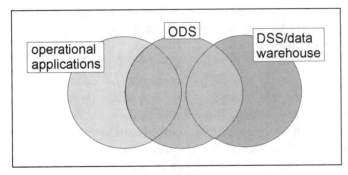

**Figure 10.1** The problem with hybrid management of the ODS environment.

The second issue with managing the ODS environment arises when the ODS environment is implemented in the form of a commercial package such as SAP, BAAN, or Oracle Financials. The commercial package almost always carries with it consultants, who in turn bring their own work ethic and work habits to the organization. The result is that the ODS in the commercial form stretches the established patterns of work flow and processes within the organization.

# Skill Sets

One way to look at ODS management is in terms of the skill set required for installing and managing the ODS. The development skills required for the installation and initial implementation of the ODS include

- Requirements gathering
- Design
- Project management
- Programming
- Testing
- Systems integration
- Application (if the ODS is a commercial application)

The types of positions required include

- Project management
- Database administration
- Data modeling and data administration
- Programming
- Metadata specialist
- Testing and systems integration

The challenge facing people filling these roles is that, in almost every case, the individual will have come from a background of either operational development or decision support data warehouse development. In order to do their job properly, there must be a blend of both types of skills. Therefore a certain amount of forgetting the past is required, as well as preparing for the future with a new mindset. Finding people with the mental and professional agility to balance the needs peculiar to the ODS is rare indeed. The activities and skills required for ongoing maintenance of the ODS are similar in many regards to the skill sets required for installation, with a few exceptions. In order to accomplish the task of ongoing maintenance of the ODS, the following skills are required:

- Training
- End-user interface
- Systems monitoring
- Systems integration
- Database administration
- Data administration and data modeling
- Metadata management
- Systems programming

## ODS Staff Size

How large should the ODS organization be? As a rule, the size of the organization depends on two factors:

- Is the ODS being built or is the ODS in a maintenance state?
- Is the ODS being built on a custom basis or is the ODS of a commercial variety?

Table 10.1 shows some suggested ranges for the size of the staff assigned to the ODS. These ranges can vary significantly, depending on factors such as

- The size of the ODS.
- The number of legacy sources.
- The degree of integration of the legacy sources.
- The geographic distribution of the corporation.
- The experience level of the developers.
- The competency level of the consultants, if consultants are to be used.

**Table 10.1**   The Number of People Required for the ODS Environment

|  | DEVELOPMENT | MAINTENANCE |
|---|---|---|
| commercial | 10 to 150 | 5 to 20 |
| custom | 5 to 25 | 3 to 10 |

- The type of ODS being built. Class I ODSs are the most difficult to build, class IV are the easiest.

- The degree of mixture of DSS processing and transaction processing that is to occur in the ODS.

### Competing for Resources

The ODS staff must compete for resources, including hardware, software, and people. The ODS competes for these resources with other projects and environments such as the data warehouse, data marts, the operational environment, and so forth. In order to compete with other groups, it is recommended that the ODS staff

- Keep in the feedback loop to management

- Set doable milestones and apprise management of the achievement of those milestones

- Set measurements for the success of the ODS such as

  - Number of users active on the ODS

  - Number of transactions run per week

  - Number of reports run from the ODS

  - Volume of data growth in the ODS

  - Percent machine utilization

  - Transaction arrival rate at peak periods

The measurements need to be quantified and made over a period of time so that progress can be gauged. It is important to be able to show measurable progress to management and the organization.

## The External Interface

The external organization—finance, sales, marketing, etc.—must be shown how to exploit the ODS for decision support and analysis. This must be done with care, however, because of the fragile online nature of the ODS during daylight hours. (The ODS is most fragile during daylight hours because that is when online performance is most in demand. In order to achieve adequate online response time, each transaction must be structured so that it uses a small amount of resources and looks at a very finite amount of data. If a transaction is submitted that does not look at a small amount of data, then performance suffers across the board.)

The organization managing the ODS must support DSS processing without disrupting transaction processing. The balance that is required can be difficult to achieve. As an example, suppose an organization is running an ODS that provides 8:00 A.M. to 5:00 P.M. online service. During online service a transaction response time of two to three seconds is maintained. There are up to 250 users submitting requests during these hours.

The data warehouse administrator receives a request to run a 72-hour query by one of the organizations "free thinkers." The data warehouse administrator knows that if the request hits the ODS, regular service will be curtailed for the daily execution of the transactions against the ODS, so he attempts to divert the 72-hour request elsewhere. The administrator allows a lot of data to be siphoned off from the ODS into what is called an *exploration warehouse*. Once in the exploration warehouse, the data is greatly condensed and is optimized for exploratory processing. The exploration warehouse is created and the analyst runs the 72-hour request. There is no performance impact on the ODS, and regular users of the ODS never know that a huge analytical request is running.

The analyst finds that the first execution of the 72-hour request creates as many questions as it answers. The analyst restates the request and runs a new 72-hour request against the exploration warehouse. Again there is no impact against the regular users of the warehouse.

Now the analyst finds out that some new data needs to be added to the exploration warehouse. The data warehouse administrator slices off some more data from the ODS, adds it to the exploration warehouse, and processing continues. The analyst continues this iterative analysis against the exploration warehouse. By balancing the needs of both the regular end-user community of the ODS and the analytical community, the data warehouse administrator has solved the problem of DSS processing against the ODS and regular transaction processing.

## The Organization Chart

There are many ways the organization chart can be constructed for the creation and maintenance of the ODS. Figure 10.2 suggests one of the ways that the needs of the ODS can be met, showing that the ODS function is separate from other similar functions under the aegis of IT. The ODS function sits at the same level as the data warehouse, operating systems, database administration, and data administration. If the ODS function were placed any lower on the chart, it would be difficult for the ODS function to effectively compete for resources. On the other hand, if the ODS function were placed at a higher position on the organization chart, the communications with other functions would not be normal or effective.

Another possibility is to combine the ODS function with either the data warehouse function or the operations function. Although such a combination may seem expedient, in the long term it is not advisable. If the ODS function is combined with either operations or the data warehouse, the ODS will inevitably start to take on the flavor of the organization it is aligned with, which means that some aspect of the ODS is going to be shortchanged. When the ODS is of the commercial variety, combining it with either operations or the data warehouse

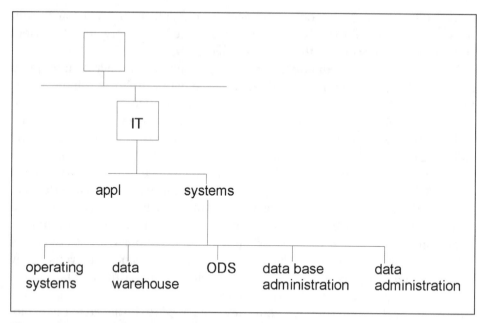

**Figure 10.2** A sample organization chart.

is usually not a problem. From an organization chart perspective, when a corporation builds a commercial ODS, the commercial ODS tends to stand by itself.

The budget for the ODS environment varies widely from one organization to another and from one ODS type to another. As a rule, commercial ODSs tend to be very expensive and may require years to implement. Custom-built ODSs tend to be much smaller and require a much smaller budget. The budget cycle for the ODS has two very distinct periods: a budget required for development and implementation, and a budget required for ongoing maintenance and operation.

## Management Feedback

Management of the ODS must periodically report to upper management about the activities taking place in the ODS environment. The reports to management should include both challenges and accomplishments. Management needs to be apprised of the positive results of the ODS so that there will be ongoing support. By the same token, when problems arise, management should be made aware of them as well, because inevitably problems require that resources be allocated. The worst thing that the ODS management staff can do is to give *no* feedback to management with regard to the ODS. The feedback process is particularly important for commercial ODSs because these take so long to implement and because they require so many resources.

Reporting to management and the organizational feedback process should be done through regular staffing channels. Reporting less than quarterly to management can prove dangerous in that management enthusiasm and support for the ODS may diminish. Reporting on a daily basis will surely tire management out, causing them to "tune out." Therefore formal reporting to upper management with regard to the ODS and the progress made must lie somewhere in between. Figure 10.3 provides a sample report made on a monthly basis by the administrator of the ODS.

---

1. Total activity against the ODS
   - 21 operating days
   - May 15
   - June 10
   - online day
   - 8:00 am to 5:00 pm, Mon – Fri
   - 165,908 day time online queries
   - average response time
   - 3.5 seconds
   - 16.7 rows per query
   - 258 online users at peak processing
   - online updates – none
   - system peak period outages – none
   - 165 load programs executed coming from the applications environment
   - addition of 726,298 rows of data
   - 294 mass downloads made against the ODS
   - 31 off peak queries satisfied
   - 35,981 (avg.) rows per query
   - largest query satisfied – 67,901 rows
   - 167 data movements to data warehouse
   - removal of 680,209 rows of data
   - data in system at report end
   - 29 tables
   - 2,897,338 rows of data
2. Extraordinary activity
   - one new table added
   - SYSQRFC
   - two tables modified
   - SYSTROW
   - SYSQUOA

3. End user comments
   - "customer retention seems to be getting better"
   - "customers are responding well to having nickname added to table"
   - "it's nice to have reliable response time"
   - "can we add customer birthdate to table? we could use that when making contact with customer on birthday."
   - "when can I train my new hires on using the system?"
   - "could we add offline reporting to some of our screens?"
4. Budget
   - hardware operating costs were $45,098
   - software operating costs were $67,220
   - there were no new capital costs
   - operational costs were $108,338
   - expenses were 1.6% over budget
5. Anticipated expenditures
   - it is anticipated that a computer upgrade is going to be required in the next six months. 6 new application areas
   - new functions anticipated in the next three months include
   - customer historical category analysis upgrade
   - customer purchase category analysis

---

**Figure 10.3** Sample ODS monthly report created by the database administrator or the data warehouse administrator.

# Return on Investment

Return on investment for the ODS can't be readily quantified. However, it can be qualitatively assessed in several ways:

- Determining what new reports are being created from the ODS data and interviewing the end user as to what is being done with the information from the report

- Determining what new users there are and interviewing them as to what they are doing

- Determining what data is being used and looking to see what is being done with it

- Determining what new transactions are being used and going to the source to find out what business need is being fulfilled by the transaction

These approaches to determining the return on investment are anecdotal rather than quantifiable. However, they lead to the down-to-earth observations that management can easily relate to.

# Summary

The ODS environment presents an organizational challenge to the IT department because there are strong elements of both operational processing and DSS processing that occur in the ODS. The ODS organization requires many classical job skills such as database administration, project management, data administration, programming, analysis, and design. The number of people required and the exact skill mix is greatly influenced by whether the ODS is a custom-built or a commercial ODS. The ODS organization is typically positioned under the IT organization, at a same level as the data warehouse.

# The Role of Standards

Much of the activity in today's computer environment is driven by standards and the open systems movement. Standardization is of keen interest for the builder of an ODS, because it can provide the interoperability needed to access legacy environments and to deliver information to end users. It is also important because of the portability that standards bring. Because an ODS is developed iteratively, it will tend to grow over time. Portability at the server level allows the ODS to be retargeted to new platforms to take advantage of new price/performance levels as time goes by. While retargeting an ODS is not something that is typically desirable, it is often necessary as the ODS outgrows the performance and function of the platform it is on. If, for instance, an ODS started as a class III and grew into a class I, a different platform might be needed to support the increase in function.

## An Open World?

In the beginning of data processing, standards were needed to allow for the transfer of data from one computer system to another. Applications were batch and mostly stand-alone. Standard tape formats permitted data to be shared between applications, systems, and, on rare occasions, companies. As technology evolved, there was a growing need to share data, applications, and people throughout the environment. Standards came relatively easily at first because there was one dominant vendor who could drive the process.

In the late 1980s, the world began to change as people migrated away from a single-vendor model. It was the promise of standards that were used to promote this approach. The computer industry is repeating a process seen in many other forms of technology. Stereos and other consumer electronics have taken the same path and it is in this context that the current state of standards becomes clear. When video recording was first undertaken, it was a very expensive commercial venture. Entire studios were built by a single vendor with numerous components linked together by proprietary interconnections. As time went by, the interfaces between various types of equipment were standardized by bodies such as the IEEE. Much of the standards work evolved from existing implementations, which made it easy for some vendors to support them. In the same way that computers have now been defined to be a collection of components such as disk, tape, and memory, video production was made up of cameras, recorders, character generators, and so on. Standardization led to specialization such that vendors would build a single component and, by thus focusing on specific products, could build superior products to vendors who tried to do everything.

In the early 1980s, the consumer video market blossomed. Home video recorders and cameras became popular and, as volumes rose, prices came down. Even though this equipment was not suitable for much of the commercial marketplace, there were many jobs that could be downsized to organizations using subprofessional equipment. This, combined with the reduced cost of components such as integrated circuits and tubeless cameras, drove costs down for commercial production facilities.

Clearly the computer industry has taken a similar tack with standards and the emergence of a consumer market driving component costs lower. Open standards allow an organization to off-load work that is less than mission critical to lower-cost platforms and still present an integrated computing environment.

## A Simple Example

Assume that an organization has a new application to build. The organization wants to evaluate platforms that might host this application. The organization comes to the conclusion that the application should be built in a client-server fashion using PC clients and a UNIX server as platforms. This conclusion seems logical, since UNIX is an open operating system that runs on many hardware platforms and adheres to published interfaces. In order to have complete portability, a relational database management system is chosen that runs on many platforms and allows the application to be built in a portable development environment.

Under this model a sizable application is developed that supports the business very well. As the years pass, a problem arises; the application needs to grow in a way that the chosen platform cannot support. For instance, the organization may be going to a 7-day, 24-hour environment and the database environment requires nightly downtime for maintenance. In addition, there is a list of other enhancements that the users need that cannot be met by the current software platform.

While the organization has built in the ability to change hardware platforms, it is locked into a software environment. It might turn out that the organization has written thousands of lines of code in a development environment that only targets one database management system or has used proprietary features of the system that pose an obstacle to porting. In effect, the organization would have to trade hardware dependence for software dependence at a time when the price of software is skyrocketing and the price of hardware is dropping.

The point of this is twofold: First, "open" is not something you buy; it is something you do. It is very possible to become locked into an environment that conforms to every standard available because vendors add features to make themselves unique in the marketplace. Users may find that these features are so powerful that they must use them, but they should do so knowing the impact on portability. Second, the open market is still maturing. While it is well defined at the lower levels of a computer system, it is still being defined at the higher levels, as shown in Figure 11.1. It is interesting to note that where standards are in place and working, prices have fallen dramatically, but at the higher levels vendors can still demand high margins.

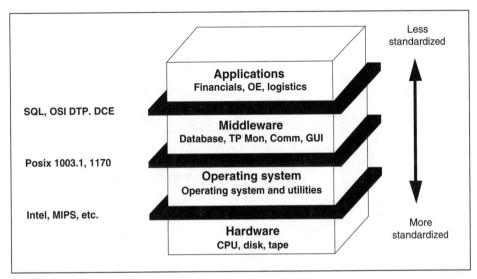

**Figure 11.1**  Standards are evolving from the lower layers of a computer to the applications.

# Portability of an Operational Data Store

With the previous example in mind, I will next focus on what is required to maintain both hardware and software portability when building an ODS. It turns out that this is not very difficult when compared with the challenge of making an operational application portable. This is because today's standards for accessing data are more defined than those used to update it. In an ODS, updating is the responsibility of the transformation software, rather than being embedded in every application, as it is in an operational application.

Portability in an ODS should be thought of as a definition of interfaces rather than implementation. As shown in Figure 11.2, choosing to standardize on an implementation rather than an interface restricts the available solution. Instead, an approach where the interfaces between the major components of an ODS are defined allows various implementations of technology to be used. In an ODS, these interfaces happen at two points, as shown in Figure 11.2.

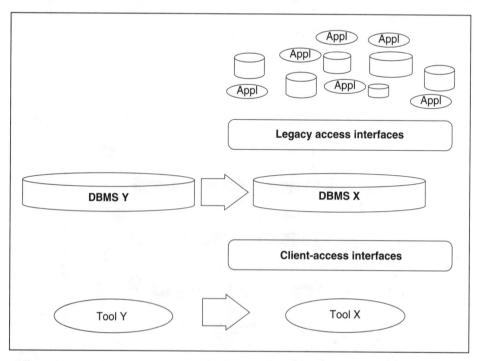

**Figure 11.2** The key points where standards are applied to an ODS are the interfaces rather than the implementations. This allows implementations to be changed.

# Client Access

End users typically access an ODS from a client platform running an application or tool. This client could be a traditional PC or it could be mainframe-based software. In the latter case, the networking environment and geography of the users could dictate that the mainframe be used as a client, as shown in Figure 11.3. Mainframe clients are sometimes the only feasible solution for the clerical users.

If the client is a workstation or departmental server, there are a number of database access standards available. Middleware products often support numerous database management systems but in the past provided their own APIs, so tools and applications had to be ported to them. This led to the larger database vendors having the widest support. In recent years, standards such as those created by the SQL Access Group (SAG) have been implemented by workstation software vendors. Soon it will be difficult to buy a workstation operating system without an installed database driver such as DAL (Macintosh) or ODBC (Windows). These interfaces are being offered now for virtually all middleware and database management systems. Using the native call-level interface of an operating system typically gives access to the widest variety of tools and applications.

If the client is the legacy host environment, standards may be more difficult to find. In this case, the most common call-level interface may be the dynamic query facility of the legacy platform. Indeed, some middleware products such as IBI's Enterprise Data Access emulate this interface to allow host-based software to issue queries to the ODS. The alternative to this is to build the ODS on the same platform with the legacy environment. Although this may not align with many organizations' strategic plans, it can simplify access from older terminals and terminal emulators.

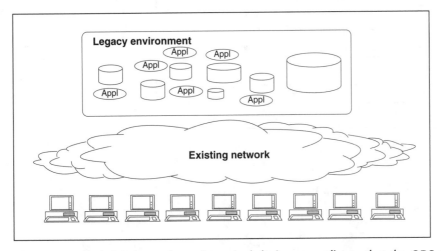

**Figure 11.3** Existing networks and terminal devices may dictate that the ODS applications and tools reside in the legacy environment.

# Legacy Data Access

The legacy interconnect is often a dedicated high-speed connection used to propagate data from the current system of record to the ODS. Depending on the size and class of the ODS, this connection may be a simple communications line or it may require a proprietary interconnect such as a mainframe channel attach or enterprise system connections (ESCON) link. This interconnect is the foundation for the transformation layer, so dependence on a proprietary technology may mean trading performance for portability.

In order to apply updates to the ODS, both a data manipulation and a transaction control interface are needed. The data manipulation interface will most likely be the native interface to the database management system and the TP interface will likely belong to a TP monitor. Both of these will be accessed by the transformation layer, as seen in Figure 11.4. This arrangement allows the database to maintain integrity by either locking or presenting consistent images to the user until groups of updates are committed. Database standards defined by ANSI are helpful, but are not as implementation specific as the workstation call-level

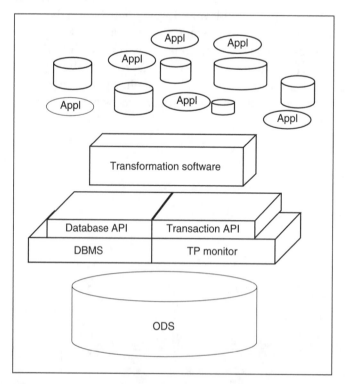

**Figure 11.4** The transformation layer will access the ODS through database and transaction interfaces.

interfaces mentioned earlier. Adhering to standards such as these can minimize but not eliminate the effort to port transformation code to a new database management system. In addition, standards for transaction control are still being defined. Currently the standards body governing this area has agreed to include three different APIs in the standard and is considering adding more. This, combined with the budding open TP monitor market, makes standardization difficult.

The lack of standards definition is not tragic so long as this is taken into account in the design of the transformation layer. Calls to the database management system and TP environments on the ODS platform should be kept in a minimum of locations. Isolating this logic to a single module of software with an internally developed API is one way to accomplish this. The other approach that can mitigate this issue is to use a tool for transformation that supports numerous ODS platforms. Doing this shifts the burden of portability to the tools provider, but can result in third-party dependency.

## The Process of Portability

Achieving a high degree of portability requires planning and process. It is desirable to put a process in place that will ensure portability. Portability requires that guidelines be set when architecting the ODS that will suggest the standards and practices to be used. An approach that some have undertaken is to create a portability plan. This is a document that defines the steps required to port from the selected environment to a new platform. This document should include plans for the replacement of all relevant components including hardware, database management communications, and so forth. It is wise to ask the vendor of any selected product to provide this plan. For instance, vendors of database management systems can be asked to deliver documents detailing how the ODS might be ported to different database management system technology as a part of their proposal. This practice leverages the knowledge of the vendors and assists in the selection of standards.

Once a plan is developed, someone must watch over it. While it is possible to designate someone as the gatekeeper of standards, it is often adequate to integrate the concept into the process of building the ODS. Standards are governed by reviewing new developments for portability in regular status meetings and design reviews. For smaller projects, this is often preferable to designating people to act as standards police.

## Summary

Building an ODS that conforms to standards can provide the ability to continually move to new technology. This is particularly important to the ODS because it is an entity that evolves over time and is likely to grow and have changing requirements. In many ways the computer industry is still evolving through a process of standardization that other industries have already been through.

It is possible to build an ODS on a platform that supports open standards and not achieve portability if standards are not adhered to. With this in mind, there are two major areas that require attention to standards in an ODS. One is client access standards that typically reside on a workstation or on the legacy environment. The other is the set of standards that affect legacy data access.

Putting a process in place that defines standards for an ODS implementation is key to a good design effort. Once this is done, it is important to designate an ongoing process to ensure conformance to standards as the ODS evolves.

**CHAPTER**

**12**

# Reengineering and the Operational Data Store

Many companies are finding that they must reengineer their systems to better support their current business process. It is a daunting task to architect and engineer systems that not only match the company's new business processes but are flexible enough to deal with change. Much has been written about this task and how best to achieve it. As difficult as this is, it is nowhere near as difficult as implementing this change in an existing mission-critical environment without missing a beat. Someone once said that the reason God could create the world in seven days was because He had no installed base. Reengineering produces a similar situation. Most organizations are too large to simply rebuild to a new plan. It turns out that taking a current inventory and designing the way it should be is minimal next to the task of actually migrating. The process of migrating from old to new is lengthy and requires the maintenance of a dual infrastructure. This has proven to be too challenging for some organizations.

## Short-Term Relief

The role that an ODS plays in reengineering is similar to that of an aspirin—it can quickly relieve some of the pain of change but it does not solve the underlying problem. One of the symptoms of the need to reengineer is that users are trying to deal with a changed business model and find that they cannot get the information they need for proper decision making or to support daily activities.

As an example, 10 years ago many financial institutions were very account-centric, as shown in Figure 12.1. This resulted from growing up in an environment where they offered a narrowly defined service, such as long-term loans. Over the last 10 years, many of these organizations have changed their business

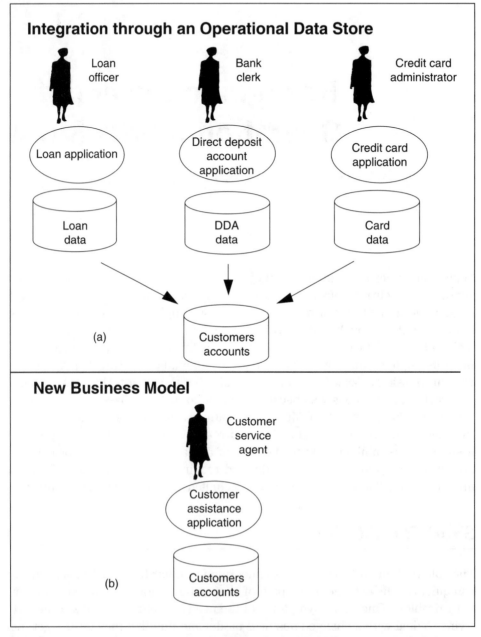

**Figure 12.1**  A comparison of the results of (a) integrating data with an ODS and (b) actually reengineering the business.

model and now offer a wider range of financial products. As a result, financial institutions are finding that the account-centric view of the world is no longer sufficient because they have customers with numerous accounts of different types. If systems were built over the years for each new business, by now they might have long-term loan systems, card service systems, and consumer savings systems that are perfectly suited to their respective functions but are not integrated. Since the various systems evolved over many years, they are probably on different technology bases. As the organizations move to a customer-centric view of the world they are not equipped to compete. If the new business model calls for an account manager who services a customer in every way, this person might end up with three terminals on his or her desk.

In the same way that a data warehouse can help an organization get an integrated view of their customers for strategic objectives, an ODS can help in tactical ways. In an ODS, a customer's current status could be integrated into a common view that would show all current balances, recent history, demographics, and so on to support various operations in the new model. In this way a customer wishing to open a new line of credit but who is delinquent on a mortgage and having bounced nine checks would be identifiable on the spot.

From a technology standpoint, building an ODS and a data warehouse can be helpful to the reengineering effort in a number of ways. It can provide an opportunity to deal with many of the challenges that will be encountered during reengineering in a less mission-critical environment. Much of the process and technology for each are the same, but an ODS implementation can often be more forgiving than a reengineering effort. Reengineering and building an ODS both require the following:

**The organization must assess its data.** The system of record must be identified by finding the best source for each and every data element in the enterprise. When data exists in multiple locations, rules must be defined to reconcile it.

**A new data design must be made.** The organization must cast its legacy environment in an integrated, subject-oriented design that reflects the new business model. A reengineered operational environment and an ODS will have some differences (to be discussed later), but the process of design is quite reusable.

**A mapping must be made of the old data model as it applies to the new.** Transformations must be defined that will apply technology changes as well as business rules to create the new data store from the old. This involves dealing with platform differences and decoding, as well as changes that will require the new rules of the business to calculate new data from old.

**The infrastructure must be built that will maintain a level of synchronization between the operational and query environments.** As is often the case, the technology is a minor part of this effort. What is often

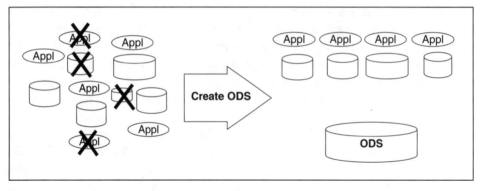

**Figure 12.2** Often the legacy environment will contain data extracted for query processing. By building a structured DSS environment, much of this can be eliminated, leaving a smaller, more manageable reengineering project.

most challenging is building the skills and practices that must be in place to make synchronization work.

**New technology must be encountered.** Moving to a reengineered environment and building an ODS often takes advantage of new technology. While this is not a requirement, many organizations are using distributed computing, object-oriented programming, and so on in their ODS implementations and would likely do the same in an operational reengineering effort.

By building an ODS, an IS organization can overcome many of these challenges in an environment that is less mission critical than a reengineered production environment. In doing so they will be better equipped to deal with reengineering. This is an indirect benefit of an ODS but there is a direct benefit as well: The ODS and the data warehouse will relieve the legacy environment of a great deal of data and processes. As shown in Figure 12.2, most legacy environments have already implemented a number of query support systems in the form of extracts, data propagations, and operational queries. Query support systems add to the overall complexity of reengineering. By removing data and query processing from the legacy environment, the task of reengineering can thus be reduced.

## The Operational Data Store and the Ideal System of Record

So far this chapter has dealt with the relationship between the ODS and the current system of record. Discussion has centered around the need for change in the existing environment to enable better decision making. Indeed, the ODS was conceived to help deal with many of the shortcomings of today's legacy environment, such as the lack of integration and the process-oriented nature of many systems. If reengineering is to be considered, a look at the relationship between an ODS and an ideal system of record is needed. This will help us understand the role of an ODS in a true reengineering effort.

The ODS has much in common with a well-reengineered environment, since both are intended to address many of the same issues. This holds true at the logical level, but there are some differences at the physical level that one should be aware of. These similarities and differences are shown in Figure 12.3.

## Integration

Most reengineering efforts involve an effort to better integrate lines of business or functional systems that may have been designed at different times on different technology bases. One of the early steps in most reengineering efforts is to develop a corporate data model that can be used as a foundation for new applications. This is a commonality with an ODS, which also seeks to interpret the current environment in an integrated fashion.

## Subject Orientation

Many systems are process oriented and therefore do not support the enterprise's way of viewing the various subjects it deals with. Both reengineering and an ODS typically express the current data in a manner that is grouped around the major subjects of the enterprise. Subject-oriented data goes hand in hand with integration.

| Similarities | Differences |
| --- | --- |
| • Integrated data | • Level of normalization |
| • Subject oriented | • Data content |
| • Periodicity | • Methodology |
| • User community | |
| • Technology base | |

**Figure 12.3**  Similarities and differences between an ODS and the ideal system of record.

## Periodicity of Data

Periodicity is defined as the time range of data that is maintained. Periodicity is measured in two ways. The first is the degree to which the data is in synch with the real world. Throughout most of the 1980s, organizations have worked to move from batch processing to online transaction processing. This movement was fueled by lower-cost technology and an explosion in data capture capability. Today most organizations can capture data at the moment events occur but often cannot use the data as well as they can capture it. This occurs for two reasons: capture technology, such as point-of-sale and bar-code devices, has progressed much faster than query processing technology, and cost justifying query processing systems can be challenging. This implies that the ideal operational database will have a close level of synchronization with the real world such that at the moment an item is purchased or a part manufactured, the corporation's data stores will represent it. A class I ODS works in a similar way. Data is propagated from the operational environment in a near-synchronous manner.

The second measure of periodicity of data is the length of time that it remains in the data store before being archived to off-line or near-online media. In both an ideal system of record and an ODS, the data is maintained as long as it serves an operational purpose. This may be 30 days for some industries or much longer or shorter periods for others. Neither the ODS nor the reengineered data stores should be designed to store long-term data as in a data warehouse.

## User Community

The user community for the ODS is typically made up of clerical users and a smaller number of information analysts. The clerical community has a profile similar to the users of a system of record. There may be a relatively large number of users doing short transactions. The users may also be distributed geographically. The users of an ODS are usually a subset of the current users of a system of record and are sometimes moved from the system of record to the ODS to gain its benefits.

## Technology Base

Comparing underlying technology needed to support an ODS and a system of record, we find that they can be very similar when the ODS in question is class I in nature. A class II or class III ODS is substantially less demanding of technology. The ODS platform may be a superset in functionality of the one needed to support a system of record. Both need to be able to perform all of the OLTP functions mentioned earlier, while the ODS also needs to have the ability to perform high-performance query. Today they are often hosted on a relational database capable of performing both OLTP and DSS. They have similar availability profiles and need to support similar workloads and numbers of users.

## Normalization

Normalization represents the first difference between the ODS and an ideal system of record. OLTP systems are often highly normalized into a third normal form (3NF). DSS is often best performed on a relatively denormalized structure called a *star schema*. Star schemas are structures pioneered by Ralph Kimball where the majority of the data in a subject area is contained in a single fact table that is surrounded by numerous small supporting tables. Organizing data in this way provides a structure that is much easier for the user to understand and access. There are also a number of reasons why relational database management technology will perform well in this environment, particularly for the large "lunking" queries typical of ad hoc analytical users.

## Data Store Content

The second potential difference between the ODS and an ideal system of record is the content of the data stores. It can be seen in Figure 12.4 that the ODS may use pointers to data currently in the operational system and therefore it may not have the level of detail that lies in a system of record. Often the ODS is

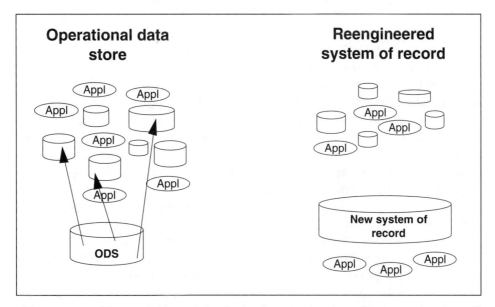

**Figure 12.4** While an ODS is a minimalist implementation that references some data still in the legacy environment, reengineering requires that the detail be moved to the new database.

designed using the current system of record as a starting point. One of the first modifications that is made is to jettison data that is not required to support integrated decision making. This activity leads to a more sparsely populated model than that of an operational database.

## Methodology

There is a fundamental difference in the methodology used to create an ODS versus a new system of record. The ODS is grown iteratively as subject areas are added to it. Flexibility is a key benefit of an ODS. As described in Chapter 6, the methodology used to develop an ODS lies somewhere between the SDLC model used for operational systems and the CLDS model used for data warehouses. A dual methodology is needed to support both the DSS analyst and the clerical users who access the ODS (see Chapter 11).

# Migrating the System of Record

When thinking about the relationship between building an ODS and building a new system of record, the obvious thought is to migrate the current system of record over time to the ODS. Application migration is possible, but it requires an ODS design that is conducive to migration. The movement of the system of record dictates certain things be considered in the design of the ODS. With careful planning, migration is feasible and should be considered in situations where major reengineering is imminent because of changing business processes. Combining a short-term ODS strategy with a long-term reengineering effort can offer a valuable mix of instant gratification and long-term change. This multistep approach is shown in Figure 12.5, where data elements B and C are eventually moved to the ODS platforms along with certain applications.

The first assumption is that the starting point is a class I ODS. This assumption provides the design criteria that more closely matches a reengineering effort. The class I ODS will share many of the platform requirements since the online propagation of data drives the need for an OLTP-capable platform and trickle-capable transformation software.

The database design of an ODS tends to be more normalized if it is destined to be a system of record at some time. Since this can have a negative impact on the large queries typical of information analysts, it is important to consider who the primary users of the ODS will be. If information analysts are the primary users, then it is not a good candidate for eventual reengineering because of the level of normalization that will have to occur to support the operational environment. If the ODS will support mostly clerical queries, it will be more conducive. This is often the case in a reengineering effort since clerical query processing will be off-loaded from the legacy environment.

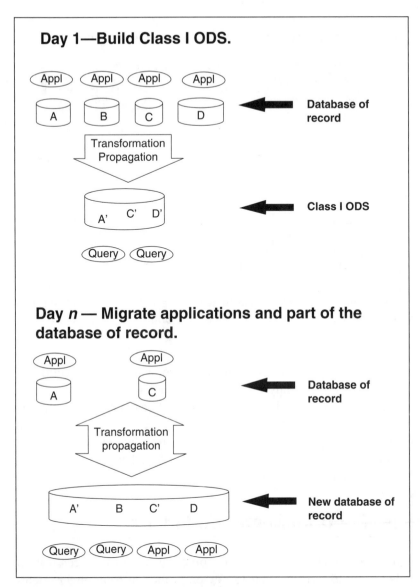

**Figure 12.5** Evolving an ODS into a new system of record.

The ODS used to support reengineering could eventually contain an enormous amount of detailed data that is not needed for pure ODS function. Much of the data that will be left behind in most ODS implementations will eventually find its way to the system to support a new system of record. This is a blessing as well as a curse, since it can have a very positive impact on response time because of the locality of the data, but will no doubt make the migration more challenging.

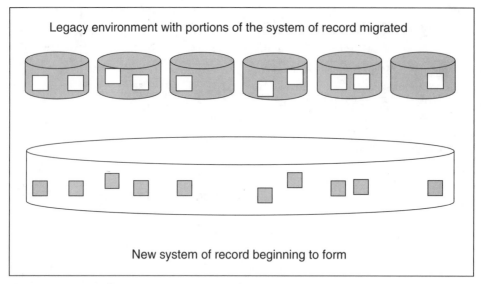

**Figure 12.6**    Reengineering requires the ability to deal with a system of record that is partially migrated to new technology. Elements of data exist in both environments.

One of the keys to making this work is data synchronization. It is essential to understand that the legacy systems will be in place for some time. It is likely that they will never go away entirely because there will be existing applications and databases that serve their purpose and do not need to change. This results in a requirement to deal with a system of record that has data elements spread over more than one platform, as shown in Figure 12.6. Synchronizing these data sources with integrity is necessary for success.

## Case Study: The Data Migration Engine

Some time ago a major telecommunications company came to the realization that they needed to migrate from their legacy environment to a newer client-server environment. This started a project that led to the creation of a concept known as the *data migration engine* (DME). (Unfortunately, at about the same time, the Open Software Foundation coined the same acronym to mean *distributed management environment*. These two terms have no relationship and in this text DME will refer to the data migration engine).

Conceptually DME is an architecture that deals with the issue of living with a system of record split across old and new platforms for the purpose of reengineering. A goal of DME is to blur the distinction between old and new databases, allowing them to appear as one virtual database. It was implemented as a successful pilot using a framework of products from a virtual corporation formed by Information Builders, Tandem Computers, Apertus Technologies, Potomac Scheduling, and Computer Network Technologies (CNT). The essence of this concept is to create an ODS with applications being reengineered onto it. It provides a graceful way to implement the changes driven by business process reengineering while continuing to support existing business systems.

A fundamental guideline of this project was that the new environment would be implemented in a client-server fashion. New application logic would reside on midtier departmental servers and desktop PCs. Data was migrated to a parallel processing SQL engine attached to the legacy environment, as shown in Figure 12.7.

Conceptually there are three types of data maintained by the transformation layer in the architecture:

**New data.** This is data that did not previously exist in the legacy environment. This data is created as a result of new functionality being added to the current environment.

**Pass-through data.** This is data that remains on the legacy environment and does not exist on the new platform.

**Controlled redundant data.** This is data that resides on both platforms and is synchronized by the transformation layer, which in this case was known as the scrubber/propagator. The term *redundant* here should not be con-

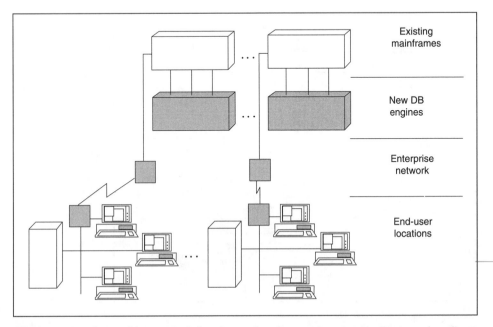

**Figure 12.7**  The architecture of the data migration project was built around a client-server model with new database engines being implemented in front of the system of record.

strued to mean that the data is merely copied, since it is transformed into an integrated, subject-oriented data store on the fly. This immediate transformation and propagation designates this as a class I ODS.

The definition of new data should be self-evident and pass-through data is relatively simple. For this project, traditional database middleware was modified to provide a high-performance link to the legacy databases. The implementation required access to mainframe-based IMS, DB2, and VSAM data. New application logic was able to access the named legacy environments when needed due to the middleware's distributed schema awareness and routing capabilities. This is illustrated in Figure 12.8.

The bulk of the work done was required to build a robust, yet high-performance transformation layer. This software was implemented to capture changes made to the system of record by capturing audits as they are created and reformatting them into a database of change. As this change is captured it is fed directly through the scrubber/propagator, which uses a rules-based system to determine the required change on the non-system-of-record database, as shown in Figure 12.9. These transformations deal with the differences in the

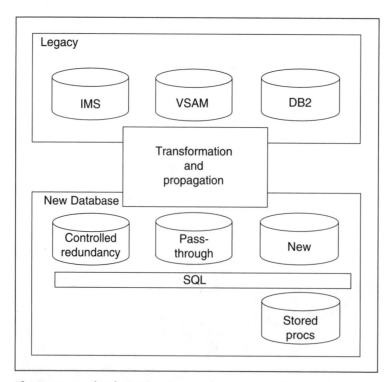

**Figure 12.8** The data migration engine project defined three types of data that interoperated with the legacy environment.

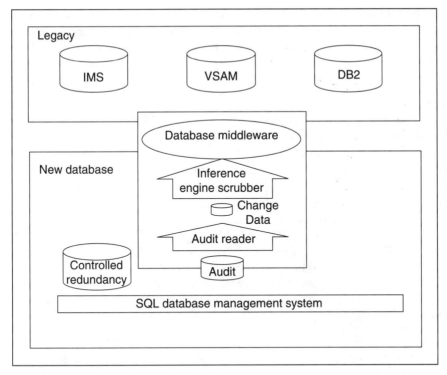

**Figure 12.9**  Controlled redundant data was near-synchronously fed through the transformation layer. As changes are applied to the new database of record, any impact on legacy data is automatically applied. This feedback to the legacy environment is the key difference between the ODS and the data migration project.

physical storage between the platforms as well as the logical database design differences. The change was then applied to the second database using the middleware mentioned earlier. In order to achieve performance that could support a large production environment (this company had numerous large mainframes), elements of the transformation layer were written as low-level communications programs called *sockets*.

The effect of this was that the ability to synchronize a class I ODS with a database design radically different from the legacy environment was achieved. The relationship between the legacy and the ODS can be expressed as rules in the transformation layer and implemented in near real time. In addition, the transformation layer was designed in such a way as to enable two-way propagation of data. New applications could be built to use the new database, and any data elements needing to be shared between the legacy and the new platform would be synchronized. Data synchronization is one of the reasons that a rules engine was used for transformation. In order to make the environment work, one must be able to deal with collisions where users simultaneously update the same data element on both platforms. While collisions are infrequent in the real world, it is a possibility and must be dealt with. Clearly collisions are not a trivial issue and careful consideration must be given to whether they will be allowed. In the DME pilot, collisions were detected and written to a log file, but automated resolution of those conflicts was not implemented. This is slated for a follow-on implementation.

This project was a proof of the concept and to date has been tested for both performance and functionality. Overall the results were exceptional. Performance was better than expected and proved that adding a new layer of processing to the environment in the form of the ODS and associated middleware actually caused a performance improvement. The transformation layer was extremely effective. Two key results were as follows:

- Pass-through data was tested by executing concurrent inserts, updates, and reads against the legacy databases, first directly and then passing through the target ODS platform, as shown in Figure 12.10. The result was that the average response time was significantly better when passing through due to better efficiency in the network utilization and the general "box carring" of transactions.

- Controlled redundancy was tested by running concurrent inserts and updates against the new relational data structures on the DME platform,

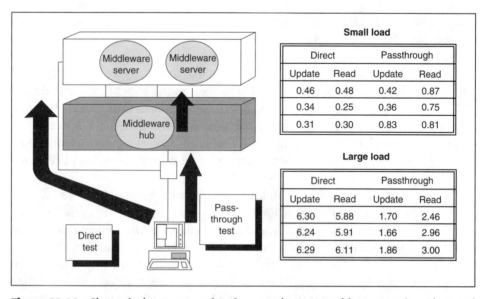

**Small load**

| Direct | | Passthrough | |
|--------|------|--------|------|
| Update | Read | Update | Read |
| 0.46 | 0.48 | 0.42 | 0.87 |
| 0.34 | 0.25 | 0.36 | 0.75 |
| 0.31 | 0.30 | 0.83 | 0.81 |

**Large load**

| Direct | | Passthrough | |
|--------|------|--------|------|
| Update | Read | Update | Read |
| 6.30 | 5.88 | 1.70 | 2.46 |
| 6.24 | 5.91 | 1.66 | 2.96 |
| 6.29 | 6.11 | 1.86 | 3.00 |

**Figure 12.10** Shown is the response time in seconds measured for transactions that read and update the legacy databases. When testing access directly to host legacy data compared to pass-through, the direct access was actually slower once the system was under load.

which were then interpreted by the translation software and applied against a legacy IMS data structure on the mainframe. Propagation was set to near-synchronous and the result was that all updates to the new system of record were translated and propagated to the legacy system of record within two seconds. Also tested was the ability to capture collisions by having the translation layer compare before images.

## Summary

Many organizations are now finding a need to reengineer their legacy environment. This is often in an effort to create systems that support a business environment that has changed since the systems were built. While the design of new systems is possible, migrating a system of record while continuing to support the enterprise can be very difficult.

An exploration of the relationship between an ODS and a reengineered environment shows that there are a number of similarities. The similarities lead to the idea of using an ODS as a basis for reengineering. In this scenario, after a class I ODS has been populated, applications would be migrated from the legacy environment to the ODS.

There are three potential differences that must be addressed before this can happen. The database design may have to be more normalized than if the ODS were not going to be used as a system of record. This may impact strategic query processing by the information analyst. More data will have to be moved to the ODS rather than using pointers to legacy data and a different methodology must be used. A careful balance of CLDS in the early ODS development with a concurrent SDLC for OLTP functionality must be used.

The key component required to make a migration of the system of record work is robust and efficient translation software. This software must be able to deal with the synchronization of the old and new system of record and deal with exceptions such as collisions that occur when both databases are updated simultaneously.

# Operational Data Store Development Methodology

The operational data store development methodology is divided into the following sections (see Figure A.1):

1. **Project management steps.** These steps are for general project planning, sizing and phasing of the project, project evaluation, and ODS maintenance.

2. **Prerequisite steps.** Steps taken to ensure that the technical environment is established and ready when needed, that capacity has been estimated, and that the first cut at data and application requirements has been made.

3. **Process design steps.** Steps used to develop the operational processing of the ODS. They include development of a high-level process model, generation of detailed process requirements, analysis of existing operational code for reusability, generation of pseudocode, and the application code itself for the first phase of the ODS project.

4. **Data design steps.** These steps are used to create the ODS database. They include the creation of a subject area diagram, the logical and physical data models, mapping of the source system of record, and population of the ODS database.

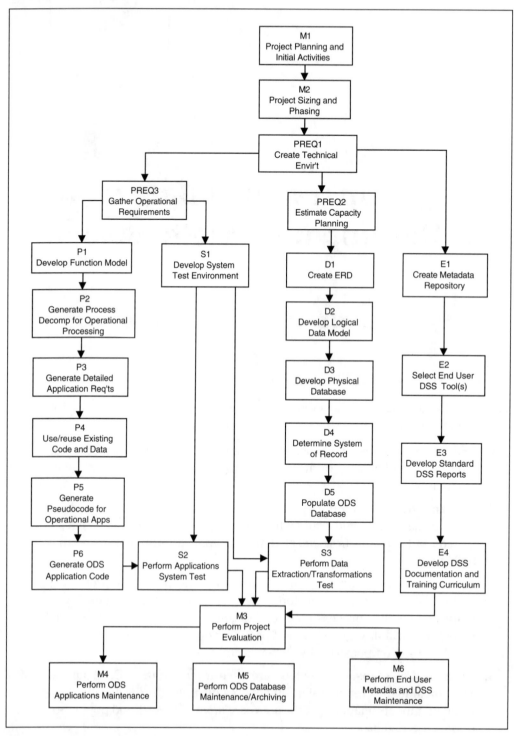

**Figure A.1**   Methodology flow chart.

5. **System testing steps.** These are the steps used to test the interaction between the ODS applications and database. These include unit, system, acceptance, and stress tests for the ODS applications, and data quality and acceptance tests for the ODS database.

6. **End-user environment steps.** These steps are used to create the end-users' environment and metadata repository. The environment contains the ability to generate analytical queries as well as standard reports and interfaces to the data.

# Project Management Step 1—Project Start

**Preceding Activity:** Decision to build the ODS.

**Following Activity:** Project Management Step 2—Determine General Sizing.

**Time Estimate:** Three weeks.

**Normally Executed Once or Many Times:** Once.

**Special Considerations:** The project plan is continually updated with changes and completed deliverables throughout the project.

**Deliverables:** The following deliverables are part of the project start step:

- A project scope document is created that includes the goals and objectives of the project, executive sponsorship, a description of the business problem to be solved, what is in scope and what is out, initial procurement requirements, and so on. If the company has a strategic business plan, it makes sense to establish how the ODS requirements relate to the overall strategy by describing this relationship in the scope document. The strategic business plan may help the company struggling with the scope of its first ODS by setting specific goals for it, establishing its business purpose, describing the organizational changes to be implemented, and so forth. Please visit the web site www.intelligentsolutions.com to obtain a free scope document outline for an ODS project.

- A detailed project plan must be developed before the project can go forward. The plan includes the activities, tasks, their deliverables and milestones, resource assignments, and time frames. Once the project plan is established, it is updated weekly with perturbations and/or the actual dates of task performance and completion.

- The appropriate end users are selected and a schedule of their participation is established. This ensures not only their involvement but also notifies them of the time they will have to set aside for the project.

- Other project start step activities include reviewing and updating the existing corporate guidelines and standards (e.g., naming and modeling standards, existing methodologies, etc.), developing change control procedures, and identifying any security requirements.

- The project plan, the scope document, and the end-user schedule are reviewed with the executive team for sign-off.

**Parameters of Success:** When performed correctly, the project start activities reduce the overall ambiguity of the project and establish a clear course of action to deliver the ODS. The scope is reasonably set defining both what is in scope as well as what is not in scope, specific and measurable goals are determined, and the resources needed for the project are understood. The political as well as the technical components of the project are well defined. The sponsoring organization is identified as well.

# Project Management Step 2—Determine General Sizing

**Preceding Activity:** Project Management Step 1—Project Start.

**Following Activity:** Project Management Step 3—Develop Project Phases.

**Time Estimate:** One and one-half weeks.

**Normally Executed Once or Many Times:** Once, then revisited for each phase of development.

**Special Considerations:** None.

**Deliverables:** Identification of the overall size of the ODS.

- Estimates of transaction, database, and network volumes are developed during this step and the hardware and software requirements are documented.

- The general functional requirements are gathered in an informal manner and sized. These requirements generally fall into two areas: the operational area and the DSS area.

- The hardware and software requirements are documented.

**Parameters of Success:** The goal is to continue the ODS development process in increments that are both economical and workable and with a technological base that is scalable.

# Project Management Step 3—Develop Project Phases

**Preceding Activity:** Project Management Step 2—Determine General Sizing.

**Following Activity:** Prerequisite Step 1—Develop ODS Architecture.

**Time Estimate:** Half a week.

**Normally Executed Once or Many Times:** Once.

**Special Considerations:** None.

**Deliverables:** Manageable phases of ODS development.

- If the ODS to be developed is quite large, it makes sense to break it up into different phases of a more manageable size and duration.
- The different development phases must be prioritized and organized into a meaningful sequence so that the second phase builds upon the work performed in the first phase, and so on. For example, if the ODS is a integrated customer information system, it may make sense to develop the commercial customers first, then residential customers, then governmental ones, etc.
- The output of this step is the breakup of general requirements into workable, manageable phases and the general hardware and software requirements needed to support the phases.

**Parameters of Success:** A series of smaller phases in a logical sequence.

# Prerequisite Step 1—Develop ODS Architecture

**Preceding Activity:** Project Management Step 3—Develop Project Phases.

**Following Activity:** Prerequisite Step 2—Select Hardware and Software.

**Time Estimate:** One and one-half weeks.

**Normally Executed Once or Many Times:** Once.

**Special Considerations:** An understanding of the entire corporate information factory architecture is necessary to determine how the ODS fits into the entire technical architecture.

**Deliverables:** The ODS vision and recommended changes to the current technology.

- The ODS vision contains the high-level architectural direction that the corporation needs to support its own strategic plans. The vision contains the overall architecture of the entire corporate information factory, including the data warehouse, data marts, metadata, and so on.

- The mechanisms to publish and subscribe data to and from the ODS is determined.

- The current technology is assessed for its role in the overall architecture.

- Finally, any changes needed to the current technology to support the vision are documented and approved.

**Parameters of Success:** A clear vision of the future architecture and documentation of the needed changes to the current technology to support this future vision.

# Prerequisite Step 2—Select Hardware and Software

**Preceding Activity:** Prerequisite Step 1—Develop ODS Architecture.

**Following Activity:** Prerequisite Step 3—Construct Technical Environment.

**Time Estimate:** Three weeks.

**Normally Executed Once or Many Times:** Once.

**Special Considerations:** Because the technical environments vary from company to company, this step may or may not be needed.

**Deliverables:** Contracts for the hardware and software.

- This step starts with an understanding of the ODS information cycle. Data enters from the legacy environment, is transformed, and is placed in the ODS. There the data is used both in a repetitive (operational) manner and in an ad hoc (DSS) manner. The pattern of usage, expected response time, volume of data, and number of users all go into the selection of the technology. The technology must also consider peak-period processing, worst-case scenarios, and scalability.

- Technology selection should include the hardware platform, network requirements, middleware, database management system technology, metadata infrastructure, and development tools.

- The technical support resources available to the project should be identified and scheduled. Their role in the construction of the ODS is critical but may not be a full-time position on the team; therefore their availability must be scheduled at the appropriate points in the project.

- Determining hardware, software, and tool requirements aids in the selection of the vendors for these products. A list of required features should be generated before interviewing and evaluating potential suppliers. Licenses and contracts are negotiated and products are ordered.

- Test criteria (goals of the testing, test tools to be used, other resources needed, etc.) for the ODS should be established. Potential test dates are scheduled.

- Note: It is recommended that this step be performed early on in the project because delivery times of hardware and software can be lengthy. In addition to this lead time, the "burn-in" time must be accounted for to ensure that proper resources are in place in time for the ODS implementation.

**Parameters of Success:** A thoroughly thought out technical environment will eliminate many problems that could have been avoided.


# Prerequisite Step 3—Construct Technical Environment

**Preceding Activity:** Prerequisite Step 2—Select Hardware and Software.

**Following Activity:** Prerequisite Step 4—Estimate Capacity Requirements.

**Time Estimate:** Two weeks.

**Normally Executed Once or Many Times:** Once.

**Special Considerations:** Depending on the environment selected, the IT staff may require training on the technology.

**Deliverables:** A fully installed and functioning technical environment.

- The hardware, software, communications, network links, and test environment are installed, tested, and ready for use.

- The staff is fully trained and knowledgeable about the technical environment.

**Parameters of Success:** Timely installations and training are crucial to the success of any technical project.


# Prerequisite Step 4—Estimate Capacity Requirements

**Preceding Activity:** Prerequisite Step 3—Construct Technical Environment.

**Following Activity:** Process Design Steps, Data Design Steps, System Testing Steps, and End-User Environment Steps.

**Time Estimate:** Depends on the size of the system being built, but it should not take more than a week.

**Normally Executed Once or Many Times:** Once per phase of development.

**Special Considerations:** Capacity planning has a history of confusing issues and the inclusion of extraneous factors that do not merit special attention. It is important to keep the capacity planning portion of the development process focused and to the point. Otherwise the exercise can become a roadblock to progress.

**Deliverables:** Storage requirements for both disk and near-line media, connectivity software, growth patterns, and initial allocations are developed.

- The gross amounts of resources consumed by the project need to be determined at this phase of development. In particular, the following should be considered:
  - Disk consumption
  - CPU consumption
  - I/O utilization
  - Memory requirements
  - Network/channel utilization

- In addition to these raw requirements, the arrival rate of transactions, peak-period processing, patterns of processing, response time requirements, and mean time to failure requirements are factored in.

- The output of this phase is the assurance that the required resources are in place. In addition, both peak-period online processing and off-peak batch loading/monitoring are included. Monitoring plans are developed as well.

**Parameters of Success:** No surprises when it comes to resources being in place, including the lead-time needed to acquire resources and the amount of resources needed.

## Prerequisite Step 5—Document ODS Requirements for Phase 1

**Preceding Activity:** Prerequisite Step 3—Construct Technical Environment.

**Following Activity:** Process Design Steps, Data Design Steps, System Testing Steps, and End-User Environment Steps.

**Time Estimate:** Three to four weeks.

**Normally Executed Once or Many Times:** Once per phase of development.

**Special Considerations:** None.

**Deliverables:** Documented, formal requirement specifications.

**Parameters of Success:** Done properly, this stage of analysis transforms all the gathered ideas into workable, formal requirements.

# Process Design Step 1—Develop High-Level Function Model

**Preceding Activity:** Prerequisite Step 4—Estimate Capacity Requirements and Prerequisite Step 5—Document ODS Requirements for Phase 1.

**Following Activity:** Process Design Step 2—Generate Process Decomposition.

**Time Estimate:** Two weeks.

**Normally Executed Once or Many Times:** Once and reviewed for each phase.

**Special Considerations:** None.

**Deliverables:** High-level function model.

- The first step in developing the operational aspects of the ODS is to create a high-level function model. If the enterprise has already generated this model, then the functions to be developed for the ODS should be selected from that model and further developed in the steps following this one.

- The major functions of the corporation are modeled from the highest level of abstraction. This diagram is equivalent to the entity-relationship diagram (ERD) in data modeling (see Data Design Step 1). Typical examples of the functions found in this model are maintain human resources, create product, sell product, market product, support customers, and so on. Generally, there are between 8 and 12 major functions identified in this model.

- The functions are defined and documented. Enough detail is given to have a firm understanding of the functions, but the developer should be careful not to try to go into excruciating detail for each and every one. That detail will be found in the process decomposition (see Process Design Step 2). For this project, concentrate on the functions to be developed during this phase only.

- The functions to be further developed for this first phase of the ODS are selected from the model. The end users participate in this selection and should sign off on the choices.

**Parameters of Success:** All major functions are identified at the highest level of abstraction. Further development efforts will focus exclusively on the selected functions for this phase.

# Process Design Step 2—Generate Process Decomposition

**Preceding Activity:** Process Design Step 1—Develop High-Level Function Model.

**Following Activity:** Process Design Step 3—Generate Detailed Application Requirements.

**Time Estimate:** Depends on the size of the system, but as a rule this step should not take more than three weeks.

**Normally Executed Once or Many Times:** Once per function.

**Special Considerations:** This is generally an iterative process of developing the decomposition and reviewing it with end users. Note: This specification applies only to the operational component of the ODS and not the DSS component.

**Deliverables:** Complete process decomposition of the selected functions.

- If the enterprise has already created a fully decomposed process model, then a review of the selected processes with the end users is all that is needed.

  - The process decomposition takes the broad function selected for the first phase of the ODS and breaks it down into a series of successively detailed processes. The processes are further decomposed into primitive activities. The primitive activities constitute the lowest level of detail for the model.
  - These lower levels of processes and activities correspond to the logical data model in the data design steps (see Data Design Step 2).
  - Reviews by the end users are critical to validate the accuracy of the processes and activities modeled.
  - The output of this step is a large decomposition model describing the processes and activities to be performed by the ODS.

**Parameters of Success:** The process decomposition reflects entirely and only the processes and activities to be implemented in this phase of the ODS. Factored into the designs are the considerations of other functions and processes that serve or will serve as building blocks. The document produced should be understandable, organized, and complete.

# Process Design Step 3—Generate Detailed Application Requirements

**Preceding Activity:** Process Design Step 2—Generate Process Decomposition.

**Following Activity:** Process Design Step 4—Use/Reuse Existing Code and Data.

**Time Estimate:** One hour per activity.

**Normally Executed Once or Many Times:** Once per activity.

**Special Considerations:** This is an iterative step as well and applies only to the operational component of the ODS.

**Deliverables:** Data flow diagrams of each process.

- The detailed process requirements are further documented by process descriptions, data flow diagrams, structure charts, workflows, and so on.

- For each primitive activity in the process decomposition, a data flow diagram (DFD) is drawn. The DFD indicates the inputs to an activity, the outputs, and the data stores needed to support the activity.

- Structure charts are generated to give more detail for the overall design to the programmers. Workflow diagrams show how the activities work together in cohesive units.

- Finally, descriptions are written defining each of the activities being performed.

**Parameters of Success:** The system or phase of the system is described in detail in terms of inputs, outputs, data stores, structure charts, and so on. No ambiguity is left to interpretation by the programming staff.

# Process Design Step 4—Use/Reuse Existing Code and Data

**Preceding Activity:** Process Design Step 3—Generate Detailed Application Requirements.

**Following Activity:** Process Design Step 5—Generate Pseudocode for Applications.

**Time Estimate:** Done very quickly, usually no more than two weeks.

**Normally Executed Once or Many Times:** Once.

**Special Considerations:** This step is one of the best ways to ensure code and data reusability. It is crucial to the integration of the environment.

**Deliverables:** Reusable code and data.

- In an architected environment, every project should use as much of the existing code and data as it can.

- This project should prepare for future projects that may use its code and data as well.

- If existing code is to be modified, the modifications are identified as a regular part of the system development requirements. If conversion of the code or data is required, the conversion becomes a component of the development effort as well.

- It should be noted that this step applies primarily to the operational aspects of the ODS. The extract/transformation code may be considered for reuse as well (especially if a data warehouse already exists that uses the same data as the ODS), but it generally must be created from scratch.

**Parameters of Success:** This step should identify any code or data that can be used as a building block for the project and it should identify all code and data that must be built in recognition of future efforts.

# Process Design Step 5—Generate Pseudocode for Applications

**Preceding Activity:** Process Design Step 4—Use/Reuse Existing Code and Data.

**Following Activity:** Process Design Step 6—Generate ODS Application Code.

**Time Estimate:** Varies, from five minutes to two days per activity at the primitive level.

**Normally Executed Once or Many Times:** Once per activity.

**Special Considerations:** If CASE or automated code generators are used, this step may not be necessary.

**Deliverables:** Programmer pseudocode.

- The algorithms and program specifications are further refined into pseudocode. The designer ensures that all needed data for operational processing is available.

- All variables, calculations, derivations, transformations, and so on are identified and defined in detail.

- Performance at the design level is factored in by using the following techniques:

  - Breaking a long-running program into a series of shorter ones
  - Requiring a program to access smaller amounts of data
  - Shortening the time a unit of data is locked
  - Changing a lock from update to access only
  - Using log/journal tapes as input.

**Parameters of Success:** The final step before coding begins includes the following evaluation:

- Completeness of design

- Order of execution of programs

- All cases required

- All contingencies covered (error handling and exception conditions)

- Structure of coding

# Process Design Step 6—Generate ODS Application Code

**Preceding Activity:** Process Design Step 5—Generate Pseudocode for Applications.

**Following Activity:** Systems Testing Step 2—Perform Applications System Testing.

**Time Estimate:** Varies, from one day per activity to several days per activity.

**Normally Executed Once or Many Times:** Once per activity.

**Special Considerations:** None.

**Deliverables:** Source code for the operational applications.

- The programmers translate the pseudocode into source code. The source code is compiled and errors corrected.

- The compiled code is thoroughly unit tested by the programmer responsible for the code.

**Parameters of Success:** The source code is a complete and efficient translation of the pseudocode, including in-line documentation. All operational requirements previously identified are satisfied.

# Data Design Step 1—Create Corporate Subject Area Diagram

**Preceding Activities:** Prerequisite Step 4—Estimate Capacity Requirements; Prerequisite Step 5—Document ODS Requirements.

**Following Activity:** Data Design Step 2—Create Logical Data Model.

**Time Estimate:** Half a week.

**Normally Executed Once or Many Times:** Once for each phase.

**Special Considerations:** For even the largest systems, one week or less should suffice if the designers are knowledgeable about the corporation. Otherwise the time may be much longer.

**Deliverables:** Corporate subject area diagram, selected subject areas for the first phase.

- If an enterprise has already created a subject area diagram, then the subject areas to be developed in the first phase of the ODS should be selected from the model and further developed in the next step (see Data Design Step 2—Create Logical Data Model).
  - The corporation's data needs are distilled down to the essential subject areas. These are typically the highest level of abstraction. Typical subject areas are CUSTOMER, PRODUCT, ORDER, and PART. This model is at the same level of abstraction as the high-level process model (see Process Design Step 1—Develop High-Level Function Model) and contains the data necessary to support the process model.
  - The major relationships between the subject areas are also identified, as well as the cardinality of the relationships. It should be noted that not all relationships are modeled; only those that are of significance at this high level of abstraction are shown in the model.
  - The subject areas to be implemented for this phase are selected from the subject area diagram. These subject areas will be used to support the operational applications being developed in the Process Design Steps as well as the DSS requirements being met in the End-User Environment Steps.

**Parameters of Success:** All major subject areas are identified at the highest level of abstraction. Further modeling efforts will focus exclusively on the selected subject areas for this phase. Note: Because this is an iterative methodology, the subject area diagram should be reviewed at the beginning of each new phase for validation.

# Data Design Step 2—Create Logical Data Model

**Preceding Activity:** Data Design Step 1—Create Subject Area Diagram.

**Following Activities:** Data Design Step 3—Create ODS Physical Model; Data Design Step 4—Historical Data Conversion.

**Time Estimate:** Four weeks.

**Normally Executed Once or Many Times:** Once per phase of development.

**Special Considerations:** None.

**Deliverables:** Logical data model and data specifications document.

- Logical data modeling concentrates on the selected subject areas only, documenting the gathered data requirements. The logical model contains attributes of data, the grouping of attributes, and keys. Supertypes and subtypes are identified, as are associative and characteristic entities.

- The output from this step is a normalized, logical data model for the subject areas containing only the primitive, operational data; derived or summarized data will be identified, stored, and managed elsewhere. Therefore the logical data model can serve as a basis for both operational processing needs and DSS needs.

- The logical data model will be reviewed with the end users for their validation and approval.

- Note: The modeling should continue until ODS-specific data requirements are finished. This concentration on ODS-specific data requirements allows the developer to determine when the data model is completed for this phase and this phase only. As each phase is completed, more and more of the enterprise logical data model will be filled in.

**Parameters of Success:** The normalized data model contains all primary, characteristic, associative, and subtype entities for the selected subject areas. The attributes and keys are fully identified and defined for each entity. Properly performed, this step produces documents and models that are understandable, organized, readable, and complete. The logical data model can then act as the starting point for a number of projects—data warehouses, OLTP systems, and/or further enhancements to the ODS.

## Data Design Step 3—Create ODS Physical Model

**Preceding Activity:** Data Design Step 2—Create Logical Data Model.

**Following Activity:** Data Design Step 5—Construct Physical Database.

**Time Estimate:** Two and a half weeks.

**Normally Executed Once or Many Times:** Once per phase.

**Special Considerations:** None.

**Deliverables:** A physical design of the ODS database and documented quality controls for that design.

- The ODS data requirements are mapped against the logical data model. Denormalization of the model takes place and summarized or derived elements are added.

- The data quality controls for the database are determined and documented. Quality issues are resolved or documented for further discussion.

**Parameters of Success:** A thoroughly attributed and documented physical model for the ODS and documented quality controls.

## Data Design Step 4—Historical Data Conversion

**Preceding Activity:** Data Design Step 2—Create Logical Data Model.

**Following Activity:** Data Design Step 7—Create Extraction/Transformation Programs.

**Time Estimate:** One week.

**Normally Executed Once or Many Times:** Once per phase.

**Special Considerations:** This step is an optional one depending on the nature of the ODS. If current information required by the ODS is stored in archived media, then a historical data conversion step will be necessary.

**Deliverables:** Historical data conversion requirements document.

- Historical data may be needed to complete some of the ODS requirements. If so, this data should be thoroughly studied to determine its quality, technological status, ease with which it can be extracted, and so on.

- It may take a special team and a special project aside from the main ODS project to convert historical data to usable ODS data.

**Parameters of Success:** Thoroughly studied and understood historical data requirements that can then be included in the ODS.

# Data Design Step 5—Construct Physical Database

**Preceding Activity:** Data Design Step 3—Create ODS Physical Model.

**Following Activity:** Data Design Step 6—Identify System of Record.

**Time Estimate:** Three weeks.

**Normally Executed Once or Many Times:** Once per phase of development.

**Special Considerations:** If the input to this step is ambiguous or incorrect, the amount of work required here can be much more than what is estimated. The scope of the project must be carefully governed.

**Deliverables:** ODS physical data model and an implemented database schema.

- In this step, the addition of some summarized (dynamic) and derived data is incorporated into the logical data model. The removal of data not used in the ODS occurs and the issue of physical denormalization is addressed. Denormalization techniques are used, such as:
  - Merging tables together
  - Selective introduction of redundancy
  - Creating popular derived and summarized data
  - Separating data according to its probability of access
  - Developing fact and dimension tables for analytical use.
- The physical design of the database will include:
  - Indexing/hashing
  - Physical distribution of data
  - Partitioning strategies
  - Storage (i.e., disk versus near line) strategies
  - Designation of keys
  - Clustering/interleaving
  - Management of variable length data
  - NULL/NOT NULL specification
  - Referential integrity (e.g., cascading deletes, updates, etc.)
  - The output is the actual specification of the database to the database management system. Both the operational applications and the DSS environment will use this database.

**Parameters of Success:** This stage of the analysis produces a design that will be efficient to access and update, both in terms of data and the programs that access and update the data. Performed properly, this step ensures efficient resource utilization and a workable database design.

# Data Design Step 6—Identify System of Record

**Preceding Activity:** Data Design Step 5—Construct Physical Database.

**Following Activity:** Data Design Step 7—Create Extraction/Transformation Programs.

**Time Estimate:** Three weeks.

**Normally Executed Once or Many Times:** Once per subject area.

**Special Considerations:** None.

**Deliverables:** Identification of the system of record for each attribute in the ODS data model.

- Once the ODS model has been developed, the next activity is to identify the source data in the existing OLTP environment. Most of the issues of integration are brought to the fore during this analysis, including
  - Key structure/key resolution as data passes from existing systems into the ODS
  - Attribution
  - What if there are multiple sources to choose from?
  - What if there are no sources to choose from?
  - What transformations—encoding/decoding, conversions, and so on—must be made as data passes into the ODS?
  - How current will data be in the ODS?
  - How will the ODS structure differ from the existing systems' structures?
- The output of this step is the mapping of the data from the existing systems to the ODS. The volume of data coming from the legacy environment is estimated. If a journal tape is to serve as a source, that too is specified.

**Parameters of Success:** When determining the source system of record, the analyst should consider

- The timeliness of the source data
- The completeness of the source data
- The accuracy of the source data

- How well the source data conforms to the structure of the ODS
- How near to the source the data comes from
- How efficient the source data is to access
- In addition, the means by which the ODS data will be transformed from the legacy environment technology to the ODS technology is addressed

# Data Design Step 7—Create Extraction/Transformation Programs

**Preceding Activity:** Data Design Step 6—Identify System of Record.

**Following Activity:** Data Design Step 8—Populate Database.

**Time Estimate:** Four to six weeks depending on the complexity of the programs.

**Normally Executed Once or Many Times:** Once per phase of development.

**Special Considerations:** If an extraction/transformation tool is not obtained, the time frame for this step must be extended to accommodate technical metadata creation.

**Deliverables:** Extraction/transformation programs, and accompanying metadata, batch software drivers (e.g., job control programs and scripts).

- Once the interface between the existing systems and the ODS has been outlined, the next step is to formalize the interface in terms of program specifications. The transformation flow plan allows the extraction and integration of data to be programmed efficiently and as simply as possible.
- Entry of the extraction and transformation information into the tool will be relatively simple. If entered correctly, verification and processing will go smoothly with minimal problems.

**Parameters of Success:** The code generated from this step should be

- Efficient
- Documented
- Easily changed
- Accurate
- Complete

# Data Design Step 8—Populate Database

**Preceding Activity:** Data Design Step 7—Create Extraction/Transformation Programs.

**Following Activity:** System Testing Step 3—Perform Data Extraction/Transformation Testing.

**Time Estimate:** Three weeks.

**Normally Executed Once or Many Times:** Once per phase of development.

**Special Considerations:** None.

**Deliverables:** Populated ODS.

- The final step in the Data Design Steps is the execution of the extraction and transformation programs and subsequent loading of the ODS data into the ODS database. The programs will use the test data created in System Testing Step 1—Develop Test Scripts and Testing Environment. Any problems with loading or data quality are fixed and the data is loaded again.

**Parameters of Success:** The result of executing these programs is an accessible and understandable ODS database that serves the needs of the operational community. The data will be thoroughly tested in System Test Step 3—Perform Data Extraction/Transformation Testing.

# System Test Step 1—Develop Test Scripts and Testing Environment

**Preceding Activity:** Prerequisite Step 5—Document ODS Requirements.

**Following Activity:** System Test Step 2—Perform Applications System Testing; System Test Step 3—Perform Data Extraction/Transformation Testing.

**Time Estimate:** Two to three weeks.

**Normally Executed Once or Many Times:** Once per phase of development.

**Special Considerations:** None.

**Deliverables:** System test plans for operational applications and for the data extraction/transformation programs as well as a test database.

- The scripts used in system testing are developed based on the documented end-user requirements. These scripts will be used to test the operational applications only. Other means of testing will be used to test the quality of the data being loaded into the ODS database by the extraction/transformation programs.

- Test data is developed to support the testing of extraction/transformation programs and is populated into the system test environment. This test data should mimic the types of data to be loaded into the ODS from the various legacy systems; the data is a small, controllable subset of all the data found in the legacy systems that can be used over and over to test the extraction/transformation programs.

- The extraction/transformation programs create the data needed to support the operational applications test scripts (i.e., the integrated, subject-oriented ODS database).

**Parameters of Success:** The system test scripts for the operational applications are developed with the philosophy that they will test the most used functions and data fields. The unit tests performed by the programmers should test the boundaries and extremes of the functions and data.

The test database will contain real examples of data as described by the end users and the analysis of the source systems, including known errors and other data problems. However, the test database will only be a small subset of the actual data to be used in the full population of the ODS.

# System Test Step 2—Perform Applications System Testing

**Preceding Activity**: Process Design Step 6—Generate ODS Application Code; System Test Step 1—Develop Test Scripts and Testing Environment.

**Following Activity:** Project Management Step 4—Perform Project Evaluation.

**Time Estimate:** Varies with complexity of code but is usually two to four weeks.

**Normally Executed Once or Many Times:** Once per phase of development.

**Special Considerations:** None.

**Deliverables:** System-tested application code.

- The unit-tested code is moved into the system test environment where the test scripts are run. This testing ensures the integration of the compiled code with other modules.

- The final system tests are run with the entire set of application modules to ensure that the system works as a whole.

- The output of this step is thoroughly tested applications ready for execution by the end-user community.

**Parameters of Success:** The code that passes system testing has program logic correctly specified. Furthermore, all conditions are tested including error and exception handling, before the code is moved into acceptance testing by the end users.

# System Test Step 3—Perform Data Extraction/Transformation Testing

**Preceding Activity:** Data Design Step 8—Populate Database; System Test Step 1—Develop Test Scripts and Test Environment.

**Following Activity:** Project Management Step 4—Perform Project Evaluation.

**Time Estimate:** Two to three weeks.

**Normally Executed Once or Many Times:** Once per phase of development.

**Special Considerations:** None.

**Deliverables:** Thoroughly tested, extracted, and transformed ODS data.

- Each of the sources of data (created in System Test Step 1—Develop Test Scripts and Test Environment) is tested for the ability of the programs to extract and transform the data correctly into the integrated ODS database.

- The quality of the data extracted and transformed must be examined. Using the test data, summarization, derivation, code translation, and all other data transformations are tested for their accuracy.

- The ability to load the data into the database is tested as well. The mechanisms used to load the data are thoroughly examined for possible errors and reliability as well as the ability to roll back the data should a fatal error be encountered.

- Finally, the error handling capability in the extraction/transformation programs is tested. The severity of errors, use of appropriate defaults, error messages logged, and so on are all part of the data extraction/transformation testing routines.

**Parameters of Success:** Fully tested data in the ODS database, error-handling routines in the extraction/transformation programs, and roll-back procedures in place.

# End-User Environment Step 1—Develop Metadata Repository and Access

**Preceding Activity:** Prerequisite Step 5—Document ODS Requirements.

**Following Activity:** End-User Environment Step 2—Select End-User Access Tools.

**Time Estimate:** Three weeks.

**Normally Executed Once or Many Times:** Once per phase of development.

**Special Considerations:** None.

**Deliverables:** Metadata repository and access to it.

- A crucial piece of the ODS architecture is the metadata describing the sources and targets of the ODS data, the transformations, summarizations, and derivations used, as well as the definitions, aliases, extract history, quality indicators, etc., of the data found in the ODS.

- The metadata gathered from the creation of the ODS database (transformation and extraction information), CASE tool entries, manual entries, and documentation developed for the ODS applications themselves must be organized and coordinated through the metadata architecture chosen (either centralized or distributed).

- The end-user access to this metadata must be built with ease of use and simplicity of access in mind. This access is thoroughly tested and approved by the end users.

**Parameters of Success:** A robust metadata architecture and access method.

# End-User Environment Step 2—Select End-User Tools

**Preceding Activity:** End-User Environment Step 1—Develop Metadata Repository and Access.

**Following Activity:** End-User Environment Step 3—Create Standard Reports.

**Time Estimate:** Two to three weeks.

**Normally Executed Once or Many Times:** Once.

**Special Considerations:** The end-user tools for this particular phase may or may not be appropriate for the next group of end users. The corporation may need different tool suites depending on the types of DSS reporting each group performs.

**Deliverables:** A suite of appropriate end-user tools.

- The OSD team and end users should create a list of prioritized requirements to be met by the access tool or suite of tools. This list should take into consideration:
  - Amount of ad hoc reporting needed
  - Sophistication of the end users in terms of SQL capability
  - Price
  - Database management systems to be interfaced with
  - Interface to other end-user tools (spreadsheets, word processors, etc.)
  - Ease of use
  - Hardware platforms to be supported
  - Availability of query governors
- The requirements should also consider the types of end users who will use these tools and the type of reporting they will perform, such as
  - Basic reporting—repetitive, rarely changing
  - Variance reporting—relatively routine but slightly more complicated
  - Complex reporting—multiple sets of data retrieved
  - Multidimensional and analytical reporting—complicated and somewhat heuristic
- An analysis of the tools available for the ODS and metadata access is performed based on the list of requirements generated. A list of potential vendors is created and vendor demos or site visits occur.
- A final set of tools is selected and the contracts developed. The end users should have the final say in the access tool decision.

**Parameters of Success:** A suite of end-user tools that permits the end user to have easy access to both the metadata and the ODS data.

# End-User Environment Step 3— Create Standard Reports

**Preceding Activity:** End-User Environment Step 2—Select End-User Tools.

**Following Activity:** End-User Environment Step 4—Develop End-User Documentation.

**Time Estimate:** Two to three weeks.

**Normally Executed Once or Many Times:** Once per phase of development.

**Special Considerations:** None.

**Deliverables:** A set of prioritized reports generated against the ODS data.

- A list of standard ODS reports may be created for the end users. The idea is to create a small number of typical DSS reports (10 or less) to show the end user how to generate his or her own reports.

- These reports should be of high priority for the end users, be commonly used by the end users, have a standard format, and be run at predetermined intervals (e.g., a daily report on the top selling product by market segment).

- The reports should be as parameter driven as possible, for example, in the sales report described above, the parameters may be the top X product in the Y market segment, based on dollar amount sold, units sold, and so on.

**Parameters of Success:** End users have a set of highly useful and flexible reports that they may use as examples from which to build their own set.

# End-User Environment Step 4— Develop End-User Documentation

**Preceding Activity:** End-User Environment Step 3—Create Standard Reports.

**Following Activity:** End-User Environment Step 5—Develop Initial Training/ Help Desk Function.

**Time Estimate:** One week.

**Normally Executed Once or Many Times:** Once per phase of development.

**Special Considerations:** None.

**Deliverables:** Documentation for the metadata repository, ODS usage, data models in business terms, and the help function.

- From the end-users' perspective, this phase of the project may be the most important one; icons and menus are generated for the end users to navigate the ODS and its applications.

- End-user documentation is created for all parts of the system. This documentation may be in the form of a manual, online help, and/or some form of help desk assistance. The documentation must be tested for clarity, ease of use, and correctness.

**Parameters of Success:** End-user documentation is fully functional.

## End-User Environment Step 5—Develop Initial Training/Help Desk Function

**Preceding Activity:** End-User Environment Step 4—Develop End-User Documentation.

**Following Activity:** Project Management Step 4—Perform Project Evaluation.

**Time Estimate:** Two to three weeks.

**Normally Executed Once or Many Times:** Once per phase of development.

**Special Considerations:** None.

**Deliverables:** A training curriculum, trained end users, and a help desk function.

- The training curriculum must be created and scheduled. The training includes not only the ODS applications themselves but also the DSS capabilities and access tools.

- The end users must also receive training on understanding and accessing the metadata.

- Finally, a help desk function should be established and the help desk personnel fully trained on their responsibilities as well as the ODS itself.

**Parameters of Success:** Fully trained and productive end users.

## Project Management Step 4—Perform Project Evaluation

**Preceding Activities:** System Test Step 2—Perform Applications System Testing; System Test Step 3—Perform Data Extraction/Transformation Testing; End-User Environment Step 5—Develop Initial Training/Help Desk Function.

**Following Activity:** Project Management Step 5—Convert Prototype to Production.

**Time Estimate:** Two to three weeks.

**Normally Executed Once or Many Times:** Once per phase of development.

**Special Considerations:** None.

**Deliverables:** Acceptance tested system and project evaluation.

- The final step before converting the system to production is to perform all the acceptance tests and to evaluate the overall project.

- The end-user community performs acceptance tests of the resulting system, making the critical Go/No Go decision for future phases.

- A review of the project methodology and project plan is performed to determine where steps could have been performed better or more efficiently. The plan and methodology are repeatable processes that will be used in future phases so a postproject evaluation could be quite helpful in the future.

**Parameters of Success:** The result is a satisfied end-user community and the go-ahead for future phases.

# Project Management Step 5—Convert Prototype to Production

**Preceding Activity:** Project Management Step 4—Perform Project Evaluation.

**Following Activities:** Project Management Step 6—Plan Next ODS Phase; Project Management Step 7—Perform ODS Applications Maintenance; Project Management Step 8—Perform Database Maintenance/Archiving; Project Management Step 9—Perform End-User Environment Maintenance.

**Time Estimate:** Two weeks.

**Normally Executed Once or Many Times:** Once per phase of development.

**Special Considerations:** None.

**Deliverables:** ODS is fully in production mode.

- To some extent, implementation into production is an ongoing activity with no end. Some of the activities typical in this step are
  - Migrating programs into the production environment
  - Initial loading of ODS data into the production database
  - Establishing monitoring utilities
  - Establishing configuration management processes
  - Implementing backup/recovery and reorganization procedures

**Parameters of Success:** Fully functional production ODS.

# Project Management Step 6—Plan Next ODS Phase

**Preceding Activity:** Project Management Step 5—Convert Prototype to Production.

**Following Activity:** None.

**Time Estimate:** Half a week.

**Normally Executed Once or Many Times:** Once per phase of development.

**Special Considerations:** None.

**Deliverables:** Selected subject areas for next phase and an updated project plan.

- A review of the subject area diagram is performed with the end users and the next set of subject areas and applications are chosen.
- An updated project plan is created and the next phase of the ODS implementation is begun.

**Parameters of Success:** Confident project team and end users going into the next phase.

# Project Management Step 7—Perform ODS Applications Maintenance

**Preceding Activity:** Project Management Step 5—Convert Prototype to Production.

**Following Activity:** None.

**Time Estimate:** Ongoing.

**Normally Executed Once or Many Times:** Ongoing.

**Special Considerations:** A team must be in place to perform the maintenance activities. This team is usually separate from the development team.

**Deliverables:** Fully maintained operational applications.

- The procedures for making enhancements or fixing problems within the application software are established and functioning. These include
  - Maintaining the development, test and production environments
  - Establishing a problem/enhancement reporting and tracking system
  - Implementing version control for the applications
  - Updating all documentation, metadata, and training curricula
  - Revising the testing mechanisms to test new changes while verifying no new problems with prior applications requirements (regression testing)
- All changes to the existing operational software must be reviewed and approved by the end-user community.
- Performance issues may be identified while using the operational applications and are resolved by Project Management Step 8—Perform Database Maintenance/Archiving.

**Parameters of Success:** A smoothly running procedure for identifying enhancements and problems and correcting the operational applications of the ODS.

# Project Management Step 8—Perform Database Maintenance/Archiving

**Preceding Activity:** Project Management Step 5—Convert Prototype to Production.

**Following Activity:** None.

**Time Estimate:** Ongoing.

**Normally Executed Once or Many Times:** Ongoing.

**Special Considerations:** A team must be in place to perform the maintenance activities. This team is usually separate from the development team.

**Deliverables:** A maintained ODS database.

- The procedures for maintaining the ODS database are established. These include
    - Procedures for updating all models (Subject Area Diagram, Logical Data Model, and ODS Physical Model) with changes
    - Maintenance of metadata and other database-related documentation
    - Performance tuning, backup, and recovery, and disaster recovery procedures
    - Version control procedures for the database
    - A problem/enhancement reporting and tracking system
    - Revised testing mechanisms to test new changes while verifying no new problems with prior database requirements (regression testing)
    - All changes to the existing ODS database must be reviewed and approved by the end-user community.
    - Performance tuning will ensure the best response time for the operational application aspects of the ODS as well as the DSS reporting aspects.
    - Version control will take into account the need to keep the database in sync with the enhancements or corrections occurring in the operational applications as well as the changing DSS requirements. Versioning must also maintain the history of the various versions so that end users may recall data from previous versions.

**Parameters of Success:** An ODS database that supports both operational applications and DSS requirements.

# Project Management Step 9—Perform End-User Environment Maintenance

**Preceding Activity:** Project Management Step 5—Convert Prototype to Production.

**Following Activity:** None.

**Time Estimate:** Ongoing.

**Normally Executed Once or Many Times:** Ongoing.

**Special Considerations:** A team must be in place to perform the maintenance activities. This team is usually separate from the development team.

**Deliverables:** Updated metadata and end-user tool access.

- The metadata repository and DSS functionality are updated with new enhancements or corrections. The procedures to perform this maintenance include

  - Establishing a problem/enhancement reporting and tracking system
  - Updating all documentation and training curricula to reflect changes
  - Changing the metadata database to reflect new or changed metadata requirements
  - Establishing version control for the metadata repository
  - Creating new or enhancing existing DSS reports based on end-user requests
  - All changes to the existing metadata and DSS functionality must be reviewed and approved by the end user community.
  - The metadata repository must keep in sync with the changes occurring within the operational applications and DSS reporting arena. It should be versioned while maintaining its history just like the ODS database is versioned.
  - Access to the metadata and the ODS database must be updated as well to reflect changes. Existing DSS applications or reports must be updated to incorporate these new changes.
  - All documentation, such as user manuals, help files, and training materials, must also be maintained.

**Parameters of Success:** A metadata repository that reflects, in a timely manner, all changes occurring in the operational applications. DSS functionality must be accurately maintained to support the ODS database changes that occur.

APPENDIX

# B

# ODS Development Project Milestones

## ODS PROJECT PLAN

| TASK NAME | DURATION | PREDECESSORS | MILESTONE |
|---|---|---|---|
| **ODS Project Plan** | **156.5 days** | | **No** |
| **Project Management Steps** | **18.5 days** | | **No** |
| **Project start** | **14.5 days** | | **No** |
| Develop mission and guiding principles | 1 day | | No |
| Create criteria for measures of success | 0.5 days | 5 | No |
| Review/create standards and guidelines | 2 days | 6 | No |
| Identify end user group | 0.5 days | 7 | No |
| Set up end user schedule | 0.5 days | 8 | No |
| Define metadata delivery mechanisms | 1 day | 5 | No |
| Identify security requirements | 2 days | 7 | No |
| Define development methodology | 2 days | 7 | No |
| Document test criteria | 2 days | 7 | No |
| Create scope document | 4 days | 5,6,10,12 | No |
| Develop detailed project plan | 2 days | 14 | No |
| Review scope and project plan with executive team | 1 day | 15 | Yes |
| Develop archive requirements | 1 day | 16 | No |
| Develop change control procedures | 2 days | 16 | No |
| Define communications process | 0.5 days | 16 | No |

| Task | Duration | No. | Critical |
|---|---|---|---|
| **Determine general sizing** | **6 days** | | **No** |
| Estimate transaction volumes | 2 days | 16 | No |
| Estimate database volumes | 2 days | 16 | No |
| Estimate network volumes | 2 days | 16 | No |
| Determine system requirements | 1 day | 24 | No |
| Document hardware & software requirements | 3 days | 25 | No |
| **Develop Project Phases** | **2 days** | | **No** |
| Determine project phases | 1 day | 25 | No |
| Revise scope document | 0.5 days | 29 | No |
| Review with end users and executives | 0.5 days | 30 | Yes |
| **Prerequisite Steps** | **39 days** | | **No** |
| **Develop ODS architecture** | **7.5 days** | | **No** |
| Define ODS vision | 2 days | 31 | No |
| Assess current technology | 4 days | 35 | No |
| Document changes to current technology | 1 day | 36 | No |
| Review with end users & executives | 0.5 days | 37 | No |
| **Select hardware and software** | **14 days** | | **No** |
| Develop RFI | 3 days | 38 | No |
| Evaluate and select vendors | 8 days | 41 | No |
| Negotiate licenses | 2 days | 42 | No |

| TASK NAME | DURATION | PREDECESSORS | MILESTONE |
|---|---|---|---|
| Order hardware/software | 1 day | 43 | Yes |
| **Construct technical environment** | **9 days** | | **No** |
| Install hardware/software | 3 days | 44 | No |
| Install communications links | 3 days | 47 | No |
| Install network communication links | 2 days | 47 | No |
| Install test environment | 2 days | 47,48,49 | No |
| Construct PC environment | 3 days | 47,48,49 | No |
| Implement changes to current technology | 3 days | 47,48,49 | No |
| **Estimate Capacity Requirements** | **3.5 days** | | **No** |
| Determine response time requirements | 1 day | 46 | No |
| Determine peak/off peak requirements | 1 day | 46 | No |
| Determine disk storage needs | 2 days | 56,55 | No |
| Determine near line storage needs | 2 days | 56,55 | No |
| Order needed storage | 0.5 days | 58 | No |
| **Document ODS Requirements for Phase 1** | **18 days** | | **No** |
| Conduct facilitation sessions | 3 days | 16 | No |
| Review existing documents | 3 days | 62 | No |
| Document facilitation sessions | 1 day | 63 | No |
| Define data quality requirements | 2 days | 64 | No |

| Task | Duration | ID | Milestone |
|---|---|---|---|
| Define data correction process | 0.5 days | 64 | No |
| Review documentation with end users | 2 days | 66,64,65 | No |
| Distill ODS requirements | 3 days | 67 | No |
| Create requirements specification document | 2 days | 68 | No |
| Review requirements specification with end users | 2 days | 69 | Yes |
| **Process Design Steps** | **97 days** | | **No** |
| **Develop high-level function model** | **9 days** | | **No** |
| Analyze operational requirements for functions | 3 days | 70 | No |
| Develop draft function model | 5 days | 74 | No |
| Review with end users | 0.5 days | 75 | No |
| Select function(s) for phase 1 ODS | 0.5 days | 76 | Yes |
| **Generate process decomposition** | **18 days** | | **No** |
| Develop processes for selected function(s) | 6 days | 77 | No |
| Develop primitive activities for processes | 6 days | 80 | No |
| Develop process and activity descriptions | 3 days | 81 | No |
| Define process quality controls | 1 day | 82 | No |
| Review diagrams with end users | 2 days | 83 | Yes |
| **Generate detailed application requirements** | **23 days** | | **No** |
| Develop data flow diagrams | 6 days | 84,127 | No |
| Develop DFD descriptions | 6 days | 87 | No |

| TASK NAME | DURATION | PREDECESSORS | MILESTONE |
|---|---|---|---|
| Develop structure charts/work flow diagrams | 6 days | 88 | No |
| Produce user specifications document | 3 days | 89 | No |
| Review application requirements with end users | 2 days | 90 | Yes |
| **Use/Reuse existing code and data** | **10 days** | | **No** |
| Analyze existing code and data for reusability | 3 days | 91 | No |
| Identify modifications needed to code and data | 2 days | 94 | No |
| Modify existing code and data | 3 days | 95 | No |
| Test modifications to code and data | 2 days | 96 | No |
| **Generate pseudocode for applications** | **14 days** | | **No** |
| Interpret detail designs into application pseudocode | 5 days | 91,97 | No |
| Document processing cycles | 2 days | 100 | No |
| Document performance issues | 3 days | 101 | No |
| Review pseudocode with programmers | 4 days | 102 | No |
| **Generate ODS application code** | **23 days** | | **No** |
| Translate pseudocode into source code | 15 days | 103 | No |
| Generate process quality code | 3 days | 106 | No |
| Perform unit tests | 5 days | 107 | Yes |
| Develop application documentation | 2 days | 107 | No |
| Develop system meta data | 2 days | 107 | No |

| Task | Duration | | |
|---|---|---|---|
| Develop application help functions | 3 days | 107 | No |
| **Data Design Steps** | **96 days** | | **No** |
| **Create Corporate Subject Area Diagram** | **3.5 days** | | **No** |
| Develop draft of corporate subject area diagram | 2 days | 70 | No |
| Review subject area diagram with end users | 0.5 days | 115 | No |
| Generate final subject area diagram | 0.5 days | 116 | No |
| Select subject area(s) from model for Phase 1 | 0.5 days | 117 | Yes |
| **Create Logical Data Model** | **19 days** | | **No** |
| Map end user requirements to subject area(s) | 4 days | 118 | No |
| Document archive requirements | 2 days | 118 | No |
| Document refreshment cycle | 2 days | 118 | No |
| Review existing data models | 5 days | 118 | No |
| Construct draft logical data model | 10 days | 121,124 | No |
| Review logical data model with end users | 2 days | 125 | No |
| Produce final logical data model | 2 days | 126 | Yes |
| **Create ODS Physical Model** | **11.5 days** | | **No** |
| Map ODS requirements to logical data model | 4 days | 16,127 | No |
| Create draft ODS physical data model | 4 days | 130 | No |
| Review with end users | 0.5 days | 131 | No |
| Create final ODS physical model | 1 day | 132 | Yes |
| Document data quality controls | 2 days | 133 | No |

| TASK NAME | DURATION | PREDECESSORS | MILESTONE |
|---|---|---|---|
| **Historical Data Conversion** | **5 days** | | **No** |
| Gather historical data conversion requirements | 3 days | 127 | No |
| Document historical data conversion requirements | 2 days | 137 | No |
| **Construct Physical Database** | **15 days** | | **No** |
| Design physical database | 4 days | 133 | No |
| Implement physical database | 2 days | 141 | No |
| Develop backup/recovery processes | 2 days | 142 | No |
| Test backup/recovery processes | 2 days | 143 | No |
| Design/test security processes | 3 days | 144 | No |
| Revise physical environment | 2 days | 145 | Yes |
| **Identify System of Record** | **12 days** | | **No** |
| Map historical operational sources to ODS database | 3 days | 146 | No |
| Map on-going operational sources to ODS database | 5 days | 146 | No |
| Map future operational sources to ODS database | 2 days | 146 | No |
| Document extraction/transformation rules | 5 days | 149,150,151 | No |
| Review rules with end users | 2 days | 152 | Yes |
| **Create extraction/transformation programs** | **26 days** | | **No** |
| Document/plan transformation flow | 5 days | 153 | No |
| Review transformation flow | 2 days | 156 | No |

| Task | Duration | Ref | Status |
| --- | --- | --- | --- |
| Train team on tools | 3 days | 157 | No |
| Generate data acquisition code | 15 days | 158 | No |
| Generate control language | 3 days | 156 | No |
| Generate data quality code | 2 days | 160 | No |
| Generate program schedules | 1 day | 159,161 | No |
| **Populate Database** | **12 days** | | **No** |
| Transfer code & control language to source | 2 days | 159 | No |
| Execute data acquisition programs | 5 days | 165 | No |
| Load data to target environment | 3 days | 166 | Yes |
| Generate audit and control reports | 2 days | 167 | No |
| **System Testing Steps** | **107 days** | | **No** |
| **Develop test scripts and testing environment** | **11 days** | | **No** |
| Document test criteria for ODS | 2 days | 70 | No |
| Schedule test dates | 0.5 days | 172 | No |
| Develop test scripts for applications | 5 days | 172 | No |
| Develop data quality test scripts | 3 days | 172 | No |
| Develop error detection/correction test scripts | 3 days | 172 | No |
| Develop test databases | 4 days | 174,176 | No |
| Create systems test environment | 3 days | 175,174 | Yes |

| TASK NAME | DURATION | PREDECESSORS | MILESTONE |
|---|---|---|---|
| **Perform applications system testing** | **10 days** | | **No** |
| Transfer code to test environment | 2 days | 108,178 | No |
| Execute test scripts for applications | 8 days | 181 | No |
| Execute error detection/correction test scripts | 3 days | 181 | No |
| Document application test results | 2 days | 183 | Yes |
| **Perform data extraction/transformation testing** | **10 days** | | **No** |
| Execute data quality test scripts | 8 days | 167,178 | No |
| Document data quality test results | 2 days | 187 | Yes |
| **End User Environment Steps** | **122.5 days** | | **No** |
| **Develop meta data repository and access** | **15 days** | | **No** |
| Develop meta data requirements | 2 days | 70 | No |
| Design meta data database | 3 days | 192 | No |
| Implement meta data database | 2 days | 193 | No |
| Load the meta data | 2 days | 194 | No |
| Develop meta data access | 3 days | 195 | No |
| Test access to meta data | 2 days | 196 | No |
| Review with end users | 1 day | 197 | Yes |
| **Select end user access tool(s)** | **12 days** | | **No** |
| Develop end user access requirements | 2 days | 198 | No |

| Task | Duration | Predecessors | Critical |
|---|---|---|---|
| Select list of potential vendors | 1 day | 201 | No |
| Conduct demos/site visits | 5 days | 202 | No |
| Order access tool(s) | 1 day | 203 | No |
| Receive training on tool(s) | 3 days | 204 | Yes |
| **Create standard reports** | **12.5 days** | | **No** |
| Conduct analytical requirements sessions | 2 days | 70 | No |
| Review requirements with end users | 2 days | 208 | No |
| Prioritize analytical reports | 0.5 days | 209 | No |
| Create standard analytical reports | 4 days | 210 | No |
| Create data quality reports | 2 days | 208 | No |
| Test reports | 2 days | 212,211 | No |
| Review standard reports with end users | 2 days | 213 | Yes |
| **Develop End User Documentation** | **5 days** | | **No** |
| Develop end user menus and icons | 4 days | 184,188 | No |
| Develop end user manual | 3 days | 184,188 | No |
| Develop end user online help | 3 days | 184,188 | No |
| Test end user documentation | 2 days | 219 | No |
| **Develop Initial Training/Help Desk Function** | **13.5 days** | | **No** |
| Develop end user training schedule | 0.5 days | 220 | No |
| Create/train help desk function | 5 days | 223 | No |

| TASK NAME | DURATION | PREDECESSORS | MILESTONE |
|---|---|---|---|
| Create end user training curriculum | 3 days | 224 | No |
| Test end user training curriculum | 2 days | 225 | No |
| Perform end user training | 3 days | 226 | Yes |
| **Project Management Steps (continued)** | **22 days** | | **No** |
| **Perform project evaluation** | **12 days** | | **No** |
| Perform applications acceptance testing | 5 days | 188 | No |
| Perform analytical acceptance test | 5 days | 188 | No |
| Tune database for performance | 3 days | 231,232 | No |
| Perform post project evaluation | 2 days | 233 | No |
| Document evaluation results | 2 days | 234 | Yes |
| **Convert prototype to production** | **7 days** | | **No** |
| Develop conversion plan | 2 days | 235 | No |
| Implement conversion plan | 5 days | 238 | Yes |
| Implement back/recovery processes | 2 days | 235 | No |
| Implement security processes | 2 days | 235 | No |
| **Plan next ODS phase** | **3 days** | | **No** |
| Select next subject area(s) | 1 day | 237 | No |
| Review with end users | 1 days | 244 | No |
| Update project plan for Phase 2 | 1 day | 245 | Yes |
| **Perform ODS applications maintenance** | **0 days** | | **No** |

| Task | Duration | | Complete |
|---|---|---|---|
| Maintain problem/enhancement tracking system | 0 days | 237 | No |
| Establish version control for applications | 0 days | 237 | No |
| Maintain system test scripts and results | 0 days | 237 | No |
| Maintain application documentation | 0 days | 237 | No |
| **Perform database maintenance/archiving** | **0 days** | | **No** |
| Maintain database problem/enhancement tracking | 0 days | 237 | No |
| Maintain ODS data models | 0 days | 237 | No |
| Maintain data quality scripts | 0 days | 237 | No |
| Maintain ODS database | 0 days | 237 | No |
| Maintain ODS database performance and tuning | 0 days | 237 | No |
| Perform database backups/versions | 0 days | 237 | No |
| Perform data archiving | 0 days | 237 | No |
| **Perform end user environment maintenance** | **0 days** | | **No** |
| Maintain documentation and training curriculum | 0 days | 237 | No |
| Maintain problem/enhancement tracking | 0 days | 237 | No |
| Maintain meta data database | 0 days | 237 | No |
| Perform meta data backups/versions | 0 days | 237 | No |
| Maintain meta data access | 0 days | 237 | No |
| Maintain help and documentation | 0 days | 237 | No |
| Maintain/create standard reports | 0 days | 237 | No |
| Maintain access and security | 0 days | 237 | No |

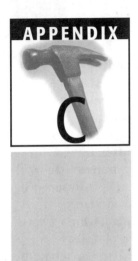
# Glossary

**access**   the operation of seeking, reading, or writing data on a storage unit.

**access method**   a technique used to transfer a physical record from or to a mass storage device.

**access mode**   a technique in which a specific logical record is obtained from or placed onto a file assigned to a mass storage device.

**access pattern**   the general sequence in which the data structure is accessed (e.g., from tuple to tuple, from record to record, from segment to segment, etc.).

**access plan**   the control structure produced during program preparation and used by a database manager to process SQL statements during application execution.

**access time**   the time interval between the instant an instruction initiates a request for data and the instant the first of the data satisfying the request is delivered. Note that there is a difference—sometimes large—between the time data is first delivered and the time when *all* the data is delivered.

**active data dictionary**   a data dictionary that is the sole source for an application program insofar as metadata is concerned. A data dictionary that is used interactively and on a mandated basis for the development of a system, where all development and all maintenance passes through the dictionary.

**ad hoc processing**   onetime only, casual access and manipulation of data on parameters never before used and possibly never used again.

**address**   an identification (e.g., number, name, storage location, byte offset, etc.) for a location where data is stored, usually on DASD.

**addressing**   assigning storage data to a specific storage location, thereby allowing the data to be retrieved by checking the location. Addressing is usually done on the basis of the contents of the key of the data.

**after image**   the snapshot of data placed on a log upon the completion of a transaction.

**AIX**   Advanced Interactive eXecutive—IBM's version of the UNIX operating system.

**algorithm**   a set of statements organized to solve a problem in a finite number of steps.

**alias**   an alternative label used to refer to a data element or entity.

**analytical processing**   the use of the computer to produce an analysis for management decision, usually involving trend analysis, drill-down analysis, demographic analysis, profiling, etc. Also called informational processing.

**ANSI**   American National Standards Institute.

**API**   application program interface—the common set of parameters needed to connect the communications between programs.

**application**   a group of algorithms and data interlinked by common code in order to support an organizational requirement.

**application blocking of data**   grouping into the same physical unit of storage multiple occurrences of data controlled at the application level.

**application database**   a collection of data organized to support a specific application (almost always an "operational application").

**archival database**   a collection of data of a historical nature. As a rule, archival data cannot be updated. Each unit of archival data is relevant to a moment in time, now passed.

**artifact of a relationship**   a design technique used to represent referential integrity in the data warehouse, DSS environment.

**atomic**   (1) data stored in the current detail level of a data warehouse; (2) the lowest level of process analysis.

**atomic database**   a database made up of primarily atomic data; current-level detail in the data warehouse; a DSS foundation database.

**atomic-level data**   data with the lowest level of granularity. Atomic-level data sits in a data warehouse at the current level of detail and is time variant (i.e., accurate as of some moment in time, now passed).

**attribute**   a property that can assume values for entities or relationships. Entities can be assigned several attributes (e.g., a tuple in a relationship consists of values). Some systems also allow relationships to have attributes.

**audit trail**   data that is available to trace system activity, usually update activity.

**availability**   a measure of the reliability of a system, indicating the fraction of time when the system is up and available divided by the amount of time the system should be up and available. Note that there is a difference between a piece of hardware being available and the systems running on the hardware also being available.

**back-end processor**  a database machine or an intelligent disk controller.

**back up**  to restore the database to its state as of some previous moment in time.

**backup**  a file serving as a basis for the activity of backing up a database. Usually a snapshot of a database as of some previous moment in time.

**backward recovery**  a recovery technique that restores a database to an earlier state by applying before images.

**batch**  computer environment in which programs (usually long-running, sequentially oriented) access data exclusively and user interaction is not allowed while the activity is occurring.

**batch environment**  a sequentially dominated mode of processing; input is collected and stored for future processing. Once collected, the batch input is transacted sequentially against one or more databases.

**batch window**  the time at which the online system is available for batch or sequential processing. The batch window typically occurs during nonpeak processing hours.

**bill of materials**  a listing of the parts used in a manufacturing process along with the relation of one product to another insofar as assembly of the final product is concerned. The bill of materials is a classical recursive structure.

**bind**  (1) to assign a value to a data element, variable, or parameter; (2) the attachment of a data definition to a program prior to the execution of the program.

**binding time**  the moment in time when the data description known to the dictionary is assigned to or bound to the procedural code.

**bit**  binary digit; the lowest level of storage. A bit can be in a 1 state or a 0 state.

**bit map**  a specialized form of an index indicating the existence or nonexistence of a condition for a group of blocks or records. Bit maps are expensive to build and maintain but provide very fast comparison and access facilities.

**block**  (1) a basic unit of structuring storage; (2) the physical unit of transport and storage. A block usually contains one or more records (or contains the space for one or more records). In some database management systems a block is called a page.

**block splitting**  the data management activity in which a filled block is written into two unfilled blocks, leaving space for future insertions and updates in the two partially filled blocks.

**blocking**  the combining of two or more physical records so that they are physically colocated together. The result of their physical colocation is that they can be accessed and fetched by a single execution of a machine instruction.

**buffer**  an area of storage that holds data temporarily in main memory while data is being transmitted, received, read, or written. A buffer is often used to compensate for the differences in the timing of transmission and execution of devices. Buffers are used in terminals, peripheral devices, storage units, and CPUs.

**byte**   a basic unit of storage made up of 8 bits.

**C**   a programming language.

**call**   to invoke the execution of a module.

**cardinality (of a relation)**   the number of tuples (i.e., rows) in a relation. See also **degree of a relation.**

**CASE**   computer aided software engineering.

**catalog**   a directory of all files available to the computer. A form of metadata.

**character**   a member of the standard set of elements used to represent data in the database.

**character type**   the characters that can represent the value of an attribute.

**checkpoint**   an identified snapshot of the database or a point at which the transactions against the database have been frozen or have been quiesced.

**checkpoint/restart**   a means of restarting a program at some point other than the beginning; for example, when a failure or interruption has occurred. *N* checkpoints may be used at intervals throughout an application program. At each of those points sufficient information is stored to permit the program to be restored to the moment in time the checkpoint was taken.

**CICS**   Customer Information Control System; an IBM teleprocessing monitor.

**CIO**   chief information officer; an organizational position managing all of the information processing functions.

**CLDS**   the facetiously named system development life cycle for analytical, DSS systems. CLDS is so named because it is the reverse of the classic system development life cycle, SDLC.

**cluster**   (1) in Teradata, a group of physical devices controlled by the same AMP; (2) in DB2 and Oracle, the practice of physically colocating data in the same block based on the content of data.

**cluster key**   the key around which data is clustered in a block (DB2/Oracle).

**coalesce**   to combine two or more sets of items into any single set.

**COBOL**   common business oriented language; a computer language for the business world. A very common language.

**CODASYL model**   a network database model that was originally defined by the Data Base Task Group (DBTG) of the Conference on Data System Language (CODASYL) organization.

**code**   (1) to represent data or a computer program in a form that can be accepted by a data processor; (2) to transform data so that it cannot be understood by anyone who does not have the algorithm used to decode the data prior to presentation (sometimes called "encode").

**collision**   the event that occurs when two or more records of data are assigned the same physical location. Collisions are associated with randomizers or hashers.

**column** a vertical table in which values are selected from the same domain. A row is made up of one or more columns.

**commit** a condition raised by the programmer signaling to the database management system that all update activity done by the program be executed against a database. Prior to the commit, all update activity can be rolled back or canceled with no ill effects on the contents of the database.

**commit protocol** an algorithm to ensure that a transaction is successfully completed.

**communication network** the collection of transmission facilities, network processors, and so on which provides for data movement among terminals and information processors.

**compaction** a technique for reducing the number of bits required to represent data without losing the content of the data. With compaction, repetitive data is represented very concisely.

**component** a data item or array of data items whose component type defines a collection of occurrences with the same data type.

**compound index** an index over multiple columns.

**concatenate** to link or connect two strings of characters, generally for the purpose of using them as a single value.

**concurrent operations** activities executed simultaneously, or during the same time interval.

**condensation** the process of reducing the volume of data managed without reducing the logical consistency of the data. Condensation is different from compaction.

**contention** the condition that occurs when two or more programs try to access the same data at the same time.

**continuous time-span data** data organized so that a continuous definition of data over a span of time is represented by one or more records.

**control character** a character whose occurrence in a particular context initiates, modifies, or stops an operation.

**control database** a utilitarian database containing data not directly related to the application being built. Typical control databases are audit databases, terminal databases, security databases, etc.

**CPU** central processing unit.

**CPU-bound** the state of processing in which the computer can produce no more output because the CPU portion of the processor is being used at 100 percent capacity. When the computer is CPU-bound, typically the memory and storage processing units are less than 100 percent utilized. With modern database management systems, it is much more likely that the computer will be I/O-bound rather than CPU-bound.

**CSP** cross system product; an IBM application generator.

**CUA** common user access. Specifies the ways in which the user interface to systems is to be constructed.

**current value data**    data whose accuracy is valid as of the moment of execution, as opposed to time-variant data.

**cursor**    (1) an indicator that designates a current position on a screen; (2) a system facility that allows the programmer to thumb from one record to the next when the system has retrieved a set of records.

**cylinder**    the area of storage of DASD that can be read without the movement of the arm. The term originated with disk files, in which a cylinder consisted of one track on each disk surface so that each of these tracks could have a read/write head positioned over it simultaneously.

**DASD**    see **direct access storage device.**

**data**    a recording of facts, concepts, or instructions on a storage medium for communication, retrieval, and processing by automatic means and presentation as information that is understandable by human beings.

**data administrator (DA)**    the individual or organization responsible for the specification, acquisition, and maintenance of data management software and the design, validation, and security of files or databases. The data models and the data dictionary are classically the charge of the DA.

**data definition**    the specification of the data entities, their attributes, and their relationships in a coherent database structure to create a schema.

**data definition language (DDL)**    also called a **data description language;** the language used to define the database schema and additional data features that allows the database management system to generate and manage the internal tables, indexes, buffers, and storage necessary for database processing.

**data description language**    see **data definition language.**

**data dictionary**    a software tool for recording the definition of data, the relationship of one category of data to another, the attributes and keys of groups of data, and so forth.

**data division (COBOL)**    the section of a COBOL program that consists of entries used to define the nature and characteristics of the data to be processed by the program.

**data-driven development**    the approach to development that centers around identifying the commonality of data through a data model and building programs that have a broader scope than the immediate application. Data-driven development differs from classical application-oriented development. The development done for the ODS is data-driven development.

**data-driven process**    a process whose resource consumption depends on the data on which it operates. For example, a hierarchical root has a dependent. For one occurrence there are two dependents for the root. For another occurrence of the root there are 1,000 occurrences of the dependent. The same program that accesses the root and all its dependents will use very different amounts of resources when operating against the two roots, although the code will be exactly the same.

**data element**   (1) an attribute of an entity; (2) a uniquely named and well-defined category of data that consists of data items and that is included in a record of an activity.

**data item**   a discrete representation having the properties that define the data element to which it belongs. See **data element.**

**data item set (DIS)**   a grouping of data items, each of which directly relates to the key of the grouping of data in which the data items reside. The data item set is found in the midlevel model.

**data manipulation language (DML)**   (1) a programming language that is supported by a database management system and is used to access a database; (2) language constructs added to a higher-order language (e.g., COBOL) for the purpose of database manipulation.

**data model**   (1) the logical data structures, including operations and constraints provided by a database management system for effective database processing; (2) the system used for the representation of data (e.g., the ERD or relational model).

**data record**   an identifiable set of data values treated as a unit, an occurrence of a schema in a database, or a collection of atomic data items describing a specific object, event, or tuple.

**data security**   the protection of the data in a database against unauthorized disclosure, alteration, or destruction. There are different levels of security.

**data set**   a named collection of logically related data items, arranged in a prescribed manner, and described by control information to which the programming system has access.

**data storage description language**   (DSDL) a language to define the organization of stored data in terms of an operating system and device-independent storage environment. See also **device media control language.**

**data structure**   a logical relationship among data elements that is designed to support specific data manipulation functions (e.g., trees, lists, and tables).

**data volatility**   the rate of change of the content of data.

**data warehouse**   a collection of integrated subject-oriented databases designed to support the DSS function, where each unit of data is relevant to some moment in time. The data warehouse contains atomic data and lightly summarized data.

**database**   a collection of interrelated data stored (often with controlled, limited redundancy) according to a schema. A database can serve single or multiple applications.

**database administrator (DBA)**   the organizational function charged with the day-to-day monitoring and care of databases. The DBA function is more closely associated with physical database design than the DA is.

**database key**   a unique value that exists for each record in a database. The value is often indexed, although it can be randomized or hashed.

**database machine**   a dedicated computer that provides data access and management through total control of the access method, physical storage, and data organization. Often called a **back-end processor.** Data is usually managed in parallel by a database machine.

**database management system**   a computer-based software system used to establish and manage data.

**database record**   a physical root and all of its dependents (in IMS).

**DatacomDB**   a database management system by CA.

**dBase III**   a microprocessor database management system by Ashton-Tate.

**DB2**   a database management system by IBM.

**DB/DC**   database/data communications.

**DBMS language interface (DB I/O module)**   software that applications invoke in order to access a database. The module in turn has direct access with the database management system. Standards enforcement and standard error checking are often features of an I/O module.

**deadlock**   see **deadly embrace.**

**deadly embrace**   the event that occurs when transaction A desires to access data currently protected by transaction B, while at the same time transaction B desires to access data that is currently being protected by transaction A. The deadly embrace condition is a serious impediment to performance.

**decision support system (DSS)**   a system used to support managerial decisions. Usually DSS involves the analysis of many units of data in a heuristic fashion. As a rule, DSS processing does not involve the update of data.

**decompaction**   the opposite of compaction; once data is stored in a compacted form, it must be decompacted to be used.

**decryption**   the opposite of **encryption.** Once data is stored in an encrypted fashion, it must be decrypted in order to be used.

**delimiter**   a flag, symbol, or convention used to mark the boundaries of a record, field, or other unit of storage.

**denormalization**   the technique of placing normalized data in a physical location that optimizes the performance of the system.

**derived data**   data whose existence depends on two or more occurrences of a major subject of the enterprise.

**derived data element**   a data element that is not necessarily stored but can be generated when needed (e.g., age given current date and date of birth).

**design review**   the quality assurance process in which all aspects of a system are reviewed publicly prior to the striking of code.

**device media control language (DMCL)**   a language used to define the mapping of the data onto the physical storage media. See **data storage description language.**

**direct access**   retrieval or storage of data by reference to its location on a volume. The access mechanism goes directly to the data in question, as is generally required with online use of data. Also called **random access** or hashed access.

**direct-access storage device (DASD)** a data storage unit on which data can be accessed directly without having to progress through a serial file such as a magnetic tape file. A disk unit is a direct-access storage device.

**directory** a table specifying the relationships between items of data. Sometimes a table or index giving the addresses of data.

**distributed catalog** a distributed catalog is needed to achieve site autonomy. The catalog at each site maintains information about objects in the local databases. The distributed catalog keeps information on replicated and distributed tables stored at that site and information on remote tables located at another site that cannot be accessed locally.

**distributed database** a database controlled by a central database management system but in which the storage devices are geographically dispersed or not attached to the same processor. See **parallel I/O.**

**distributed free space** space left empty at intervals in a data layout to permit insertion of new data.

**DL/1** IBM's Data Language One, for describing logical and physical data structures.

**domain** the set of legal values from which actual values are derived for an attribute or a data element.

**download** the stripping of data from one database to another based on the content of data found in the first database.

**drill-down analysis** the type of analysis where examination of a summary number leads to the exploration of the components of the sum.

**dual database** the practice of separating high-performance, transaction-oriented data from decision-support data.

**dual database management systems** the practice of using multiple database management systems to control different aspects of the database environment.

**dumb terminal** a device used to interact directly with the end user where all processing is done on a remote computer. A dumb terminal acts as a device that gathers and displays data.

**dynamic SQL** SQL statements that are prepared and executed within a program while the program is executing. In dynamic SQL, the SQL source is contained in host language variables rather than being coded into the application program.

**dynamic storage allocation** a technique in which the storage areas assigned to computer programs are determined during processing.

**dynamic summary data** a summarization whose components of calculation are subject to change.

**EDI** electronic data interchange.

**EIS (executive information systems)** systems designed for the top executive, featuring drill-down analysis and trend analysis.

**embedded pointer** a record pointer (i.e., a means of internally linking related records) that is not available to an external index or directory. Embedded pointers are used to reduce search time, but require maintenance overhead.

**encoding** a shortening or abbreviation of the physical representation of a data value (e.g., male = "M", female = "F").

**encryption** the transformation of data from a recognizable form to a form unrecognizable without the algorithm used for the encryption. Encryption is usually done for security reasons.

**enterprise** the generic term for the company, corporation, agency, or business unit. Usually associated with data modeling.

**entity** a person, place, or thing of interest to the data modeler at the highest level of abstraction.

**entity-relationship-attribute (ERA) model** a data model that defines entities, the relationship between the entities, and the attributes that have values to describe the properties of entities and/or relationships.

**entity-relationship diagram (ERD)** a high-level data model; the schematic showing all the entities within the scope of integration and the direct relationship between those entities.

**event** a signal that an activity of significance has occurred. An event is noted by the information system.

**event-discrete data** data relating to the measurement or description of an event.

**expert system** a system that captures and automates the use of human experience and intelligence.

**external data** (1) data originating from other than the operational systems of a corporation; (2) data residing outside the central processing complex.

**external schema** a logical description of a user's method of organizing and structuring data. Some attributes or relationships can be omitted from the corresponding conceptual schema or can be renamed or otherwise transformed. See **view.**

**extract** the process of selecting data from one environment and transporting it to another environment.

**file** a set of related records treated as a unit and stored under a single logical filename.

**first-in-first-out (FIFO)** a fundamental ordering of processing in a queue.

**first-in-last-out (FILO)** a standard order of processing in a stack.

**flag** an indicator or character that signals the occurrence of some condition.

**flat file** a collection of records containing no data aggregates, nested repeated data items, or groups of data items.

**floppy disk** a device for storing data on a personal computer.

**foreign key**   an attribute that is not a primary key in a relational system, but whose values are the values of the primary key of another relation.

**forward recovery**   a recovery technique that restores a database by reapplying all transactions using a before image from a specified point in time to a copy of the database taken at that moment in time.

**fourth-generation language**   language or technology designed to allow the end user unfettered access to data.

**functional decomposition**   the division of operations into hierarchical functions (i.e., activities) that form the basis for procedures.

**granularity**   the level of detail contained in a unit of data. The more detail there is, the lower the level of granularity. The less detail there is, the higher the level of granularity.

**graphic**   a symbol produced on a screen representing an object or a process in the real world.

**hash**   to convert the value of the key of a record into a location on DASD.

**hash total**   a total of the values of one or more fields, used for purposes of auditability and control.

**heuristic**   the mode of analysis in which the next step is determined by the results of the current step of analysis. Used for decision-support processing.

**hierarchical model**   a data model providing a tree structure for relating data elements or groups of data elements. Each node in the structure represents a group of data elements or a record type. There can be only one root node at the start of the hierarchical structure.

**hit**   an occurrence of data that satisfies some search criteria.

**hit ratio**   a measure of the number of records in a file expected to be accessed in a given run. Usually expressed as a percentage: number of input transactions/number of records in the file times 100 = hit ratio.

**homonyms**   identical names that refer to different attributes.

**host**   the processor receiving and processing a transaction.

**IDMS**   a network database management system from Computer Associates.

**IEEE**   Institute of Electrical and Electronics Engineers.

**image copy**   a procedure in which a database is physically copied to another medium for the purposes of backup.

**IMS**   Information Management System; an operational database management system by IBM.

**index**   the portion of the storage structure maintained to provide efficient access to a record when its index key item is known.

**index chains**   chains of data within an index.

**index point**   a hardware reference mark on a disk or drum, used for timing purposes.

**index sequential access method (ISAM)**   a file structure and access method in which records can be processed sequentially (e.g., in order, by key) or by directly looking up their locations on a table, thus making it unnecessary to process previously inserted records.

**indirect addressing**    any method of specifying or locating a record through calculation (e.g., locating a record through the scan of an index).

**information**    data that human beings assimilate and evaluate to solve a problem or make a decision.

**information center**    the organizational unit charged with identifying and accessing information needed in DSS processing.

**information engineering (IE)**    the discipline of creating a data-driven development environment.

**Informix**    a Unix-based database management system.

**input/output (I/O)**    the means by which data is stored and/or retrieved on DASD. I/O is measured in milliseconds (i.e., mechanical speeds) whereas computer processing is measured in nanoseconds (i.e., electronic speeds).

**instance**    a set of values representing a specific entity belonging to a particular entity type. A single value is also the instance of a data item.

**integrity**    the property of a database that ensures that the data contained in it is as accurate and consistent as possible.

**intelligent database**    a database that contains shared logic as well as shared data and automatically invokes that logic when the data is accessed. Logic, constraints, and controls relating to the use of the data are represented in an intelligent data model.

**interactive**    a mode of processing that combines some of the characteristics of online transaction processing and batch processing. In interactive processing the end user interacts with data over which he or she has exclusive control. In addition, the end user can initiate background activity to be run against the data.

**interleaved data**    data from different tables mixed into a simple table space where there is commonality of physical colocation based on a common key value.

**internal schema**    the schema that describes logical structures of the data and the physical media over which physical storage is mapped.

**interpretive**    a mode of data manipulation in which the commands to the database management system are translated as the user enters them (as opposed to the programmed mode of process manipulation).

**intersection data**    data that is associated with the junction of two or more record types or entities, but which has no meaning when disassociated with any records or entities forming the junction.

**inverted file**    a file structure that uses an inverted index, where entries are grouped according to the content of the key being referenced. Inverted files provide for the fast spontaneous searching of files.

**inverted index**    an index structure organized by means of a nonunique key to speed the search for data by content.

**inverted list**  a list organized around a secondary index instead of around a primary key.

**I/O**  input/output operation. Input/output operations are the key to performance because they operate at mechanical speeds, not at electronic speeds.

**I/O bound**  the point after which no more processing can be done because the I/O subsystem is saturated.

**ISAM**  see **indexed sequential access method.**

**is a type of**  an analytical tool used in abstracting data during the process of conceptual database design (e.g., a cocker spaniel is a type of dog).

**ISO**  International Standards Organization.

**item**  see **data item.**

**item type**  a classification of an item according to its domain, generally in a gross sense.

**iterative analysis**  the mode of processing in which the next step of processing depends on the results obtained by the existing step in execution; heuristic processing.

**JAD (joint application design)**  an organization of people—usually end users—to create and refine application system requirements.

**join**  an operation that takes two relations as operands and produces a new relation by concatenating the tuples and matching the corresponding columns when a stated condition holds between the two.

**judgment sample**  a sample of data where data is accepted or rejected for the sample based on one or more parameters.

**junction**  from the network environment, an occurrence of data that has two or more parent segments. For example, an order for supplies must have a supplier parent and a part parent.

**justify**  to adjust the value representation in a character field to the right or to the left, ignoring blanks.

**keeplist**  a sequence of database keys maintained by the database management system for the duration of the session.

**key**  a data item or combination of data items used to identify or locate a record instance (or other similar data groupings).

**key, primary**  a unique attribute used to identify a single record in a database.

**key, secondary**  a nonunique attribute used to identify a class of records in a database.

**key compression**  a technique for reducing the number of bits in keys; used in making indexes occupy less space.

**label**  a set of symbols used to identify or describe an item, record, message, or file. Occasionally a label may be the same as the address of the record in storage.

**language**  a set of characters, conventions, and rules used to convey information and consisting of syntax and semantics.

**latency**   the time taken by a DASD device to position the read arm over the physical storage medium. For general purposes, average latency time is used.

**least frequently used (LFU)**   a replacement strategy in which new data must replace existing data in an area of storage; the least frequently used items are replaced.

**least recently used (LRU)**   a replacement strategy in which new data must replace existing data in an area of storage; the least recently used items are replaced.

**level of abstraction**   the level of abstraction appropriate to a dimension. The level of abstraction that is appropriate is entirely dependent on the ultimate user of the system.

**line**   the hardware by which data flows to or from the processor. Lines typically go to terminals, printers, and other processors.

**line polling**   the activity of the teleprocessing monitor in which different lines are queried to determine whether they have data and/or transactions that need to be transmitted.

**line time**   the length of time required for a transaction to go either from the terminal to the processor or the processor to the terminal. Typically line time is the single largest component of online response time.

**linkage**   the ability to relate one unit of data to another.

**linked list**   a set of records in which each record contains a pointer to the next record on the list.

**list**   an ordered set of data items.

**living sample**   a representative database typically used for heuristic statistical analytical processing in place of a large database. Periodically the very large database is selectively stripped of data so that the resulting living sample database represents a cross-section of the very large database as of some moment in time.

**load**   to insert data values into a database that was previously empty.

**local site support**   within a distributed unit of work, a local site update allows a process to perform SQL update statements referring to the local site.

**local transaction**   in a distributed database management system, a transaction that requires reference only to data that is stored at the site where the transaction originated.

**locality of processing**   in a distributed database, the design of processing so that remote access of data is eliminated or reduced substantively.

**lockup**   the event that occurs when update is done against a database record and the transaction has not yet reached a commit point. The online transaction needs to prevent other transactions from accessing the data while update is occurring.

**log**   a journal of activity.

**logging**   the automatic recording of data with regard to access of the data, updates to the data, and so on.

**logical representation**   a data view or description that does not depend on a physical storage device or a computer program.

**loss of identity**   when data is brought in from an external source and the identity of the external source is discarded, loss of identity occurs. A common practice with microprocessor data.

**LU6.2**   logical unit type 6.2; peer-to-peer data stream with network operating system for program-to-program communication. LU6.2 allows midrange machines to talk to one another without the involvement of the mainframe.

**machine learning**   the ability of a machine to improve its performance automatically based on past performance.

**magnetic tape**   (1) the storage medium most closely associated with sequential processing; (2) a large ribbon on which magnetic images are stored and retrieved.

**main storage database (MSDB)**   a database that resides entirely in main storage. Such databases are very fast to access but require special handling at the time of update. Another limitation of MSDBs is that they can manage only small amounts of data.

**master file**   a file that holds the system of record for a given set of data (usually bound by an application).

**maximum transaction arrival rate (MTAR)**   the rate of arrival of transactions at the moment of peak-period processing.

**message**   (1) the data input by the user in the online environment that is used to drive a transaction; (2) the output of a transaction.

**metadata**   (1) data about data; (2) the description of data's structure, content, keys, indexes, and so forth.

**metalanguage**   a language used to specify other languages.

**microprocessor**   a small processor serving the needs of a single user.

**migration**   the process by which frequently used items of data are moved to more readily accessible areas of storage and infrequently used items of data are moved to less readily accessible areas of storage.

**mips (million instructions per second)**   the standard measurement of processor speed for minicomputers and mainframe computers.

**mode of operation**   a classification for systems that execute in a similar fashion and share distinctive operational characteristics. Some modes of operation are operational, DSS, online, and interactive.

**modulo**   an arithmetic term describing the remainder of a division process— 10 modulo 7 is 3. Modulo is usually associated with the randomization process.

**multilist organization**   a chained file organization in which the chains are divided into fragments and each fragment is indexed. This organization of data permits faster access to the data.

**multiple-key retrieval**   a query that requires searches of data on the basis of the values of several key fields (some or all of which are secondary keys).

**MVS** Multiple Virtual Storage; IBM's mainline operating system for mainframe processors. There are several extensions of MVS.

**Named Pipes** program-to-program protocol with Microsoft's LAN manager. The Named Pipes API supports intra- and intermachine process-to-process communications.

**natural forms**

**first normal form** data that has been organized into two-dimensional flat files without repeating groups.

**second normal form** data that functionally depends on the entire candidate key.

**third normal form** data that has had all transitive dependencies on data items other than the candidate key removed.

**fourth normal form** data whose candidate key is related to all data items in the record and that contains no more than one nontrivial multivalued dependency on the candidate key.

**natural join** a join in which the redundant logic components generated by the join are removed.

**natural language** a language, generally spoken, whose rules are based on current usage and not explicitly defined by a grammar.

**navigate** to steer a course through a database, from record to record, by means of an algorithm that examines the content of data.

**network** a computer network consists of a collection of circuits, data switching elements, and computing systems. The switching devices in the network are called "communication processors." A network provides a configuration for computer systems and communication facilities within which data can be stored and accessed and within which database management systems can operate.

**network model** a data model that provides data relationships on the basis of records, and groups of records (i.e., sets) in which one record is designated as the set owner, and a single member record can belong to one or more sets.

**nine's complement** transformation of a numeric field calculated by subtracting the initial value from a field consisting of all nines.

**node** a point in the network at which data is switched.

**nonprocedural language** syntax that directs the computer as to what to do, not how to do it. Typical nonprocedural languages include RAMIS, FOCUS, NOMAD, and SQL.

**normalize** to decompose complex data structures into natural structures.

**null** an item or record for which no value currently exists or possibly may ever exist.

**numeric** a representation using only numbers and a decimal point.

**occurrence** see **instance.**

**offset pointer** an indirect pointer. An offset pointer exists inside a block and the index points to the offset. If data must be moved, only the offset pointer in the block must be altered; the index entry remains untouched.

**online storage**   storage devices and storage media where data can be accessed in a direct fashion.

**operating system**   software that enables a computer to supervise its own operations and automatically call in programs, routines, languages, and data as needed for continuous operation throughout the execution of different types of jobs.

**operational data**   data used to support the daily processing a company does.

**operational data store (ODS)**   the architectural construct where collective integrated operational data is stored. The ODS contains only very current data.

**operations**   the department charged with running the computer.

**optical disk**   a storage medium using lasers as opposed to magnetic devices. Optical disk is typically write only, is much less expensive per byte than magnetic storage, and is highly reliable.

**ORACLE**   a database management system by ORACLE Corp.

**order**   to place items in an arrangement specified by such rules as numeric or alphabetic order. See **sort.**

**OS/2**   the operating system for IBM's Personal System/2.

**OSF**   Open Software Foundation.

**OSI**   Open Systems Interconnection.

**overflow**   (1) the condition in which a record or a segment cannot be stored in its home address because the address is already occupied (in this case, the data is placed in another location referred to as "overflow"); (2) the area of DASD where data is sent when the overflow condition is triggered.

**ownership**   the responsibility for update for operational data.

**padding**   a technique used to fill a field, record, or block with default data (e.g., blanks or zeros).

**page**   (1) a basic unit of data on DASD; (2) a basic unit of storage in main memory.

**page fault**   a program interruption that occurs when a page that is referred to is not in main memory and must be read in from external storage.

**page fixed**   the state in which programs or data cannot be removed from main storage. Only a limited amount of storage can be page fixed.

**paging**   in virtual storage systems, the technique of making memory appear to be larger than it really is by transferring blocks (pages) of data or programs into external memory.

**parallel data organization**   an arrangement of data in which the data is spread over independent storage devices and is managed independently.

**parallel I/O**   the process of accessing or storing data on multiple physical data devices.

**parallel search storage**   a storage device in which one or more parts of all storage locations are queried simultaneously for a certain condition or under certain parameters.

**parameter**   an elementary data value used as a criterion for qualification, usually of searches of data or in the control of modules.

**parent**   a unit of data in a 1:n relationship with another unit of data called a "child," where the parent can exist independently, but the child cannot exist unless there is a parent.

**parsing**   the algorithm that translates syntax into meaningful machine instructions. Parsing determines the meaning of statements issued in the data manipulation language.

**partition**   a segmentation technique in which data is divided into physically different units. Partitioning can be done at the application or the system level.

**path length**   the number of instructions executed for a given program or instruction.

**peak period**   the time when the most transactions arrive at the computer with the expectation of execution.

**performance**   the length of time from the moment a request is issued until the first of the results of the request are received.

**periodic discrete data**   a measurement or description of data taken at a regular time interval.

**physical representation**   (1) the representation and storage of data on a medium such as magnetic storage; (2) the description of data that depends on such physical factors as length of elements, records, and pointers.

**pipes**   vehicles for passing data from one application to another.

**plex or network structure**   a relationship between records or other groupings of data in which a child record can have more than one parent record.

**plug-compatible manufacturer (PCM)**   a manufacturer of equipment that functionally is identical to that of another manufacturer (usually IBM).

**pointer**   the address of a record or other groupings of data contained in another record so that a program may access the former record when it has retrieved the latter record. The address can be absolute, relative, or symbolic, and hence the pointer is referred to as absolute, relative, or symbolic.

**pools**   the buffers made available to the online controller.

**populate**   to place occurrences of data values in a previously empty database. See **load.**

**precision**   the degree of discrimination with which a quantity is stated. For example, a three-digit numeral discriminates among 1,000 possibilities, from 000 to 999.

**precompilation**   the processing of source text prior to compilation. In an SQL environment, SQL statements are replaced with statements that will be recognized by the host language compiler.

**prefix data**   data in a segment or a record used exclusively for system control, usually unavailable to the user.

**primary key**   an attribute that contains values that uniquely identify the record in which the key exists.

**primitive data**   data whose existence depends on only a single occurrence of a major subject area of the enterprise.

**privacy**   the prevention of unauthorized access and manipulation of data.

**privilege descriptor**   a persistent object used by a database management system to enforce constraints on operations.

**problems database**   the component of a DSS application where previously defined decision parameters are stored. A problems database is consulted to review characteristics of past decisions and to determine ways to meet current decision-making needs.

**processor**   the hardware at the center of execution of computer programs. Generally speaking, processors are divided into three categories: mainframes, minicomputers, and microcomputers.

**processor cycles**   the hardware's internal cycles that drive the computer (e.g., initiate I/O, perform logic, move data, perform arithmetic functions, etc.).

**production environment**   the environment where operational, high-performance processing is run.

**program area**   the portion of main memory in which application programs are executed.

**progressive overflow**   a method of handling overflow in a randomly organized file that does not require the use of pointers. An overflow record is stored in the first available space and is retrieved by a forward serial search from the home address.

**projection**   an operation that takes one relation as an operand and returns a second relation that consists of only the selected attributes or columns, with duplicate rows eliminated.

**proposition**   a statement about entities that asserts or denies that some condition holds for those entities.

**protocol**   the call format used by a teleprocessing monitor.

**punched cards**   an early storage medium on which data and input were stored. Today punched cards are rare.

**purge date**   the date on or after which a storage area may be overwritten. Used in conjunction with a file label, it is a means of protecting file data until an agreed-upon release date is reached.

**query language**   a language that enables a user to interact directly with a database management system to retrieve and possibly modify its data.

**queue time**   the amount of time a transaction spends after being transmitted to the processor and before going into execution. Queue time depends on many factors: the system load, the level of integrity of processing required, the priority of the transaction, and so on. Queue time can become the most important factor in poor online response time.

**random access**   to obtain data directly from any storage location regardless of its position with respect to the previously referenced information.

**random access storage** a storage technique in which the time required to obtain information is independent of the physical location of the information most recently obtained or accessed. This strict definition must be qualified by the observation that we usually mean relatively random. The magnetic drum storage devices are relatively nonrandom access in nature when compared with magnetic cores for main memory, but are relatively random access when compared with magnetic tapes for file storage.

**record** an aggregation of values of data items or elements.

**record-at-time processing** access of data a unit at a time (i.e., sequential processing).

**record type** the category to which an instance of a record belongs, as defined by the record format in the database schema.

**recovery** the restoration of a database to its status at a previous moment in time, where transactions can be rerun against the database.

**recursion** the definition of something in terms of itself, such as a bill of materials or an organization chart.

**reorganization** the process of unloading data in one state and reloading the data in a proper and organized state.

**repeating group** a collection of data that can occur multiple times within a given record.

**response time (user)** the amount of time the user has to wait from the time a transaction is entered until the first of the response comes back to the originator of the transaction. Response time is a result of many factors, such as line time, I/O time, queue time, buffer time, and execution time.

**rolling summarization** the practice of compacting details of data based on the age of the data. The more current the data, the more details there are.

**row** a nonempty sequence of values in a table. The smallest unit of data that can be physically stored in a table.

**scope of integration** a statement of the boundaries of the data model.

**SDLC** the classical system development life cycle, where requirements are gathered and where system implementation results.

**secondary index** an index on other than the primary key of the table or database.

**secondary key** the column of data on which a secondary index is based.

**secondary storage** storage facilities not forming an integral part of the computer facilities.

**security** protection provided to prevent unauthorized or accidental access/ manipulation of a database.

**set-at-a-time processing** the access and manipulation of data by groups of data having a commonly identifiable characteristic.

**snapshot** a database dump or archiving of data as of some past moment in time.

**sort** to sequence data according to some set of criteria.

**static summary data**   summary data whose variables will not be subject to change.

**stress test**   a test to determine how many resources are consumed during different levels of input processing.

**subject database**   a database organized around the major entities of the corporation.

**system of record**   the final authority as to the accuracy of any given occurrence of data.

**table**   a relation that consists of a set of columns with a heading and a set of rows.

**time-variant data**   data whose content is accurate as of some moment in time. The common forms of time-variant data are continuous, discrete, and periodic discrete.

**transaction**   a command, message, or input record that explicitly or implicitly calls for a processing action. A transaction is atomic with respect to recovery and concurrency.

**transition data**   data exhibiting both primitive and derived characteristics.

**"type of" relationship**   the grouping of attributes according to subsets of data.

**update**   the process of altering the contents of a database.

**variable field**   a field that may or may not occur.

**variable-length field**   a field whose length may vary.

**view**   an external relation that consists of attributes retrieved or derived from one or more base relations joined and projected as given in the view definition.

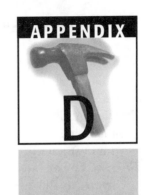

# Articles of Interest

Adelman, Sid. 1996. The Data Warehouse Database Explosion. *Data Management Review*, December. [A very good discussion of why volumes of data grow as fast as they do in the data warehouse environment and what can be done about it.]

Ashbrook, Jim. 1993. Information Preservation. *CIO Magazine*, July. [An executive's view of the data warehouse.]

Bair, John. 1996. It's About Time! Supporting Temporal Data in a Warehouse. *INFODB*, February. [A good discussion of some of the aspects of time variant data in the DSS/data warehouse environment.]

Ballinger, Carrie. 1993. TPC's Emerging Benchmark for Decision Support. *DBMS*, December. [A description of the extension of the TPC benchmark to include DSS.]

Bluhata, Donelle, and Tricia Spencer. 1997. The Business Value of Data Warehousing. *Enterprise Systems Journal*, June. [A discussion of the business merits of data warehousing.]

Coffing, Tom. 1998. TPC-D Tests. *Data Management Review*, January. [An analysis of TPC-D benchmarking.]

Discount Store News. 1992. Retail Technology Charges Up at KMart. *Discount Store News*, February 17. [A description of the technology employed by Kmart for their data warehouse, ODS environment.]

Engebretson, Joan. 1997. The Cost of Entry. *Telephony*, August 11. [Do telecommunications need data warehouses in order to be competitive?—yes, it seems.]

Frawley, Andy. 1997. Marketing Warehouse ROI. *Data Management Review*, June. [A discussion of how marketing data warehouses can get you closer to your customer.]

Fryman, Lowell, and Joyce Norris-Montanari. 1998. Gaining Insight into Your Day to Day Business. *Data Management Review*, July\August. [A description of the business uses of the different types of ODS.]

Geiger, Jon. 1993. Information Management for Competitive Advantage. *Strategic Systems Journal*, June. [A discussion of how the data warehouse and the Zachman framework have advanced the state of the art.]

Geiger, Jon. 1996. Data Element Definition. *Data Management Review*, December. [A good description of the definitions required in the system of record.]

Geiger, Jon. 1996. What's In a Name. *Data Management Review*, June. [A discussion of the implications of naming structures in the data warehouse environment.]

Geiger, Jon. 1997. Data Integration: Salad or Juice? *Data Management Review*, January. [A discussion of the issues of integration with an interesting metaphor of a fresh vegetable salad.]

Geiger, Jon. 1997. Data Stewardship Using the Zachman Framework. *Data Management Review*, December. [A discussion of the issues of data stewardship and the Zachman framework.]

Geiger, Jon. 1997. Importance of Recognizing the Model View. *Data Management Review*, June. [A description of the relationship between the subject area model and the business model.]

Geiger, Jon. 1997. Why Five Types of Data Models? *Data Management Review*, May. [An identification of the different types of data models needed to create the architected environment.]

Geiger, Jon. 1998. Call It Sam. *Data Management Review*, July/August. [A discussion of the naming of the ODS construct.]

Gilbreath, Roy, 1995. Health Care Data Repositories: Components and a Model. *Journal of the Healthcare Information and Management Systems Society*. Spring. [An excellent description of information architecture as it relates to health care.]

Gilbreath, Roy. Informational Processing Architecture for Outcomes Management. [A description of the data warehouse as it applies to health care and outcomes analysis.]

Gilbreath, Roy, Jill Schilp, and Robt Pickton. 1996. Towards an Outcomes Management Informational Processing Architecture. *HealthCare Information Management*, Spring. [A discussion of the architected environment as it relates to health care.]

Goldberg, Paula, Robert Lambert, and Katherine Powell. 1991. Guidelines for Defining Requirements for Decision Support Systems. *Data Resource Management Journal*, October. [A good description of how to define end-user requirements before building the data warehouse.]

Graham, Steve. 1996. The Financial Impact of Data Warehousing. *Data Management Review*, June. [A description of the cost benefit analysis report done by IDC.]

Graham, Stephen, 1996. The Foundations of Wisdom. Toronto: International Data Corp. [The definitive study on the return on investment for data warehouse, as well as the measurement of cost effectiveness.]

Grise, Mark, and Jack Sweeney. 1996. Datamart: Its Role in an Enterprise-Wide Data Warehouse. *Inside Decisions*, Winter. [Another similar perspective of the role of data marts in the DSS environment.]

Hackney, Doug. 1996. Vendors Are Our Friends. *Data Management Review*, June. [Discusses beneficial relationships with vendors.]

Hufford, Duane. 1996. Data Warehouse Quality, Part 1. *Data Management Review*, January. [A description of data warehouse quality.]

Hufford, Duane. 1996. Data Warehouse Quality—Part II. *Data Management Review*, March. [The second part of a discussion on data quality.]

Hufford, Duane. *A Conceptual Model for Documenting Data Synchronization Requirements*. AMS. [Data synchronization and the data warehouse.]

Hufford, Duane. *Data Administration Support for Business Process Improvement*. AMS. [Data warehouse and data administration.]

Imhoff, Claudia. 1996. End Users: Use 'em or Lose 'em. *Data Management Review*, November. [An excellent discussion of the ways to manage the end-user data warehouse effort.]

Imhoff, Claudia. 1998. The Operational Data Store: Hammering Away. *Data Management Review*, July\August. [A discussion of terminology, containing the famous "What's in a Name" universal Inmon/Kimball translator.]

Imhoff, Claudia, and Jon Geiger. 1996. Data Quality in the Data Warehouse. *Data Management Review*, April. [A description of the parameters used to gauge the quality of data warehouse data.]

Imhoff, Claudia, and Ryan Souse. 1997. The Information Eocsystem. *Data Management Review*, January. [A description of the corporate information factory.]

Imhoff, Claudia, and Ryan Sousa. 1997. The Information Ecosystem, Part 2. *Data Management Review*, February. [Article continuation.]

Inmon, Bill. 1995. Growth in the Data Warehouse. *Data Management Review*, December. [A description of why the data warehouse grows so fast and the phenomenon of increasing amounts of storage while decreasing the percent utilization of storage.]

Inmon, W.H. 1988. At the Heart of the Matter. *Data Base Programming/Design*, July. [Primitive and derived data and what the differences are.]

Inmon, W.H. 1990. Going Against the Grain. *Data Base Programming/Design*, July. [A description of the granularity issue and how it relates to the data warehouse.]

Inmon, W.H. 1991. The Cabinet Effect. *Data Base Programming/Design*, May. [A description of why the data warehouse centered architecture does not degenerate into the spider web environment.]

Inmon, W.H. 1992. Building the Data Bridge. *Data Base Programming/Design*, April. [Ten critical success factors in building the data warehouse.]

Inmon, W.H. 1992. Data Structures in the Information Warehouse. *Enterprise Systems Journal*, January. [A description of the common data structures found in the data warehouse.]

Inmon, W.H. 1992. Data Warehouse—A Perspective of Data Over Time. *370/390 Data Base Management*, February. [A description of the relationship of data warehouse and the management of data over time.]

Inmon, W.H. 1992. EIS and the Data Warehouse. *Data Base Programming/Design*, November. [The relationship between EIS and the data warehouse.]

Inmon, W.H. 1992. Metadata: A Checkered Past, A Bright Future. *370/390 Data Base Management*, July. [A conversation about metadata and how metadata relates to the data warehouse.]

Inmon, W.H. 1992. Neat Little Packages. *Data Base Programming/Design*, August. [A description of how data relationships are treated in the data warehouse.]

Inmon, W.H. 1992. The Need for Reporting. *Data Base Programming/Design*, July. [The different kinds of reports found throughout the different parts of the architecture.]

Inmon, W.H. 1992. Winds of Change. *Data Base Programming/Design*, January. [Data administration and the data warehouse; a description of how data administration evolved to where it is today.]

Inmon, W.H. 1993. The Structure of the Data Warehouse. *Data Management Review*, August. [This article addresses the different levels of data found in the data warehouse.]

Inmon, W.H. 1993. Untangling the Web. *Data Base Programming Design*, May. [Explores the factors that turn data into information.]

Inmon, W.H. 1994. The Data Warehouse—All Your Data at Your Fingertips. *Communications Week*, August 29. [An overview of the data warehouse.]

Inmon, W.H. 1994. Data Warehouse Lays Foundation for Bringing Data Investment Forward. *Application Development Trends*, January. [A description of data warehouse and the relation to legacy systems.]

Inmon, W.H. 1994. The Data Warehouse: Managing the Infrastructure. *Data Management Review*, December. [A description of the data warehouse infrastructure and the budget associated with it.]

Inmon, W.H. 1995. The Anatomy of a Data Warehouse Record. *Data Management Review*, July. [A description of the internal structure of a data warehouse record.]

Inmon, W.H. 1995. Data Warehouse and Contextual Data: Pioneering a New Dimension. *Data Base Newsletter*, July/August. [A description of the need for contextual data over time, as found in the data warehouse.]

Inmon, W.H. 1995. EIS and Detail. *Data Management Review*, January. [A description of how much detail is needed to support EIS and the role of summarized data in the data warehouse environment.]

Inmon, W.H. 1995. From Transactions to the Operational Data Store. *INFO DB*, December. [A discussion about how quickly transactions in the operational environment go into the operational data store.]

Inmon, W.H. 1995. Multidimensional Data Bases and Data Warehousing. *Data Management Review*, February. [A description of how current detailed data in the data warehouse fits with multidimensional database management systems.]

Inmon, W.H. 1995. Performance in the Data Warehouse Environment. *Data Warehouse Report*, Autumn. [A description of the different aspects of performance in the data warehouse environment.]

Inmon, W.H. 1995. Performance in the Data Warehouse Environment—Part 2, *Data Warehouse Report*, Winter. [A continuation of the article on data warehouse performance.]

Inmon, W.H. 1995. Profile/Aggregate Records in the Data Warehouse. *Data Management Review*, July. [A description of how profile/aggregate records are created and used in the data warehouse environment.]

Inmon, W.H. 1995. Profiling the DSS Analyst. *Data Management Review*, March. [A description of DSS analysts as farmers and explorers.]

Inmon, W.H. 1995. The Ladder of Success. *Data Management Review*, November. [Building and managing the data warehouse environment entails more than selecting a platform. This article outlines the many necessary steps required to achieve a successful data warehouse environment.]

Inmon, W.H. 1995. The Operational Data Store. *INFODB*, February. [A description of the ODS.]

Inmon, W.H. 1995. Transformation Complexity. *Data Management Review*, September. [Why automating the transformation process is a superior idea to manually programming the transformations that are required in order to build the data warehouse.]

Inmon, W.H. 1996. Choosing the Correct Approach to Data Warehousing: "Big Bang" vs Iterative. *Data Management Review*, March. [A discussion of the proper strategic approach to data warehousing.]

Inmon, W.H. 1996. Commentary: The Migration Path. *ComputerWorld*, July 29. [A brief description of some of the issues of migrating to the data warehouse.]

Inmon, W.H. 1996. Cost Justification in the Data Warehouse. *Data Management Review*, June. [A discussion of how to justify DSS and the data warehouse on the cost of reporting.]

Inmon, W.H. 1996. The Data Warehouse and Data Mining. *CACM*, November. [A description of the relationship between data mining and the data warehouse.]

Inmon, W.H. 1996. Data Warehouse Security: Encrypting Data. *Data Management Review*, November. [A description of some of the challenges of data warehouse security and industrial strength security.]

Inmon, W.H. 1996. The Future in History. *Data Management Review*, September. [A discussion of the value of historical information.]

Inmon, W.H. 1996. Knowing Your DSS End-User: Tourists, Explorers, Farmers. *Data Management Review*, October. [A description of the different categories of end users.]

Inmon, W.H. 1996. Managing the Data Warehouse Environment. *Data Management Review*, February. [Defining who the data warehouse administrator is.]

Inmon, W.H. 1996. Managing the Data Warehouse: The Data Content Card Catalog. *Data Management Review*, December. [An introduction to the notion of a data content card catalog, that is, stratification of data content.]

Inmon, W.H. 1996. Measuring Capacity in the Data Warehouse. *Enterprise Systems Journal*, August. [A discussion of how capacity should be measured in the data warehouse, DSS environment.]

Inmon, W.H. 1996. Monitoring the Data Warehouse Environment. *Data Management Review*, January. [What is a data monitor for the data warehouse environment and why would you need it.]

Inmon, W.H. 1996. Rethinking Data Relationships for Warehouse Design. *Sybase Server*, Spring. [A discussion of the issues data warehouse data relationships.]

Inmon, W.H. 1996. SAP and the Data Warehouse. *Data Management Review*, July/August. [A description of why the data warehouse is still needed in the face of SAP.]

Inmon, W.H. 1996. Security in the Data Warehouse: Data Privatization. *Enterprise Systems Journal*, March. [The data warehouse requires a very different approach to security than the traditional VIEW based approach offered by database management system vendors.]

Inmon, W.H. 1996. Summary Data: The New Frontier. *Data Management Review*, May. [A description of the different types of summary data including dynamic summary data and static summary data, lightly summarized data and highly summarized data, etc.]

Inmon, W.H. 1996. User Reaction to the Data Warehouse. *Data Management Review*, December. [A description of the different user types in data warehousing.]

Inmon, W.H. 1996. Virtual Data Warehouse: The Snake Oil of the 90's. *Data Management Review*, April. [A discussion of the virtual data warehouse and how the concept tries to attach itself to the legitimacy of the data warehouse.]

Inmon, W.H. 1997. The Data Warehouse Budget. *Data Management Review*, January. [A description of the components of a typical data warehouse budget.]

Inmon, W.H. 1997. Architecture for Information Systems. *Data Management Review*, June. [The difference between a blueprint, an architecture, and implementation of an architecture.]

Inmon, W.H. 1997. Are Multiple Data Warehouses Too Much of a Good Thing? *Datamation*, April. [Multiple data warehouses are starting to pop up in corporations. Is this predictable phenomenon a good or bad thing and how should you deal with it?]

Inmon, W.H. 1997. Data Types in the Data Warehouse. *Data Management Review*, April. [A description of some of the common data types in the data warehouse.]

Inmon, W.H. 1997. Does Your Datamart Vendor Care About Your Architecture? *Datamation*, April. [A discussion of the mess that is created when the data mart is built directly against the legacy applications.]

Inmon, W.H. 1997. Dormant Data: At the Heart of Managing the Data Warehouse. *Enterprise Systems Journal*, May. [A description of the phenomenon of dormant data and how dormant data creeps into the data warehouse.]

Inmon, W.H. 1997. EIS in the ODS Environment. *Data Management Review*, March. [A description of the DSS aspects of the ODS.]

Inmon, W.H. 1997. Iterative Development In the Data Warehouse. *Data Management Review*, November. [A discussion of the reality of iterative development.]

Inmon, W.H. 1997. Managing the Data Warehouse with a Resource Governor. *Data Management Review*, December. [Resource governors leave much to be desired as a warehouse management tool. This article outlines the deficiencies of the resource governor.]

Inmon, W.H. 1997. Security in the Data Warehouse/Internet Environment. *ISAC Journal*, vol. IV. [A description of the issues in the data warehouse environment with regards to security.]

Inmon, W.H. 1997. A Self Assessment Test. *Data Management Review*, July/August. [A self-assessment test to measure the maturity of your data warehouse/data mart environment.]

Inmon, W.H. 1997. Tuning the Data Warehouse. *Data Management Review*, February. [A description of different activities that can be done once you have built the data warehouse.]

Inmon, W.H. 1997. Using the Data Model In the Data Warehouse Design. *Data Management Review*, May. [A description of the usage of the data model as a basis for iterative development.]

Inmon, W.H. 1997. What Happens When You Build the Data Mart First? *Data Management Review*, October. [A discussion of how to salvage as much as you can out of the disaster that is created by building the data mart before you build the data warehouse.]

Inmon, W.H. 1997. Year 2000 and Data Warehouses. *Data Management Review*, September. [Outline of a strategy to deploy data warehouses in the face the impending year 2000 problem.]

Inmon, W.H. 1998. Bottom Up Warehouse Development. *Data Management Review*, February. [One more rendition of why building data marts first is the improper thing to do.]

Inmon, W.H. 1998. Controlling Warehouse Costs. *Data Management Review*, October. [A self-administered test to determine whether you have the right to complain about the costs of your data warehouse.]

Inmon, W.H. 1998. Data Mart Does Not Equal Data Warehouse. *Data Management Review*, May. [A further discussion of why a data mart is not the same thing as a data warehouse.]

Inmon, W.H. 1998. Designing the Operational Data Store. *Data Management Review*, July/August. [A discussion on the basic design issues for an ODS.]

Inmon, W.H. 1998. Enterprise Metadata. *Data Management Review*, November. [A description of the distributed metadata environment.]

Inmon, W.H. 1998. Rating Your Data Warehouse Consultant. *Data Management Review*, March. [What should your consultant know in order to be effective. An eclectic collection of ways to look at the job your consultant is doing.]

Inmon, W.H. 1998. Really Large Data Warehouses. *Data Management Review*, September. [This article introduces the architectural component of the near-line storage and the cross-media storage manager.]

Inmon, W.H. 1998. Referential Integrity in the Warehouse. *Enterprise Systems Journal*, August. [Referential integrity is an operational concept. Applying referential integrity to the data warehouse, DSS environment requires an entirely different approach than that offered by standard database management systems.]

Inmon, W.H. 1998. The End User Community. *Data Management Review*, December. [A description of tourists, farmers, explorers, and miners.]

Inmon, W.H. 1998. The Exploration Warehouse. *Data Management Review*, June. [A description of the exploration warehouse.]

Inmon, W.H. 1998. The Fate of the Legacy Environment. *Data Management Review*, April. [A description of the migration from the legacy environment to the data warehouse environment.]

Inmon, W.H. 1998. What Data Warehousing Means to Sales Organizations. *Sales and Field Force Automation*, March. [A discussion of how data warehousing has changed the process of sales.]

Inmon, W.H. 1998. Wherefore Warehouse. *Byte Magazine*, January. [A description of the evolution of the history of data warehousing.]

Inmon, W.H. and Michael Loper. 1992. The Unified Data Architecture: A Systems Integration Solution. Auerbach Publications. [Original article suggesting that a data architecture was in order for future systems development.]

Inmon, W.H. and Sue Osterfelt. 1992. Data Patterns Say the Darndest Things. *Computerworld* February 3. [A description of the use of the data warehouse in the DSS community and how informational processing can be derived from a warehouse.]

Inmon, W.H., and Chuck Kelley. 1994. The 12 Rules of Data Warehouse. *Data Management Review*, May. [A description of the defining characteristics of data warehouse.]

Inmon, W.H., and Phyliss Koslow, 1994. Commandeering Mainframe Database for Data Warehouse Use. *Application Development Trends*, August. [A discussion of optimal data warehouse use inside the mainframe.]

Jordan, Arthur. 1996. Data Warehouse Integrity: How Long and Bumpy the Road? *Data Management Review*, March. [A discussion of the issues of data quality inside the data warehouse.]

Kador, John. 1995. One on One. *Midrange Systems*, October 27. [A discussion about data warehouses with Bill Inmon, including some of the history of how data warehouses came to be.]

Kelly, Sean. 1997. Data Marts: The Latest Silver Bullet. *Data Management Review*, January. [A description of why it is best to build the data warehouse first and data marts on top of them.]

Kimball, Ralph, and Kevin Strehlo. 1994. Why Decision Support Fails and How to Fix It. *Datamation*, June. [A good description of fact tables and star joins, with a lengthy discussion about Ralph's approach to data warehouse and decision support.]

Kimball, Ralph. 1995. Is ER Modeling Hazardous to DSS? *Data Warehouse Report*, Winter. [A dialogue on dimensional modeling versus ER modeling.]

Konrad, Walecia. 1992. Smoking Out the Elusive Smoker. *BusinessWeek*, March 16. [A description of database marketing in the advertising restricted marketing environment.]

Lambert, Bob. 1996. Data Warehousing Fundamentals: What You Need to Know to Succeed. *Data Management Review*, March. [Several significant strategies for data warehousing to guide you through a successful implementation.]

Lambert, Bob. Break Old Habits to Define Data Warehousing Requirements. *Data Management Review*, [A description of how the end user should be approached to determine DSS requirements.]

Laney, Doug. 1996. Are OLAP and OLTP Like Twins? *Data Management Review*, December. [A comparison of the two environments.]

Lebaron, Mike, and Sid Adelman. 1997. Metadata Standards. *Data Management Review*, December. [An excellent discussion of the role of metadata and standards as they apply to the warehouse environment.]

Marco, David. 1998. Data Mart Migration. *Data Management Review*, December. [A discussion of the need to migrate away from independent data marts to dependent data marts. Excellent article.]

Marco, David. 1998. Fitting Square Pegs into Round Holes. *Data Management Review*, September. [An excellent description of the issues of unintegrated metadata in the DSS environment.]

Mena, Jesus. 1997. Mining the Warehouse. *Data Management Review*, January. [An excellent article on the use of data warehouses as a foundation for data mining.]

Meyer, Al. 1997. The Case for Dependent Data Marts. *Data Management Review*, July/August. [A description of why dependent data marts are architecturally superior to independent data marts.]

Myer, Andrea. 1996. An Interview with Bill Inmon. *Inside Decisions*, March. [An interview discussing the start of data warehousing, use of data warehousing for competitive advantage, the origins of Prism Solutions, building the first data warehouse, etc.]

Neushloss, Genia. 1996. Debunking the Myth of Data Marts. *Inside Decisions*, Winter. [A discussion of the role of data marts in the DSS architecture.]

O'Mahoney, Michael. 1995. Revolutionary Breakthrough in Client/Server Data Warehouse Development. *Data Management Review*, July. [A description of older legacy development methodologies versus modern iterative methodologies.]

Osterfelt, Sue. 1997. Information Democracy. *Data Management Review*, May. [Outlines the relationship between business intelligence and data warehousing.]

Osterfelt, Sue. 1997. Neural Networks. *Data Management Review*, January. [A description of where neural networks fit.]

Powell, Ron. 1998. From the publisher. *Data Management Review*, September. [A formal challenge to Ralph Kimball for a public debate.]

Rawls, Judy. 1997. Multitiered Data Warehouses. *Data Management Review*, June. [An article that confuses the issues between data warehousing and data marts. This article is an example of a vendor defocussing users on the important and relevant issues of data warehousing.]

Rudin, Ken. 1996. Parallelism in the DataBase Layer. *Data Management Review*, December. [An excellent discussion of the differences between DSS parallelism and OLTP parallelism.]

Rudin, Ken. 1996. Who Needs Scalable Systems. *Data Management Review*, November. [A good discussion of the issues of scalability in the data warehouse environment.]

Rudin, Ken. 1997. Are Object/Relational Databases Scalable? *Data Management Review*, June. [With the advent of objects in database management systems, the issue arises as to whether the system can handle the performance demands on the technology.]

Rudin, Ken. 1997. Can Parallel Queries Save Your Warehouse's Performance. *Data Management Review*, December. [A discussion of the architectural issues of performance and parallelism in the warehouse environment.]

Rudin, Ken. 1997. Data Marts. *Data Management Review*, February. [A discussion of the issues of data marts.]

Rudin, Ken. 1997. Data Warehouse Architecture: Configuring a Balanced Hardware System. *Data Management Review*, January. [An excellent article on hardware foundations of the data warehouse.]

Rudin, Ken. 1997. NUMA Hardware: A Primer. *Data Management Review*, July/August. [A description of nonuniform memory access architecture.]

Rudin, Ken. 1997. Quantifying Scalability. *Data Management Review*, November. [A discussion of scalability in the data warehouse environment.]

Rudin, Ken. 1997. Scalable Microsoft Windows NT Platforms: Reality vs Myth. *Data Management Review*, October. [A discussion of the progress Microsoft has made and the challenges that await them.]

Rudin, Ken. 1997. Using Distributed Objects to Enhance Scalability. *Data Management Review*, May. [A discussion of the issue of capacity enhancement using distribution.]

Saylor, Mike. 1997. Five Questions IS Managers Should Ask Vendors. *Data Management Review*, June. [A discussion of administration issues in preparing the organization for a mature data warehouse.]

Sloan, Robt, and Hal Green. 1993. An Information Architecture for the Global Manufacturing Enterprise. [A description of information architecture in the large-scale manufacturing environment.]

Swift, Ron. 1996. Creating Value Through a Scalable Data Warehouse Framework. *Data Management Review*, November. [A very nice discussion of the data warehousing issues scale.]

Tanler, R., D. Hackney, and W.H. Inmon. The Intelligent Enterprise. [A white paper designed to discuss the next generation of DSS produced by Information Advantage and Pine Cone Systems.]

Tanler, Richard. 1996. Data Warehouses and Data Marts: Choose Your Weapon. *Data Management Review*, February. [A description of the differences between data marts and the current level detail of the data warehouse.]

Tanler, Richard. 1996. Taking Your Data Warehouse to a New Dimension on the Internet. *Data Management Review*, May. [A discussion of the different components of the data warehouse as they relate to the Internet.]

Thiessen, Mark. 1994. Proving the Data Warehouse to Management and Customers: Where Are the Savings? Presentation at the 1994 Data Warehouse Conference.

Wahl, D., and Duane Hufford. 1992. A Case Study: Implementing and Operating an Atomic Data base. *Data Resource Management Journal*, April. Auerbach Publications. [A description of the U.S. Army DSS data architecture.]

Welch, J.D. 1990. *Providing Customized Decision Support Capabilities: Defining Architectures*. Auerbach Publications. NY, NY [Decision support systems and architecture (based on the PacTel Cellular DSS architecture).]

Winsberg, Paul. 1996. Modeling the Data Warehouse and the Data Mart. *INFODB*, June. [A description of architecture and modeling as it relates to different types of data warehouses.]

Wright, George. 1996. Developing a Data Warehouse. *Data Management Review*, October. [A very good discussion of snapshots and the basic structures of data warehouse.]

1988. An Architecture for a Business and Information System. *IBM Systems Journal* 17: [A description of IBM's understanding of the data warehouse.]

1993. Chargeback in the Information Warehouse. *Data Management Review*, March. [Charge back in the data warehouse can be both a blessing and a curse. This article addresses the both sides of the issues.]

1993. Now Which Is Data, Which Is Information. *Data Base Programming/ Design*, May. [The difference between data and information.]

1994. Liberate Your Data. *Forbes*, March 7. [An interesting and naive article about data warehouse as viewed by the uninformed businessperson.]

1994. The Doctor of DSS. *DBMS Magazine*, July. [An interview with Ralph Kimball.]

1995. A Trillion Byte Weapon. *BusinessWeek*, July 31. [A description of some of the larger data warehouses that have been built and how they play a role in business competition.]

1996. In the Words of Father Inmon. *MIS*, February. [An interview with Bill Inmon.]

1998. An Interview with Bill Inmon. *Innovation Magazine*, Spring. [An interview with Bill Inmon.]

1998. Inmon on Data Warehousing. *Computing News and Review*, February. [An interview that covers the issues of current warehouse thinking. The interviewer did an excellent job of reporting my responses, as well as asking questions that were germane to the thinking in the field.]

1998. The Data Warehouse/Data Mart Marketplace. *Data Management Review*, January. [A taxonomy for the data warehouse DSS marketplace.]

# Prism Solutions Tech Topics

1. Time Dependent Data Structures—a discussion of the different types of data structures and their advantages and disadvantages.

2. Creating The Data Warehouse Data Model from the Corporate Data Model—the steps you need to take to create the data warehouse data model from the corporate data model.

3. Representing Data Relationships in the Data Warehouse: Artifacts of Data —design issues for the building of data relationships in the data warehouse.

4. Snapshots of Data in the Warehouse—a description of the different types of snapshots and the advantages and disadvantages of each.

5. Defining the System of Record—the design considerations of identifying and defining the system of record.

6. What is a Data Warehouse?—this tech topic defines what a data warehouse is and what its structure looks like. This is a basic discussion appropriate to anyone investigating the world of data warehouse.

7. Capacity Planning for the Data Warehouse—this tech topic discusses the issue of capacity planning and projection for both disk storage and processor resources for the data warehouse environment.

8. Operational and DSS Processing from a Single Data Base: Separating Fact and Fiction—an early notion was that a single database should serve as the basis for both operational processing and DSS analytical processing. This tech topic explores the issues and describes why data warehouse is the appropriate foundation for DSS informational processing.

9. Parallel Processing in the Data Warehouse—the management of volumes of data is the first and major challenge facing the data architect. Parallel technology offers the possibility of managing much data. This tech topic is on the issues of parallel technology in the data warehouse environment.

10. Metadata in the Data Warehouse—metadata is an important component of the data warehouse. This tech topic discusses why and what the different components of metadata are for the data warehouse.

11. Loading the Data Warehouse—at first glance, loading data into the data warehouse seems to be an easy task. It is not. This discussion is on the many different considerations of loading data from the operational environment into the data warehouse.

12. Accessing Data Warehouse Data from the Operational Environment— most flow of data is from the operational environment to the data warehouse environment, but not all. This tech topic discusses the "backward" flow of data.

13. Information Architecture for the 90's: Legacy Systems, Operational Data Stores, Data Warehouses—describes the role of operational data stores along with a description of the architecture that results when you mix an operational data store and a data warehouse.

14. Information Engineering and the Data Warehouse—the data warehouse architecture is extremely compatible with the design and modeling practices of information engineering. This tech topic describes that relationship.

15. EIS and Data Warehouse—EIS under a foundation of legacy systems is very shaky, but EIS under a data warehouse foundation is very solid, as detailed in this tech topic.

16. Client/Server and Data Warehouse—client/server processing is quite able to support data warehouse processing. This tech topic addresses the issues of architecture and design.

17. Data Warehouse and Cost Justification—a priori cost justification is a difficult thing to do for a data warehouse. This topic discusses the issues.

18. Reengineering and the Data Warehouse—many organizations are not aware of the very strong and very positive relationship between reengineering and the data warehouse. This topic identifies the relationship and discusses the ramifications.

19. The Operational Data Store—the operational counterpoint of the data warehouse is the operational data store. The ODS is defined and described in detail in this tech topic.

20. Security in the Data Warehouse—security takes on a very different dimension in the data warehouse than in other data processing environment. This tech topic describes the issues. Tech topics are available from PRISM Solutions.

21. Using the Generic Data Model—some corporations have a data model as a point of departure for the design of their data warehouse; others do not. The generic data model "jump starts" the data warehouse design and development effort.

22. Service Level Agreements in the Data Warehouse Environment—one of the cornerstones of online operations is the service-level agreement. Service-level agreements are applicable to the data warehouse but are implemented quite differently.

23. Getting Started—the data warehouse is built iteratively. This tech topic describes the first steps, in a detailed manner, you need to take.

24. Changed Data Capture—the resources required for repeatedly scanning the operational environment for the purpose of refreshing the data warehouse can be enormous. This briefing addresses an alternative way to accomplish the same thing—changed data capture.

25. Telling the Difference Between Operational and DSS—in every shop the issue arises, what is operational and what is DSS? This tech topic tells you how to tell the difference between the two environments.

26. Managing Multiple Data Warehouse Development Efforts—when the organization starts to build multiple data warehouse efforts simultaneously, a new set of design and development issues arise. This tech topic identifies and addresses those issues.

27. Performance in the Data Warehouse Environment—performance is as important in the DSS environment as it is in the OLTP environment. However, performance plays a very different role. This tech topic is all about performance in the DSS data warehouse environment.

28. The Data Warehouse Budget—This tech topic addresses the different patterns of spending and the rate at which funds are spent. In addition, some suggestions for minimizing expenses are included.

29. Explaining Metadata to the End User—when the layman first encounters metadata, the first reaction usually is "What in the world is metadata and why would I ever need it?" This tech topic addresses metadata in very plain, straightforward terms.

30. Summary Data in the Data Warehouse/Operational Data Store—summary data has its own set of unique considerations. There is, for example, dynamic summary data and static summary data. Both types of summary data require very different treatment from the designer and the end user. This tech topic creates a taxonomy for summary data and relates the different types of summary data to the data warehouse and the operational data store.

31. OLAP and Data Warehouse—lightly summarized data has always been an integral part of the data warehouse architecture. Today this construct is know as OLAP or a data mart. This tech topic addresses the relationship of OLAP and the detailed data found in the data warehouse.

PRISM Solutions
1000 Hamlin Court
Sunnyvale, CA 94089
1-800-995-6916

# Pine Cone Systems Tech Topics

1. Monitoring Data Warehouse Activity—activity in the data warehouse needs to be monitored for a variety of reasons. This tech topic describes monitoring techniques and considerations, and provides a description of why activity monitoring needs to be done.

2. Charge Back in the Data Warehouse DSS Environment—charge back is an extremely useful way to get the end user to take responsibility for the resources that are being consumed. This tech topic addresses the issues of charge back.

3. Iterative Development Using a Data Model—Data modeling is an essential part of the data warehouse design process. This tech topic explains how

iterative development can be done and at the same time how the data model is incorporated into the development process.

4. What Is a Data Mart?—Data marts are a natural product of the data warehouse. This tech topic outlines the salient characteristics of the data mart.

5. Data Mining—An Architecture—using the data warehouse is an art. This tech topic relates the underlying architecture of the data warehouse to the sophisticated way in which the data warehouse can be used.

6. Data Mining—Exploring the Data—once the data is gathered and organized and the architecture for exploitation has been built, the task remains to use the data. This tech topic addresses how data can be mined once the architecture is built.

7. Building the Data Mart or the Data Warehouse First?—while the data mart is a companion to the data warehouse, data mart vendors try to encourage people to build the data mart without building the data warehouse. This tech topic addresses the issues relevant to this important design decision.

8. Monitoring Data Warehouse Data—while activity monitoring is very important, so is monitoring the data itself in the data warehouse. The growth of the data, the quality of the data, the actual content of the data are all at stake in this issue.

9. Data Warehouse Administration—with DSS and the data warehouse comes the need to manage the environment. A new organizational function has arisen, data warehouse administration. This tech topic addresses the charter of data warehouse administration and other important data management issues.

10. Metadata in the Data Warehouse: A Statement of Vision—metadata is an important part of the data warehouse environment. Metadata has a dual, conflicting role. In some cases metadata must be shared. In other cases metadata needs to be managed autonomously. This tech topic addresses the distributed metadata architecture which allows metadata to be distributed and to be managed autonomously.

11. Data Warehouse Administration in the Organization—once the need for data warehouse administration is recognized, there is the question, Where should the DWA function be placed in the organization? This tech topic addresses the issues of the organization placement of the DWA function.

12. Managing the Refreshment Process—data periodically needs to be refreshed from the legacy environment into the data warehouse. The refreshment process is much more complex than one would ever imagine. This tech topic addresses the issues of data warehouse refreshment.

13. Data Stratification in the Data Warehouse—How do you tell someone what is inside a 1 terabyte data warehouse? How many customers? Of

what type? Of what age? Living where? Buying how much per year? This tech topic addresses the technique of stratifying data in order to create a library "table of contents" that describes what actual content of data there is inside a data warehouse.

Pine Cone Systems
303-221-4000
303-221-4010 (Fax)

# Other Notable White Papers

*Data Warehousing Performance with SMP and MPP Architectures*, Sun Micro-Systems, July 1997, Sun Database Engineering Group—an excellent paper quantifying the debate between SMP and MPP, referring to speed up, scalability, and other important performance measurements.

*Digital Data Directions*, by Fred Moore, StorageTek Corp., Louisville, CO—an excellent collection of facts and figures about disk storage and other storage media.

# Books

Berry, Michael, and Gordon Linoff. *Data Mining Techniques*, New York: John Wiley & Sons, 1997.

Brackett, Mike. *The Data Warehouse Challenge*. New York: John Wiley & Sons.

Devlin, Barry. *Data Warehouse: From Architecture to Implementation*. Reading, MA: Addison Wesley.

Hackathorn, Richard. *Web Farming for the Data Warehouse*. San Francisco: Morgan Kaufman.

*Evolution of the High Performance Database* (selected articles from Informix Tech Notes). Menlo Park, CA: Informix Press, 1997.

Inmon, W.H. *Building the Data Warehouse*. New York: John Wiley & Sons, 1990.

Inmon, W.H. *Building the Data Warehouse*, 2nd ed. New York: John Wiley & Sons, 1996.

Inmon, W.H. *Building the Operational Data Store*. New York: John Wiley & Sons, 1995.

Inmon, W.H. *Corporate Information Factory*. New York: John Wiley & Sons, 1998.

Inmon, W.H. *Data Warehouse Performance*. New York: John Wiley & Sons, 1998.

Inmon, W.H. *Information Systems Architecture: Development in the 90's*. New York: John Wiley & Sons, 1989.

Inmon, W.H. *Managing the Data Warehouse*. New York: John Wiley & Sons, 1997.

Inmon, W.H. *Rdb/VMS: Developing the Data Warehouse*. New York: John Wiley & Sons, 1994.

Inmon, W.H. *Third Wave Processing: Database Machines and Decision Support Systems*. New York: John Wiley & Sons, 1989.

Inmon, W.H. *Using the Data Warehouse*. New York: John Wiley & Sons, 1992.

Kelly, Sean. *Data Warehousing—The Key To Mass Customization*. New York: John Wiley & Sons.

Kimball, Ralph. *Practical Techniques for Building Dimensional Data Warehouses*. New York: John Wiley & Sons, 1996.

Love, Bruce. *Enterprise Information Technologies*. New York: John Wiley & Sons, 1991.

Parsaye, Kamran, and Marc Chignell. *Intelligent Database Tools & Applications*. New York: John Wiley & Sons, 1993.

Silverston, L., K. Graziano, and W.H. Inmon. *The Data Model Resource Book*. New York: John Wiley & Sons, 1997.

Tanler, Richard. *The Intranet Data Warehouse*. New York: John Wiley & Sons, 1997.

Zachman, J., J. Geiger, and W.H. Inmon. *Data Stores, Data Warehousing and the Zachman Framework*. New York: McGraw Hill, 1997.

## Book Reviews

*Information Systems Management*, Winter 1997.
Bookisms, by Paul Gray, "Mining For Data Warehouse Gems." A review of several books on data warehousing.

## Research Papers

*Successful Data Warehouses*, by Gloria Lee, September 1997. Discovery Solutions, P.O. Box 64340, Sunnyvale, CA 94086; 408-732-2390; e-mail: discsolns@aol.com. An excellent survey and interpretation covering many aspects of data warehousing. Contains discussions of both problem areas and successes. Very worthwhile reading.

# Index